WHOLE MEALS

WHOLE MEALS

Marcea Weber

PRISM PRESS

Special thanks to *The Japanese Bookshop* and *Ichibankan* for the loan of the Japanese china and artifacts in the photographs. Also thanks to Margaret and Ann for their china, plants and nick nacks.

Published in the U.K. in 1983 by
PRISM PRESS
Sherborne, Dorset

and in the U.S.A. by
PRISM PRESS
P.O. Box 778
San Leandro
California, 84577

Originally published in Australia by Doubleday Australia Pty. Limited

Production and Design: Diane Quick
Line Illustrations: Margaret Snape
Photographs: Michael Cook

© 1983 Marcea Weber

ISBN 0 907061 46 X (Hardback)
ISBN 0 907061 47 8 (Paperback)

Distributed in the U.S.A. by Interbook Inc.,
861 Lawrence Drive, Newbury Park, California 91320

Typeset by Margaret Spooner Typesetting, Dorchester, Dorset
Printed by Purnell & Sons (Book Production) Ltd., Paulton, Bristol

CONTENTS

With sincere love and
appreciation I dedicate
this book to my parents
who shared themselves
with us totally

ACKNOWLEDGEMENTS

The satisfaction of writing a book comes from the ability to share it with others. If I were not able to communicate by sharing there would be no reason to write. Of course I truly enjoy experimenting, creating new and different recipes and seeing them put into practice, but the real joy comes in giving it away. All the time devoted to teaching and 'kitchen-chemistry' would not have been possible without the help and support of many sincere and devoted friends. This book would never have made the transition from a 'dream' into reality—it would probably have never left the kitchen.

To my dear friend Susan, who sat by me, typing endlessly into the night, and who read, listened, guided me and smiled. This book would not have been born without her devotion, patience and true understanding of sharing.

To Adrienne, who took the very first draft and made sense out of my scribbles, giving me back a workable copy from which I was able to assemble a more coherent manuscript. And to Anne Marie, who inspired me after reading her whole foods cookbook.

What would the book be without those magnificent drawings which sing and bounce off each page? Margaret, I am most grateful to your ability, talent, perseverence, sincerity and friendship.

I am most grateful to Masako, a very dear friend, for her generosity, patience and love. She has a remarkable way of always being there any time of the day or night.

Many thanks also, to all those people who took time out from their busy schedules in the restaurants to share their popular recipes with you: Pam, Jill, Diane and Peter.

A special word of thanks to Bruce Gyngell, who invited us out to Australia to teach and get a first hand experience of what it is all about.

And last, but never least, my husband Daniel, who is always there listening, supporting and sharing.

All of these people, along with my students, family and friends throughout the world and of course my teachers, Michio and Aveline Kushi, Herman and Cornelia Aihara and Masahiro Oki, are responsible for this book. We all have shared in the pleasure of giving to you so that you in turn can share with others.

'He will never go to heaven
who is content to go alone'
Boethius 450 A.D.

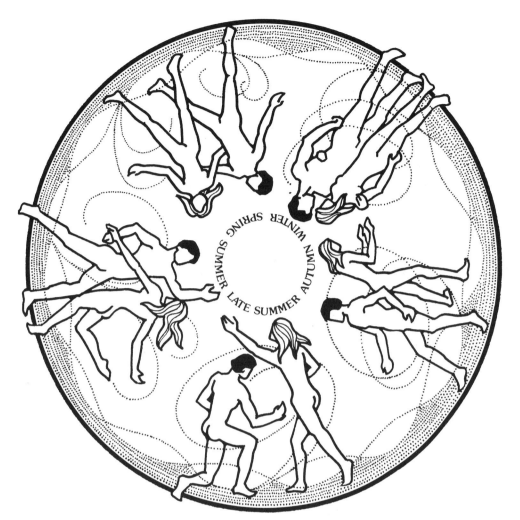

SUMMER SPRING WINTER AUTUMN LATE SUMMER

INTRODUCTION

There's no doubt in my mind that health and happiness are a matter of choice. Each time I've been confronted with this fact I have found myself somewhere near the crossroads of two very separate schools of thought. The first concerns the constant pressure of modern-day society that demands that you be a part of the 'with-it' generation—always the first in the neighbourhood to own the latest time-saving device, or be known as the best cook around when it comes to spontaneously 'throwing together' an elaborate dinner party which you know very well took weeks of planning. On the other hand, I sometimes feel a desire to become more independent of the consumer society and revert to a more natural lifestyle. This rekindling of traditional ways may be the only answer to relieving all those modern-day pressures, and once again coming in touch with the simple pleasures that nature has to offer: health and happiness.

Most of us are caught somewhere in between. In one way we are conscious of something lost in the quality of our lives, but at the same time we do not quite know what, or where to look for the answer.

The sharing of food is one of the most important social contacts and is usually considered to be a criteria of how much people care about us. With more and more meals being taken outside the home, perhaps we should begin to consider just in fact what all this really means. Could it be a contributing factor to the increasing stress found in our lives today?

I remember when I was young that everything at home seemed to revolve around the kitchen. My mother would cook and bake whilst I would sit and watch. She surrounded me with her warmth and the traditional dishes that her mother had taught her to cook. Little did I realise that these were my very first cooking lessons and how much I learned just by being there. Sharing with her those intimate moments with the pots and pans and wholesome ingredients had in some ways given me more insight than any of the cooking classes that I have attended since.

It's really a shame that so much of this ritual has faded away. Now, instead of being there with Mum, helping to lick the bowls and play with the dough, we have exchanged these experiences for frozen, processed, chemically-treated, artificially coloured and flavoured 'fast foods' that can remain edible after weeks or even months on the shelf. Foods that don't nourish, because they are so refined that the very essence of the food itself has disappeared.

There is no reason why health and happiness cannot be an integral part of everyone's life. When I was first introduced to the idea that a change in my diet might help bring about a cure for an old back injury, I was very reluctant to listen. A chiropractor tried to explain that the way to cure my back pain was to stop eating refined foods (too much animal protein and sugar) and to start a diet based on vegetables, whole grains and seasonal fresh fruits. I really thought that he was barking up the wrong tree but on the other hand, what did I have to lose. The only alternative was a back operation, which I wasn't really ready for. So reluctantly, I went along to the nearest 'whole foods' restaurant in New York and sat down to the first of many vegetarian dinners. Much to my amazement I liked it and found myself going back for seconds.

This experience had proved far greater than my expectations and the best prize of all was that I began to feel better inside myself as well. I continued my daily eating habits for several weeks following the adjustments the chiropractor had suggested and it wasn't long before I recognised that wholefoods really made a difference to me. I didn't miss refined, processed foods or sugar, dairy products and meat. When I finally got on the road to recovery I changed my diet somewhat to suit my needs and I still find that today I am constantly changing it according to where I live, the type of work that I do, the climate that I live in and how I feel.

My approach to cooking is nothing more than an understanding and respect for nature. I began to realise (thanks to Michio Kushi, Aveline Kushi, Cornelia and Herman Aihara, and Lima and George Oshawa) that everything in the universe is nothing but a system of opposites: night and day, sun and moon, man and woman, heaven and earth, fire and water. So it is that by appreciating and understanding these opposite yet complementary forces (like summer and winter, the needs and foods that accompany them, how the seasonal foods grow, their water content, shape, size and colour), we can begin to understand how and when to use them to best suit our needs.

Certainly today, when time is short and there are so many things that we must accomplish in one day, we have to take certain 'short cuts' to fit it all in, but this should not be at the expense of our health and happiness. Today, food processors and marketers have made our lives less complicated, but we have become too dependent upon them: there is crumbless bread, frozen dinners that leave no mess or bother, dehydrated or instant meals in a cup and drinks that have an endless life. In the past few decades, supermarkets have virtually dictated our food purchases by stocking the shelves with brilliantly designed packages which dazzle the eye. Manufacturers have clouded our minds with clever slogans which appeal to our emotions and billions of dollars have been spent on food advertising often implying a wholesomeness that doesn't exist.

By using slogans and jingles about convenience, pleasure and romance, food manufactures seduce the public with memories of happier times when food was 'home-made', 'country-fresh' and 'straight from the farm'.

The ultimate commodity is the good old reliable 'takeaway'. But what is really being taken-away? Even though most of us are well aware that serious doubts have been raised regarding the lack of nutrition in foods touted as 'high-energy' and 'weight-reducing', we choose to ignore the obvious.

One of the saving graces in Australia has been the tremendous influx of European migrants that have entered since World War II. By opening up small businesses (mostly ethnic), they have provided the traditional native foods of their country which are still relatively wholesome, unprocessed and natural. Goat's milk cheeses, pickles, dark breads and freshly-made pasta are just a few examples.

Asian influences have also made a distinct impression on Australian cuisine, as evidenced by the growing numbers of Chinese, Japanese, Vietnamese, Korean, Indian, Indonesian and Malaysian restaurants that have sprung up over the past few years. There are also a variety of cooking books and schools providing lessons in the different cuisines which help us to share in the various cultures; if you eat the food of the land you will experience both the land and it's people.

At a time when more and more illnesses appear related to bad eating habits, the more fats, sugars and processed foods that are dished out the less effective (in terms of quantity and quality) will vitamins and minerals be. A diet high in refined carbohydrates, sugar, and fats, combined with less activity and sedentary work habits can be beneficial to no one. By increasing the consumption of complex carbohydrates such as whole grains, vegetables and fruits and decreasing the consumption of foods high in fat, sugar, salt, additives and preservatives, the quality of our lives will increase 100 per cent.

Of all the variables affecting our health and happiness, the preparation and cooking of food is the most essential and the easiest to modify to suit our needs. The barbecue, camping out in the bush, and the family weekend picnic are all part of a strong Australian tradition. These experiences provide times for sharing and after all, what better way is there to enjoy each other's company than by eating, drinking and laughing together? Food has always been a symbol of sharing hospitality, a bridge of friendship and of caring about other human beings. Cooking is in fact a kind of external predigestion. Now I ask you: should you let anyone else digest your food for you?

GUIDE TO CHANGING YOUR DIET

You may not be ready to commit yourself to a total change in diet at this stage. That's probably very wise. Everyone has their own individual pace for making change and the slower the better. A slower but even pace actually assures a stronger foundation. A sudden change may set off a rapid elimination of toxins that can be too much for the body to handle all at once. Remember it really is better to be safe than sorry.

Try to purchase organically grown grains, fruits and vegetables whenever possible, making use of the goodness that nature provides. Eating natural, unrefined foods helps to supply your body with the essential vitamins, minerals, fats, protein and complex carbohydrates needed for your daily routine. Natural foods are *not* artificially treated *after* the growing season. However, it does not mean that they are necessarily organic (e.g. natural raisins). They provide good health, vital energy and well-being without having to resort to vitamin pills or mineral supplements. Basically speaking, vegetables and fruits are healthier for the body because they are high in vitamins, minerals, natural salts, cellulose and chlorophyll content which help digestion and clears the digestive tract. Here are some steps to follow if you wish to be successful in gradually changing your diet:

1 Choose foods that are organically grown (without chemical pesticides or fertilisers). They are both better for you and taste sweeter and richer too.

2 Use foods in their whole state—unrefined, unprocessed and unpeeled. Use both the roots and tops.

3 Eat whole grains instead of just the bran. Use whole fruits (fresh or dried) instead of too many concentrated sweeteners or fruit juices. Use sesame or sunflower seed or nuts before using oils.

4 In salad dressings, use foods that are not refined: tofu, expeller-pressed oils, miso shoyu, kuzu, and sea salt.

5 Use local produce whenever possible and *try to avoid* tropical foods in a temperate zone.

6 Depending upon the work you do, the climate in which you live and your past eating habits, choose food that is not so extreme in its nature (for example, meat and sugar) which could cause great imbalance.

7 Reduce animal food consumption to three times weekly. (This stage may take anywhere from 1–4 months.)

8 Reduce liquid intake but remember, the more animal food you eat or have eaten in the past, the more liquid you should drink. The kidneys need liquid to wash out animal toxins.

9 Eat plenty of salad to help move the animal fats through the system.

10 Try using more whole grains, beans and fresh vegetables, and make fish or chicken a supplementary food instead of your main source of protein. This will create more harmony and more nourishment.

11 Vary the food in each meal in relation to taste, colour, texture and nutrition.

12 Pay attention to quantity as well as quality. Some people need more grain and less vegetables or vice versa. Feed people according to their needs. Generally speaking, if you choose foods from a variety of categories such as grains, beans, freshly cooked and raw vegetables, nuts, seeds and occasionally fish or chicken with dessert as a special treat instead of part of your daily meal, then you will be fulfilling your family's daily requirements, needs and desires all at the same time.

13 Avoid medication whenever possible. Don't inhibit the body from eliminating toxins, instead just allow the discharging to take place naturally (itching, perspiration, blemishes and so on).

14 Do not drink while eating, because liquids dilute the gastric juices and always chew well thus aiding digestion.

15 Spend one day a week eating very little to allow the body to rest and regenerate itself.

16 Eat a combination of cooked and raw food at each meal.

17 Try to reduce foods that are harmful because they require the body to devote a great deal of time and effort to digestion. These are: coffee, tea, milk, refined flour products, refined sugar, alcohol, foods fried in butter or margarine, fatty meats, rich sauces, creams and cheeses.

18 Exercise daily to help maintain and support a healthy body.

19 Eat less and do more.

Gluten free diets

If you are on a gluten free diet there is an easy guide to follow in this book. Just look for the symbol (G) indicating which recipes contain *no* gluten. Remember that if the recipe contains shoyu you will have to substitute it with the wheat free variety. Also, if the recipe calls for miso, use the hatcho which also contains no gluten. As far as the sweeteners are concerned, only maple syrup is gluten free.

NATURAL DIETS

In order to lose weight many people think that they have to either starve themselves or go on an extreme diet for several weeks. The truth is that a slow, gradual weight loss is best, because the inevitable reaction to an extreme 'crash diet' is swinging back in full force to the old eating habits.

These types of 'crash' diets do nothing but create imbalances in the body. Overweight and underweight problems are only symptoms of physical imbalance. Most of us learnt the nutritional concepts of proteins, carbohydrates and fat; eating only from the four basic food groups such as meat and fish, fruits and vegetables, dairy products, and cereals. If we showed signs of eating too much by gaining weight in the 'wrong' places, we were told to stop eating or cut down on carbohydrates. Most of the so called 'modern' diets are based on high protein and low carbohydrate intake. Carbohydrates are necessary for energy, and proteins for body construction. Judging the correct quantity for your daily needs is the most important point to consider.

'Will I gain weight if I switch to eating high calorie carbohydrate foods like grains, beans and wholemeal bread?' If you increase your intake of whole grains such as brown rice, millet, oats, barley, rye, wheat, buckwheat and corn, and minimise your consumption of other sugars from fruits (fructose), milk products (lactose) sweeteners such as honey and cane sugar (sucrose) and fats you will re-orientate your system towards a more efficient food metabolism.

Eating less animal protein and relying on whole grain and their products plus supplementing with beans, nuts, seeds and miso will provide you with a complete vegetable protein containing all the necessary amino acids. You won't gain weight and it certainly won't break your budget either!

Excess body weight is due to an accumulation of food appearing in the form of water, protein or fat. The easiest to lose is the water weight, followed by the fat. The hardest to lose is the excess formed from proteins. (Dairy products are not advisable for weight loss because they are high in proteins, fats and milk sugars and do not metabolise as quickly as grains or vegetables.)

It is the *refined* carbohydrates that give this group of foodstuffs a bad reputation—white flour products (such as pastries and breads), sugar-filled foods, alcohol—these foods are responsible for the extra weight and digestive problems often associated with carbohydrates.

Starch is found in grains, beans and root vegetables and consists of large molecules which during digestion break down into smaller units of a simple sugar, *glucose* which is carried by the bloodstream to all our body cells. The other major dietary carbohydrates include the sugars *sucrose*, found in cane and beet sugars, honey (very small amounts also occur in fruits and vegetables) and other sweeteners, *fructose* from fruits, and *lactose* which is found in dairy products.

The problem with sucrose, fructose and lactose is that they are more rapidly digested and absorbed into the bloodstream (in some cases within one or two minutes) than maltose (starch), which goes through a much slower process of metabolism. The great advantage of consuming carbohydrates in the form of starch is that they break down into glucose much more slowly and therefore do not cause a rapid rise and fall in the blood sugar levels as do the other forms of sugar—making you crave for something sweet again! (*See 'Sweet or Sour?' page 22.*)

Another advantage of eating more whole grains is the presence of fibre or roughage (indigestible substances such as cellulose) in the bran of grains. Recent studies done in the United States have indicated the favourable effects of fibre on such conditions as cancer of the bowel, diverticulitis, varicose veins and coronary thrombosis.

With our eating habits we over-consume fats along with carbohydrate foods (buttered potatoes, creamed vegetables), thus putting on extra kilos. The trick then is to control our fat intake, and starches therefore, won't be a problem. The reducing diets that restrict carbohydrate intake do not allow for the fact that when your body's intake of carbohydrates is too low your system compensates by manufacturing *energy* from *protein*. This process will eventually leave you with a *nutritional deficit*. It's not a fair trade—body-building and repairing capabilities of protein for much needed energy. The answer to the weight problem is *moderation*. Eat only what your body can *use* and those extra kilos will cease to be a problem.

VITAMINS AND MINERALS

The market is flooded with charts, stories and descriptions telling us what we need in the way of vitamins and minerals from our daily foods. Today, one of the most common trends in 'health food' circles is the constant taking of vitamin and mineral supplements. People are taking these supplements in the same way they pop pills for a common cold. Have you ever stopped to think about whether the body can utilise all these pills that are normally taken in a haphazard manner anytime?

Nature after all, provided essential vitamins and minerals in all foods and in *proper proportions* so that the body could utilise them as needed.

Man has come along and changed these proportions through the use of unnatural methods, thereby changing the structure of foods which upset the balance of these nutrients in relation to one another. This has been done by refining, processing and altering the soil in which our foods grow and by changing the basic structure of the food itself.

There are so many different tasks that vitamins perform and so little that we know about them. We do know that they are present in food only in exceedingly small quantities and that they are absolutely essential for life and cannot be produced by the body. They must be supplied by what we eat and without them the food that we eat could not be utilised.

Most vitamins are soluble in water, hence the term 'water soluble' vitamins has been coined to describe this group. These can be carried by the blood throughout the body and absorbed by the cells where they are needed. However, they are not able to be stored and any excess vitamins in our diet are washed out in the urine; so these must be kept in fairly constant supply. The other vitamins, known as 'fat soluble' are resistant to water, so that they concentrate in the fatty tissues and can be stored by the body. However they can build up to toxic levels when taken in too large amounts often through the use of vitamin supplements.

Like vitamins, minerals play an important role in the body. In combination with organic compounds minerals are found as constituents of hormones, enzymes and vitamins as well as of cells, especially tissues of the teeth and bones.

With the stresses and pollution we encounter today, our nutritional requirements are greater than ever before. But the processed and refined foods we eat result in severe nutritional loss. To get the most out of any meal, it should be eaten in a relaxed and happy atmosphere. Be happy, laugh and enjoy your companions and this will aid in digestion, and bring about better nutrition. In the following chart, the figures set in bold type refer to the range of cooking losses in percentages.

FAT SOLUBLE

Vitamin A 0–40%[1]

Vitamin A is usually stable during medium heat but destroyed at high temperatures in the presence of oxygen, for example when deep frying or sautéeing for long periods. It is also destroyed when stored oil turns rancid. It is unstable with acid and stable to alkali.

Vitamin D 0–25%[2]

Vitamin D is stable for cooking and storage.

Vitamin E 0–55%[1]

Vitamin E losses occur in oils primarily when they go rancid or are used for deep frying. The free fatty acid derivatives (peroxides) that form under these circumstances react with the Vitamin E and destroy it. Air, light and alkalies enhance the destruction. Vitamin E is also destroyed by freezing.

WATER SOLUBLE

Vitamin C 0–100%[1]

Vitamin C, otherwise known as ascorbic acid, is more readily destroyed than the other vitamins. If it is preserved, the other nutrients in the food will be too. It decomposes quickly in the presence of heat, air, alkali and certain metals like copper and iron in pots and leaches readily into cooking water. As soon as a plant is harvested the Vitamin C content begins to diminish because the tissue damage activates an enzyme which destroys Vitamin C. Blanching inactivates this enzyme. However, this enzyme is not present in citrus fruits. Vitamin C is the most stable in acid fruits so fruit juices which are stored in the refrigerator in sealed containers will retain their Vitamin C content for several days.

Thiamin 0–80%[1]

Thiamin is one of the most easily destroyed vitamins. It is destroyed by the oxygen in the air and is unstable to heat in alkaline or neutral conditions. Baking bread results in a 15–30 per cent thiamin loss and toasting destroys an additional 10–30 per cent. Thiamin is also destroyed by sulphur dioxide which is sometimes used as a preservative.

Riboflavin 0–75%[1]

It is stable to heat in a dry or acid medium, and sensitive to light especially in high temperatures or an alkaline medium. It is destroyed in milk when it is exposed to direct sunlight in clear containers. It loses 50 per cent in two hours in sunlight and 20 per cent on an overcast day.

Niacin 0–75%[1]

Can only be lost when boiling vegetables and not using the cooking water. It is leached into the water very quickly.

Vitamin B6 0–40%[1]

Most of this vitamin is lost through refining and processing but it is also sensitive to heat and light especially in alkaline conditions.

Vitamin B12 0–30%[3]

It is lost by too much cooking because it is only stable to heat in neutral solutions. Most foods are either acid or alkaline.

Folacin 0–100%[1]

This can be destroyed by air and light so vegetables (green ones especially) should be stored in dark, cool airtight places. An average of half is said to be lost during cooking[2] and even more during reheating.

PROTEIN AND ITS ALTERNATIVES

Almost everyone nowadays has the urge to get fit. It may suddenly become necessary at the beginning of a season (usually those which demand our figure to be perfect) when we try on last season's clothing and find that they don't fit or that that extra bulge doesn't quite complement summer's new fashions.

Other people look at fitness as an on-going process—a constant and *willing* desire to maintain that good, healthy feeling and extra energy along with a slim figure that usually accompanies those who are really fit. To maintain vitality and a quality of 'aliveness' trust your experience: be more active and eat less. After all, when you were a child didn't you do more and eat less?

If you asked the average person what they thought they needed to get the most out of the food that they were eating, nine out of ten would probably say 'protein'. This judgment is based on how much activity we do and what we hear other people say. But an increase or over-consumption of protein is not the answer. If anything we should think about being over-nourished rather than under and consider that perhaps we have been eating too much meat, milk, eggs, cheese and refined foods which may have caused the problem in the first place.

[1]Harris, R. S., and von Loesecke, Harry eds., *Nutritional Evaluation of Food Processing*, Wiley, NY, 1960; [2]Bender, A. E., *Proceedings on Vitamins*, University of Nottingham;[3] FAO/WHO, *Ascorbic Acid, Vitamin B$_{12}$, folate and iron*, p. 41.

According to Hara Marano, editor of *US Medical World News* the average Australian consumes 87 kilos of red meat a year, 24 kilos of poultry, 6 kilos of fish, 294 eggs, 7 kilos of cheese and 118 kilos of other dairy products. On average, we consume twice as much protein than the recommended amount. The obligatory daily need of the average 70 kilo male is actually no more than 238 grams of protein—a peanut butter sandwich. However, no matter where you derive your protein from, their ability to supply amino-acids in proportion to the needs of the body is most essential. Over-consumption of protein can reduce the body's calcium intake. While calcium is apparently being absorbed, much is excreted in the urine.

AMINO-ACIDS

There are some amino acids that can be manufactured by the body so long as it has enough of the chemical element, nitrogen. But another group of amino-acids cannot. These must be present in foods in adequate amounts otherwise the body won't be able to produce the protein it requires. The critical difference rests in whether the quantity of each essential amino-acid is sufficient. For example, if we eat beans and wheat or rice together, these two protein sources make up for one another's amino-acid deficiencies. So you can see that grains and legumes are complementary in terms of protein, because each one makes up for the amino-acid shortages of the other.

A combination of animal and vegetable sources of protein is most suitable to meet the demands of today's stress and high-speed living. Over the next few years we will see a definite trend towards using more soy protein in our diet which will add more protein, less calories, reduce our expenditure on food costs and meet human needs on a world-wide scale.

Experts in the food industry already experimenting with soy beans are creating a whole new range of products for the future. At the present time, there are a few foods that already meet these requirements in terms of low-calorie, high-protein appetising and quick preparation foods. They have been around for hundreds if not thousands of years, and I would like to share some of them with you.

ANCIENT PROTEIN ALTERNATIVES:

Miso   Miso, like shoyu, tamari, rice vinegar and sake is made using *koji*, a culture that grows best at the temperature of the human body, produces enzymes similar to those contained in human saliva and used in the digestion of starches and proteins. The different kinds of miso can be attributed mainly to differences in the koji. Miso also contains whole soy beans, wheat, salt and water. With the addition of koji, which actually begins to digest the grain and bean mixture by producing certain enzymes, it changes the soy beans, wheat, salt and water into a living organism. The result is a complete protein, containing 17 amino-acids which enables easy digestion. In addition, the digestion-inhibiting enzyme (trypsin) which is always a problem in raw or under-cooked soy beans is destroyed during fermentation. The B-vitamins—riboflavin, niacin and B12—are each increased during fermentation of miso. Vitamin B12 only has a few known sources among vegetable foods: comfrey, sea vegetables, certain sprouts and fermented soy products.

Once you discover the way to work with miso, there will be no need to follow recipes. The combination of soy beans and grains in miso produces a highly usable protein with well-balanced amino-acids. Paste-like in appearance and texture, it looks similar to vegemite. Miso is fully fermented for at least one year and the result is that not only the essential amino-acids but also the enzymes assist directly with the digestion of other foods, as well as stimulating the secretion of fluids in the stomach. Other attributes of miso include its superior chemical balance and the alkalising affect it has upon digestion, contributing to the strength and quality of blood circulating from the intestines. It is respected as both a food and a medicine.

Hatcho miso   The highest in lactic acid of all the misos, it is also the heartiest. It has the thickest texture and has a rich, almost chocolate-like flavour. It makes an excellent soy bean base for all miso soups and goes well with peanut butter or tahini spread on wholemeal bread.

Mugi miso   This miso is made with barley koji and is introduced first to cooked barley after which it is mixed with soy beans in the kegs where the miso ferments. This is perhaps the most universally appealing of the misos in taste and suits both summer and winter cooking. It can be used quite easily in spreads, desserts, dressings and soups.

Kome miso   This kind of miso is made with rice-koji which yields the sweetest kind of miso. It is ideal for those first beginning to use miso or as a pleasant change from any of the other kinds.

Soba miso   A unique kind of 'young' miso, it is made with buckwheat, soy beans, water and salt quite rapidly yielding a light, delicious miso for warmer climates.

Natto miso   A special treat, this miso is only 30 days old and combines the subtle flavours of barley, kombu (sea vegetable), malt, ginger, koji, soy beans, and salt to produce a very unique flavour. Use it on freshly cooked rice, for salad dressings, as a spread on bread and in desserts for a very tantalising taste.

Genmai miso   Brown rice miso is very rich in glucose and other natural sugars. It has a rich and savoury salty flavour with a deep fragrance. A popular and versatile miso, it is well suited for use in all types of cookery.

Remember also that scientific studies have shown that miso has the ability to absorb, attract and discharge radioactive elements from the body such as strontium 90 and nicotine. It also helps the body to discharge toxins it would otherwise retain. As the old saying could go: 'A bowl of miso soup a day helps keep the doctor away!'

Shoyu—traditional soy sauce

Shoyu is a traditional soy sauce made from four basic ingredients: soy beans, wheat, salt and water. Koji is then inoculated into the soy beans and wheat, and incubated in a chamber where the temperature and humidity can be controlled. Then after the mould matures it is taken out and mixed with saltwater and placed in large wooden barrels. These barrels are left uncovered throughout fermentation and are stirred regularly to keep the ferment active. After the shoyu is fully aged it is pressed to yield raw shoyu. After settling for about a month it is repeatedly skimmed and then heated at 80°C for one hour.

Shoyu has a number of beneficial effects on the body. It stimulates the secretion of digestive fluids in the stomach, has a preservative effect on food and fosters the growth of healthy bacterial cultures in the intestinal tract. Further, it improves circulation and strengthens the contractions of the heart and often completes the protein balance of foods since it includes the amino-acids, usually lacking in cereal grains.

There are no set recipes for using shoyu. It can be used on foods, in foods, or as a dip. It can also be used in various cooking techniques with many different kinds of foods. The versatility of shoyu just depends upon your imagination and knowing when to use just a little in the right place.

Some suggestions for using shoyu:
1 Mixed with brown rice vinegar, the acetic acid quality of the vinegar makes the aroma and taste of shoyu fresher and more flavoursome.
2 Grated red or white radish with shoyu makes the harshness of the radish disappear. Since the sharpness in radish is neutralised by the shoyu and also assists gastric juices in the digestion of oil, grated radish mixed with shoyu is good to serve along with a tempura.
3 Lemon shoyu is just simply lemon juice and shoyu mixed together according to your own taste. It is an excellent accompaniment to shellfish, boiled cabbage, cauliflower, brussel sprouts and turnips.
4 Try adding it to oily dressings, broths, soups, or using it to baste fish or chicken in.

One last hint concerning storage. Since the chemical structure of shoyu is adversely affected by both sunlight and heat, keep it in a dark place away from the heat.

Most present day soy sauce and shoyu is the result of a mixture of mashes made from heat-controlled fermentation and hydrochloric acid treatments with additions of caramel colouring and flavouring agents. A quick test for authentic shoyu is by shaking the bottle vigorously until bubbles form in the neck of the bottle. Natural shoyu will form a thick head of foam that may take as long as fifteen minutes to settle whereas inferior shoyu will settle more quickly. Another test is to place a drop of shoyu in a glass of still water. Inferior shoyu will disperse immediately near the surface while natural shoyu will sink deep into the glass before spreading slowly.

Tempeh
Now Indonesia's most popular soy-protein food, tempeh is quickly becoming popular also in the Western world. It is an excellent diet food in that it only contains 157 calories per 100 gram serving. It is low in saturated fats and contains an abundance of lecithin plus essential polyunsaturates such as linolenic and linoleic acids. These acids perform the vital functions of emulsifying, dispersing, and eliminating deposits of cholesterol and other fatty acids that may have accumulated in the vital organs and bloodstream. One of the most versatile foods that I have come across, it can be baked, grilled or deep fried.

Tofu (soy bean cheese or curd)
Tofu, also known as bean curd, soy bean cake or cheese has been the low-cost protein food of the Asian diet for more than 2000 years. Discovered by a Chinese prince in 164 B.C., tofu is presently the single most important soy bean food for more than one billion people. About 227 grams of tofu contains 17.7 grams of protein which is 37 per cent of the average recommended daily requirement of 65 grams.

The uses are infinite; they range from a vegetable, cream sauce, cream soup, salad dressing base, dip, spread, sandwich filling or bread substitute to 'cheese-cake'. It is also ideal for those who are concerned with losing weight or maintaining it because it contains one of the lowest calorie counts of any plant food and does not increase body weight.

The high percentage of lecithin-phosphoric acid (1.64 per cent) present in the soy bean greatly enhances the oxidation of its fatty acids; therefore in spite of the high fat content of the soy bean this fat is readily oxidised by the system instead of being stored as excess weight. In countries where soy bean products are a staple food, there are seldom people overweight, let alone fat. About 100 grams of tofu contains only 60–65 calories compared to an equal weight of eggs containing three times as many calories and steak which contains four to five times as many.

The Japanese variety of tofu, usually available in most natural food shops, is mostly chemically-free*. The Chinese variety (bean curd) available in most oriental groceries uses a different coagulating agent derived from calcium sulphate (gypsum) imparting a different flavour, taste and texture as well as chemical composition. Tofu can be used in a variety of different ways and is only limited by one's own creativity, and imagination.

Net protein utilisation (NPU)

Net protein-utilisation (NPU) depends upon the food's digestibility and the degree to which the configuration of the eight essential amino-acids making up the protein match the pattern required by the body. The higher the NPU the more completely the body is able to utilise that food's protein.

Food	NPU
eggs	94
milk	82
fish	80
miso	72
brown rice	70
cheese	70
beef (steak, hamburger)	67
tofu	65
chicken	65
soy beans and soy flour	61
peanuts	43

*Look for tofu made from nigari. (Sea water extract.)

SPROUTING

The Vegetable Garden Jar

Can you think of a vegetable that will grow in any climate, at any time of the year, that usually requires neither soil nor sunshine, and rivals tomatoes in Vitamin C, matures in three to five days, has no waste preparation, has not been subjected to chemical sprays while growing, rivals meat in nutritive value and can be grown indoors within a minimum amount of space?

Sprouts from seeds, beans, and grains provide the answer. Not only are they an excellent source of protein in its purest form, but they also provide natural carbohydrates, vitamins and minerals. The starch and protein from sprouts are readily digested due to the high quality of its enzymes. However, in the first few days of sprouting, most of the starch changes to simple sugar—especially in the case of wheat berry sprouts, which begin with a composition of almost all starch. They quickly increase in sugar content, however, changing into an excellent source of quick energy. Tests have proven that when lentils, alfalfa and wheat seeds are sprouted, their nutrients increase from 50 per cent to 400 per cent. The foods become rich sources of:

Vitamin A	...	calcium
Vitamin B1	...	iron
Vitamin B2	...	phosphorus
Vitamin C	...	potassium
Vitamin D	...	sodium
Niacin	...	chlorine

Some essential amino-acids, which are difficult to find in most foods, are present in sprouts. These amino-acids are required by the body for daily functioning and must all be supplied within the same meal for best results. So, by incorporating sprouts from beans such as lentils, mung beans, chickpeas and soy beans, and grains such as unhulled barley, millet, buckwheat, oat groats, wheat, brown rice or rye, and seeds like alfalfa, sesame (unhulled), un-shelled sunflower, radish or mustard, a more complete protein can be obtained.

Some people believe that it is better to sprout two types of sprouts together such as alfalfa and wheat berries. As alfalfa is a legume, and wheat is a non-legume, they provide good polarity for each other. Also, since the rinsing and soaking water of any sprout is rich in amino-acids, save and use it for cooking.

Sprouting Instructions

Using ¼–½ cup dried beans or grains (depending upon the size of your sprouting container or tray), rinse and pick through, eliminating damaged, non-sproutable seeds, beans or grain.

Mature sprouts

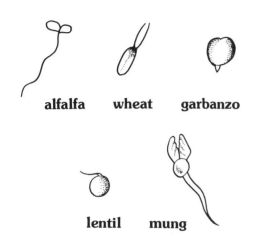

alfalfa   wheat   garbanzo

lentil   mung

First, soak the seeds, beans or grain a minimum of 12 hours (and up to 24 hours) in a glass jar or sprouting container. Rinse, drain off the water and reserve it for some other use. Cover the mouth of the jar with a material that will allow air to pass through, and secure it with string. (Muslin or cheesecloth is a good material for this.)

Place the jar on its side and keep it in a warm, dark environment. If the jar is too hot, it will cause souring; if it is too cold, it will cause stagnation. To keep the seeds moist, rinse them *every* day and drain off *all* the water to avoid fermentation of the roots. After 12 hours, the jars can be removed from the darkness into the light (not direct sunlight).

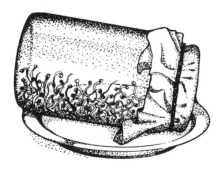

Sprouting can be achieved on a tray, plate, or in a bowl, crock or stainless steel sprouting mesh. In order to sprout unshelled sunflower seeds or unhulled grains such as buckwheat, they must be placed about 6 mm deep in moist soil on a tray. They require damp soil (sunlight is not necessary), and they should be planted about 6 mm apart from each other. In 3–5 days, the sprout will reach a height of about 13 cm.

Cut them off very close to the soil just before using. Wheat berries may also be planted this way to obtain wheat grass or sprouted in a jar to obtain little sprouts.

Before using sprouts grown in indirect sunlight, expose them to more light until they become green. This process enriches the chlorophyll and Vitamin C content.

Alfalfa is about the most alkaline plant that we have. Most diseases thrive in an acid condition within the body; alkalinity helps to balance these conditions. It contains *every* essential amino-acid required, and the protein content is 18.9 per cent, as compared to 16.5 per cent in beef, 13.1 per cent in eggs and 3.3 per cent in milk. The alfalfa plant has a deep root structure that if stretched in a straight line would measure from 42 to 82 metres. These roots are able to pick up many of the trace minerals that aid in building up the bloodstream and organs, and have ten times the mineral content of grains. A tea of alfalfa seeds is said to be beneficial for arthritis and rheumatic conditions. Steep one tablespoon of seeds in a quart of boiling water and take three times daily.

Seeds take about 3–5 days to sprout, depending upon the temperature and moisture of the environment. Alfalfa seeds are ready when they are 2.5–5 cm in length. Lentil and chickpea sprouts mature at about 1.2–2.5 cm, mung and soy beans at 1.2–2.5 cm also. Grain sprouts are ready when they are equal in length to the grain. If they grow longer it is best to use them in bread instead of soups or salads. Use organically grown seeds whenever possible, because chemicals can damage the embryo and cause the seed to rot instead of sprout.

The Chinese have a unique sprouting technique for mung and soy beans: Soak beans overnight. Place them on top of a board on a damp cloth or tea towel. Make the layer no more than 6 mm thick and cover with another damp towel or cloth. Place another board on top and a heavy weight on top of that. (The heavier the weight, the juicier and fatter the sprouts.) Wash daily and rinse out towels or cloths, wringing out all excess moisture. (Will take approximately 5–6 days.)

How to use sprouts

Sprouted seeds are quite refreshing when eaten raw in a salad or dropped into soup just before serving. They also make a nice garnish for any cooked dish, as well as complement any sandwich in taste and texture.

Bean sprouts are most suitable for cooking. Try stir-frying Chinese vegetables with mung-bean sprouts or mixing them with freshly cooked hot noodles or rice dishes. Bean sprouts also make nourishing and delicious tasting soups, thickened with arrowroot and coloured with tiny drops of beaten egg. It is best to cook most bean sprouts to aid in digesting them.

Sprouted wheat bread is the most common way to use grain sprouts; mix them into the batter along with your other ingredients. When sautéed with carrots and onion, the natural sugars from the vegetables and the sprouts will surprise any sweet tooth.

For an unusual way to prepare a natural sweetener, here is a recipe for **Grain syrup:**

Pressure cook or boil 2 cups brown rice, without salt (best to use the short grain) in 6 cups water for 45 minutes. (If boiling, soak overnight.) Cool to 45°C using a candy thermometer. Crush or blend freshly made grain sprouts. (Wheat or rice is best.)

Combine the rice and the sprouts (use 1 table-spoon sprouted grain to every $1\frac{1}{2}$ cups cooked rice), cover and keep at a constant 42–45°C for at least 4–5 hours. Remove cover and taste. If it is not sweet enough, cover and let sit another few hours, tasting until it is right. Squeeze liquid through cheesecloth into saucepan, reserving grain for breads. Add a pinch of sea salt and boil down or bake in 180°C oven until it reaches the desired consistency.

THE OIL STORY

Since there is such an enormous choice of oils on the store shelves today it seems even more confusing than ever to reach an agreement as to which is best. Some appear to be very clear and have hardly any colour, while others are very cloudy and dark. Because of the growing tendency away from animal fats and towards vegetable oils, it is necessary to understand the methods of refining and to weigh both the advantages and disadvantages of both.

Many new terms seem to have cropped up in the last few years regarding vegetable fats and oils. Some of these include: 'refined', 'expeller pressed', 'cold pressed', 'solvent-extracted', and 'bleached'. Generally an edible oil is extracted from nuts, seeds and beans. Natural oils (crude expeller pressed, unrefined or mildly-processed) differ from heavily-processed oils (refined, deodorised, solvent extracted or bleached) not only in appearance, but also smell and taste. This makes the difference in nutritional value quite apparent.

Oils contain lecithin, an important nutrient for the nervous system, as well as Vitamins A, E, K and minerals. Oil does have its good points—it is a good medium for sautéeing or deep-frying, and is sometimes a necessary ingredient in breads, pastry, and salad dressings. But unfortunately, only some oils are essential for good health whilst others are unnecessary and potentially harmful.

Saturated oils, found mainly in foods of animal origin, are solid at room temperature and are commonly called fats. Recent medical studies have shown that if fats are regularly consumed over a long period of time they tend to be deposited in the circulatory system, and can lead to heart disease, arthritis, arteriosclerosis and aid in the development of cancerous tumours. Unsaturated oils derived from seeds, break down during digestion to form unsaturated and polyunsaturated fatty acids. These unsaturated oils distribute the fat soluble vitamins around the bloodstream, supply energy, conserve body heat, build new tissue, and promote the growth of beneficial intestinal bacteria. They can actually help break down deposits of saturated fats in the body, as extraordinary as it may seem.

Most processed oils are commercially prepared by steaming them at a temperature of more than twice the boiling point of water which destroys most vitamins including Vitamin E. They are then solvent-extracted by being subjected to petroleum-based chemical solvents which allow more oil to be extracted from the grain or seed. After this the oil is deodorised and bleached.

The other more desirable method of oil extraction is done by the use of pressure which extracts only 95 per cent of the oil and is known as 'expeller-pressing'. However, after the oil has been 'expeller pressed', there is still between two and five per cent of the oil in the meal. As this is too much waste, the oil is usually sent onto the next plant for solvent extraction. The resulting product is a 'refined' oil. Unrefined oils are mechanically pressed, at a temperature below boiling point. They contain no bleaching agents or chemical solvents. Essentially they have retained Vitamin E, lecithin, chlorophyll, and trace minerals. 'Cold pressed' oils have been filtered more so they are lighter.

The best oils to use for sautéeing are sesame or safflower unrefined oil. Deep-frying and tempura are best prepared with cold pressed oils because sometimes the unrefined ones have small amounts of water left in from the pressing which tend to bubble while cooking.

Whatever your choice, the wisest course is moderation. Since our fat consumption has increased well out of proportion, most people could afford to reduce their fat and oil intake which would help unclog the system of unnecessary fatty deposits.

The following lists some recommended oils to choose from:

Corn oil   Ideal for all baking and deep-frying purposes.

Sesame oil   Fragrant and highly nutritious, for everyday frying, and salad dressings. It has the ability to remain stable and free from rancidity even in hot weather.

Safflower oil   Best for salad dressings and when combined with 30 per cent sesame oil makes the best oil for deep frying. Has the highest percentage of linoleic acid (up to 80 per cent) which tends to lower the cholesterol level in the blood.

Olive oil   Strong, dark and fruity in flavour, it can enhance any Italian pasta dish or salad. Not for everyday use.

I do not recommend the use of peanut, coconut or soy bean oil as they are too heavy for everyday use. The flavour is too over-powering and the methods of extraction are sometimes dubious.

FATS AND THEIR EFFECTS

Within the last 30 years a fourth group of fats has been discovered. These are commonly known as 'hydrogenated' fats or margarine, and have been treated with hydrogen in such a way that some or all of the unsaturated acids present are converted into saturated ones. This raises the melting point or 'hardens' the fats. The reasons for hydrogenating a fat are various—extending shelf life, getting rid of unpleasant flavours or giving it a more acceptable and pleasant texture. Basically it just makes an *edible* fat out of an *inedible* one.

Margarine was first introduced in France in 1870 when it was manufactured in the form of a low-melting fraction of suet which was stewed with milk. Over the years, margarine was constantly being improved by blending it with vegetable oils and by using starters. By 1910 margarine was being made without any animal fat, using only hydrogenated vegetable fat which lowered its cost considerably.

Margarine was considered to be inferior to butter for many reasons. One of the most outstanding reasons was demonstrated in 1922 when the Medical Officer of Christ's Hospital in England showed that the replacement of butter by margarine in the boys' diet in 1917 had corresponded with a sharp increase in the number of boys who broke their limbs. He reintroduced butter and the incidence of broken bones returned to a lower level. These breakages were mainly due to the absence of vitamins which are present in butter.

It is strange but true that our bodies actually need a certain amount of essential fatty acids. This is because a deficiency could lead to an accumulation of cholesterol in the arteries, thus clogging them and resulting in coronary and other diseases. Because these essential fatty acids occur almost wholly in vegetable oils, particularly in corn oil, neither butter nor margarine are necessary. It is also believed that the beneficial effect of these acids is counteracted if too much fat containing saturated fatty acids is eaten. This means an *increased* consumption of hydrogenated fats also contains an increased proportion of *saturated* fats.

DAIRY PRODUCTS

Mothers usually agree that they want the best for their children. Then why is it that more and more mothers are taking the easy way out and starting off their children's lives with a handicap due to poor feeding habits early in life? Most people agree that breast-fed babies naturally receive immunities to help them resist infection, because human milk contains antibodies capable of fighting infection in humans. Cow's milk obviously does not contain the necessary antibodies to fight human diseases.

In spite of all the evidence supporting the benefits of breast-feeding, the trend away from this natural method is being evidenced worldwide. Even in such countries as Africa, artificial feeding with cow's milk has become somewhat of a status symbol. An analysis of colostrum, the milk secreted during the first five days after birth shows that it is extremely rich in Vitamin A and carotene. In fact, the concentration of antibodies and antitoxins is four times higher than in the milk produced later by mothers. After this initial stage, mother's milk is 40 times richer in Vitamin E, five times in Vitamin C and twice richer in Vitamin A. Human milk also contains lecithin which cow's milk does not.

If the baby consumes cow's milk (which is three and a half times richer in protein and three times richer in sodium than mother's milk), the baby will require more cow's milk to meet his energy requirements because protein is used less efficiently by the baby than carbohydrates. As the cow's milk increases, so does the sodium and calorie intake.

Excess calories actually build extra fat cells and causes an increased rate of growth whereas excess sodium (salt) can cause water retention. Therefore, most of the children over the last twenty years have grown to be taller and fatter than ever before.

Milk is not designed for adults. No adult

animal drinks milk after weaning. Both animals and humans lose the partial or complete production of *lactase*, an enzyme necessary in the digestion of milk which may account for many people (especially the Japanese) who cannot digest milk at all.

The advertising of milk and dairy foods is very misleading. Often told that milk contains large quantities of protein and calcium, we think that by drinking milk and eating lots of dairy food we will be 'healthier and happier'. The truth is that milk only contains three per cent protein by weight compared with 50 per cent for some soy bean products, 20–25 per cent for beans and 10 per cent in grains. Oddly enough the protein in cow's milk contains the insoluble substance caseinogen, which forms a dense curd in the stomach, making it difficult to digest. More and more doctors and nutritionists are now warning that milk, cheese, butter and margarine can be contributing factors in the development of heart disease, obesity, allergies, nasal congestion, hyper-activity, irritability and fatigue. Dr Frank Oski in *Don't Drink your Milk* points out, 'It is natural to lose the lactase activity in the gastro-intestinal tract. It is a biological accompaniment of growing up.'

Soy milk

Soy milk is highly praised by both doctors and laymen alike. Many view it as an effective natural medicine and doctors in Japan prescribe it as a regular part of the diet for diabetes (because it is low in starch), high blood pressure, hardening of the arteries, kidney stones (because it is low in saturated fats, free of cholesterol and rich in linoleic acid and lecithin) and anaemia (because it is rich in iron). It is also used to strengthen the digestive system and alkalise the bloodstream.

Many Japanese people claim that it also has the ability to bring out the natural lustre in their skin, increase mother's milk supply and cure constipational disorders in children. It is also important to those suffering from an allergy to cow's milk.

Quick and easy to prepare, you can make it in less than 20 minutes in your own home. If you have no time to make it yourself, be sure that you purchase soy milk that contains no added sugar or chemicals of any kind.

The following is a chart based on 100 grams portion of soy, dairy and mother's milk.

When soy milk is prepared with the same percentage of water as that found in dairy milk, soy milk contains 51 per cent more protein, 24 per cent less fat, 12 per cent fewer calories and 16 per cent less carbohydrates. It also contains 15 times as much iron, *no* cholesterol, and a smaller amount of chemicals, if any.

Say cheese!

After glancing at some of the recipes in this book, you may wonder why there is very little cheese used in them. Our present day 'cheese' is a far cry (in most cases) from the original, simple curded milk that was coagulated by adding rennet (found in a calf's stomach) to the milk, heating the liquid to make hard cheese and then separating the curds from the whey. Unfortunately today, most cheeses are processed and flavoured by injecting moulds, bacilli and fungus into them to produce those many flavours available in the market.

One of the most simple methods of ancient cultures, the process of fermentation, has been used in a variety of ways including yogurt, pickles, vinegar, buttermilk, miso and shoyu. But, by the time we get it, cheese has been artificially-coloured and acidifying agents have been added as well as emulsifying agents and hydrocarbons. More than likely it has been covered with a wax coating with chemical additives, to prevent 'bacteria growth' and probably sprayed with some form of insecticide.

Many years ago when most families ate a great deal of cheese and dairy foods of all types, the circumstances were different. They were healthier, worked harder and ate less. If you work hard physically all day then you can handle more dairy foods, especially cheese. Consider also the climate in which you are living. Do you need extra fat for fuel to keep your body warm? Or, do you live in a climate that is mostly warm all year round and don't really need the warmth that this food will provide? An active, vigorous outdoor way of life is what you will need to use up and burn off any excess waste that these particular foods produce.

If you are going to eat cheese, choose one that is very dry, like parmesan or one made from goat's milk.

Soy milk			
	Soy milk	Dairy milk	Mother's milk
Water (g)	88.60	88.60	88.60
Protein	4.40	2.90	1.40
Calories	52.00	59.00	62.00
Fat	2.50	3.30	3.10
Carbohydrates	3.80	4.50	7.20
Ash	0.62	0.70	0.20
Calcium (mg)	18.50	100.00	35.00
Sodium	2.50	36.00	15.00
Phosphorous	60.30	90.00	25.00
Iron	1.50	0.10	0.20
Thiamine (B1)	0.04	0.04	0.02
Riboflavin (B2)	0.02	0.15	0.03
Niacin	0.62	0.20	0.20

(*Source:* Standard Tables of Food Composition (Japan))

If the animals that produced the dairy foods are fit and healthy and eat non-chemicalised food then you can occasionally partake in a good, simple food which should be used in moderation keeping in mind how active you are, your environment and your condition.

SWEET OR SOUR?

Sugar is the basic chemical unit of all carbohydrates and therefore occurs naturally in an immense amount of foods that we consume daily (see 'Sugar and their Sources' page 24). When you think of sugar, what comes to mind? Most people think that sugar is only found in a bag—usually white or brown and generally granulated. Most of the sugar in the diet of primitive man was found in fruits and vegetables. Legend has it that Hercules went about the earth searching for the golden apple and Adam and Eve, who were unable to resist the temptation of 'sweetness' from the apple, learned about the difference between good and evil the hard way!

The fact is that one's natural attraction to sweet foods bears a distinct relationship to a need that one has once hunger occurs! When blood sugar levels begin to drop we feel the need to eat and when our blood sugar is elevated the feeling disappears.

Starches are essentially nothing but sugar units that reach the bloodstream over a long period of time. As you digest wholefoods in the form of starches, there are other nutrients that are also absorbed including protein, fat, vitamins and minerals, which aid in the digestion of the starches. As the carbohydrates in the food are used up by the body to supply energy, the blood sugar gradually begins to sink again and once more you become hungry.

Since large quantities of carbohydrates are needed by the body in order for it to function fully, they are known as 'energy foods'. The same principal applies to your car. You can run a vehicle without water or oil for a time but petrol is the most essential ingredient which cannot be overlooked or taken for granted.

As people began cultivating more and more plants for food, sugar became one of the most popular. In its simplest form, sugar is the most fundamental of all foods. In converting sunlight into food, green plants first make simple sugars. The starch in a potato comes from sugar formed in the leaves of the potato plant and wood is built from sugar made in the leaves of the trees. Most foods are developed from sugar including protein in grains and oil in peanuts.

Sugar consumption

Sugar was first cultivated as early as 325 B.C. in India, but it wasn't until Colombus brought sugar cane to the Caribbean in 1493 that it became more than a luxury. Within the next hundred years, sugar became one of the most valued products of the New World. The sugar beet became popular for use when the Napoleonic Wars cut off shipments of Caribbean sugar to France. It was at this point that sugar evolved from being a household 'occasional' luxury to an integral part of the average person's diet.

Between 1900 and 1970, world production of sugar climbed from eight million to 70 million tonnes. By 1965, the average annual sugar consumption per head had reached 54 kilos from a mere four kilos in 1815. Why do we consume all this sugar? It was thought that in primitive times sweetness was nature's way of telling man which foods were safe to eat. Very often foods that tasted bitter were considered poisonous, and fruits, vegetables and grains that tasted sweet were nutritious. Thus, the word 'sweet' has come to stand for anything that is good, fresh, pure, refreshing, wholesome, clean and delicious. Advertising has used this misleading fact to push the 'sweetness' attraction, magnifying the 'sweet taste of foods.'

Eventually, people began to discover how to extract sugar from food and discard the rest of the nutritious part. This way, sugar could be eaten, satisfying the taste buds, and suppressing hunger and would not have to break down the starch into small sugar units. It would be immediately absorbed and hunger would disappear like magic!

But, when such concentrated sugars are taken alone, the body chemistry undergoes an immediate shock. Their quick absorption results in an immediate rise in blood sugar and one gets that instant 'energy rush'. This short burst of energy is followed by a period of letdown, exhaustion and weakness. This automatically leads to an uncontrollable craving for another portion of sugar and this perpetuates the cycle.

Starch vs sugar

The difference between sugar and starch can now be seen very clearly. Where sugar may give an instant thrust of energy and then an instant low, starch is gradually broken down into sugar units, giving the body little bits of usable carbohydrate spread out over several hours as opposed to minutes. This way the blood sugar doesn't drop as quickly, putting undue stress on the pancreas.

Up until 100 years ago, the process used to extract sugar from the cane or beet was too expensive and impractical. Sugar was a rare delicacy only enjoyed by royalty, but then as the process of refining sugar and extracting it from cane or beet became industrialised, it also became more widely available thus decreasing its cost to the consumer.

Raw, brown or white

When refined sugar is produced from the sugar cane, everything is extracted except *sucrose*. So, although white refined sugar is usually considered the culprit, processed sugar, whether it is 'raw', brown or white all belongs to the same family. Brown or raw sugar may look more attractive and healthier (because of its brown colour) but all sugars have been concentrated in their refining process, stripped of their essential vitamins and minerals and treated with chemicals like sulphur. The difference is minimal — white sugar is 99 per cent pure sucrose and products like raw, or brown sugar and molasses (see page 25) are about 96 per cent pure sucrose, but with a slight trace of vitamins, minerals, and protein, although in very small quantities.

Real raw sugar, is made by evaporating the water from sugar cane juice and allowing it to solidify and granulate. In other parts of the world such as India, this type of sugar is still readily available. It is almost the same as the sugar cane except for the absence of fibre and water.

Sugar refining

The manufacturing of sugar from sugar cane is an interesting process. First the cane is crushed, then pressed and the juice is treated to remove impurities. Then it is boiled down until it begins to crystallise. The liquid is then separated, leaving 'raw' sugar. At this point it has to be washed with steam because of so called 'contaminating factors'. This is the light coloured raw sugar that may contain traces of minerals but still is more than 99 per cent sucrose.

The dark, rich 'brown sugar' is made by pouring molasses that was extracted during the sugar refining process over white sugar. This may contain some minerals but the desirability of 'coloured' sugar is very much up to the individual.

Hidden sugar

Now, more than ever, we have far less control over the amounts of sugar we eat daily. A large percentage of the sugar we consume is 'hidden'. It is used not only to provide sweetness, but it also retains and absorbs moisture which prevents foods from drying out rapidly and it depresses the freezing point, making ice cream and other frozen desserts smoother. In addition, it can act as a preservative and even enhance the appearance of certain foods. It has been stated that even meat products contain nearly three per cent (by weight) of added sugar, while more than 13 per cent of processed vegetables is added sucrose.

So-called 'junk' food consists mainly of empty calories, because the metabolism of sugar will proceed only by using the vitamins, minerals and protein from the tissues in the body, which can lead to the body being deficient in important nutrients. Without the proper usage of sugar the body may be too tired to be active. Proper vitamins and minerals facilitate the metabolism of carbohydrate and some of the sugar is stored away as fat. It seems like one can literally starve to death even though one is overweight—this is the marriage of malnutrition and obesity.

There is definitely no dietary requirement for extra sugar other than that which is naturally occuring in foods such as fruits, grains and vegetables. Unless you have been fasting for several days your body has enough reserves to call upon even if you are doing a considerable amount of physical activity or sports. If you do eat sugar before exercising, the sugar will be quickly metabolised and stored with your other fuel reserves.

The worst danger of all is that as we increase our average sugar consumption there seems to be a *decrease* in the average consumption of whole grains and flours and a trend towards eating more refined foods in the form of white flour, white rice, pasta and sucrose.

There is increasing evidence to suggest that over-consumption of products containing refined sugar is a major cause of diet-related diseases. Yet, it is becoming almost impossible to find prepared food products without some kind of added sugar in them. Not only is sugar found in sweet biscuits, cakes and pastries but it is also disguised in baby food, sauces, drinks, cereals, salad dressing, so-called quick frozen foods, instant soups, some frozen or tinned vegetables, fruit yogurts and even pizzas. You must begin to scrutinise labels if you want to escape the ever-increasing risk of getting unwanted sugar in almost every prepared and pre-packaged food. (Up to 5 per cent sugar in certain prepared foods can go unlabelled.)

Sugar alternatives

Once you've gotten over the so-called 'sugar blues' you have to have a destination in mind. After all, everyone likes to have a sweet now and then. There are sweets like dried fruits which contain large amounts of another sugar called fructose (see page 24). It seems to be absorbed more slowly into the bloodstream, and now this kind of sugar is being marketed as a replacement for ordinary table sugar. However, a word of caution: if the fructose is taken in too large a quantity this can also result in the same kind of reaction as eating pure sucrose. Moderation is the key.

An increasing awareness that refined sugar is harmful to the body when taken daily has swayed many people over to the use of honey. However, there are disadvantages in using concentrated sugars of all kinds, even honey. The body apparently needs carbohydrates daily for fuel, and if sufficient amounts are not taken the body will turn to using stored proteins and fats. The danger in this is that carbohydrates are needed to be present when using proteins and fats as a substitute otherwise the residues they produce can cause problems. Therefore the most ideal form of carbohydrate other than a simple sugar is starch which is a complex sugar found in grains and beans. So, by changing starches in grains into sugars such as found in barley malt extract, maltose, grain syrup, rice honey and sprouted wheat, we can find enough sweetness to last a lifetime.

Sweetness equivalency chart
Many times when I am preparing desserts I use different sweeteners depending on the recipe and what I have on hand. Different sweeteners give different tastes. I personally find honey too overpowering for most recipes so I tend to use more maple syrup, maltose or rice syrup.

This chart will help you understand the relationship between one sweetener and another. Try different ones to see which one works best for you. Remember to *increase* or *decrease* the liquid or flour in the recipe according to the sweetener you choose.

$\frac{1}{4}$ cup maple syrup $= \frac{1}{4}$ cup honey
$\frac{1}{4}$ cup maple syrup $= \frac{1}{2}$ cup fruit purée (date, sultana or raisin)
$\frac{1}{4}$ cup maple syrup $= 1\frac{1}{4}$ cups apple juice
$\frac{1}{4}$ cup maple syrup $= \frac{1}{4}$ cup molasses
$\frac{1}{4}$ cup maple syrup $= \frac{1}{4}$ cup coconut sugar
$\frac{1}{4}$ cup maple syrup $= \frac{1}{4}$ cup palm sugar
$\frac{1}{4}$ cup maple syrup $= \frac{1}{4}$ cup date sugar
$\frac{1}{4}$ cup maple syrup $= \frac{3}{4}$ cup maltose
$\frac{1}{4}$ cup maple syrup $= \frac{3}{4}$ cup barley malt
$\frac{1}{4}$ cup maple syrup $= \frac{3}{4}$ cup rice syrup

When substituting maple syrup or honey in any recipe that may call for sugar, reduce the liquid content by $\frac{1}{4}$ cup. If no liquid is called for, add 3–5 tablespoons of flour for every $\frac{3}{4}$ cup of maple syrup or honey. Heat the maltose, barley malt or rice syrup before using as it is quite solid at room temperature. Oil the measuring cup or spoon before measuring so that it can be released from the spoon or cup quickly.

If you are using honey, store and mix in glass, ceramic ware, stainless steel or pottery because of its high acid content. Bake products con-

Sugar and their sources		
Monosaccharides (sugar molecule) fructose galactose glucose	Fruit sugar or laevulose in many of the more complex carbohydrates Constituent of lactose and many plant polysaccharides Also dextrose or grape sugar. Principle constituent starch and others	honey, most fruits milk, most vegetables root vegetables, green leafy vegetables
Disaccharides (two molecules) lactose maltose raffinose sucrose	Otherwise known as milk sugar and unique to mammals. Glucose and galactose From breakdown of starch in malting of barley. Glucose and glucose This is a trisaccharide of fructose. Glucose and galactose Beet sugar, cane sugar, glucose and fructose	milk, butter cheeses, yoghurt barley, beers, maltose, grain syrup, malt molasses cane, beet
Polysaccharides (many molecules) cellulose glycogen pectin sea vegetables (agar-agar) starch	(plant fibre) tasteless Animal starch as opposed to plant Useful setting and jellying properties Jelly forming used in place of animal geletine Made up of many glucose molecules in the form of granules. Swell in moist heat becoming more soluble and more digestible. Broken down into maltose, then glucose	all green plant vegetables vegetables, liver, shellfish many fruits, root and green vegetables seeds and roots of many vegetables and grains—including potatoes, parsnip, rice, corn

taining honey at a lower temperature because high temperature can adversely affect the flavour of honey. (Always allow extra baking time.)

HARMONISERS

Barley malt extract
All barley malt extract is made by a sprouting process. The barley is steeped in water to soften it, then germinated and at the moment the germination process has reached its peak the process is stopped by applying heat. This dries the malt and brings out the flavour.

The final product is a malt syrup that contains maltose, dextrins, protein, dextrose and minerals. In some malts you can find the enzyme *diastase*, which helps to convert starch to sugar and thereby aiding in digestion. If you have the malt that contains this enzyme and want to use it for sweetening in baking or cooking, just bring the malt to a boil and hold 2–3 minutes. Cool and use. This will inactivate the enzyme and make it more suitable for cooking and baking.

Maltose
Unlike barley malt extract, maltose is usually made by a fermentation process. Wheat, rice or barley is sprouted then added to freshly cooked rice and set aside at a fairly constant warm temperature. This enables the starch in the rice to ferment into a sugar. Because it is more concentrated than barley malt it is usually sweeter.

Rice syrup
This newly introduced product is a bit difficult to find and may be listed under several names. It is sometimes referred to as Yinnie Syrup or Rice honey. Made from rice, it is fermented in a similar process to maltose. It tends to be a little less sweet, but has the same consistency. Both maltose and rice syrup should be heated in a jar or container before using.

Maple syrup
Tapped from the maple trees of North America and Canada, it takes 200 litres of maple sap to produce four litres of maple syrup. It is a completely natural food which contains calcium, phosphorus, potassium and sodium. When changing over from sugar to another sweetener maple syrup, used in *moderation*, is one of the better sweeteners to use.

Sorghum molasses
Sorghum molasses is a step closer to a wholefood that is both natural and nutritious. It is the boiled down juice of the sorghum plant (related to the maize family) without anything being taken away except water.

Dried fruit purée
By using whole dried fruits and reconstituting them by cooking them in water until a purée is formed, a natural wholesome sweetener can be obtained. However, not every recipe will accept this sweetener, as there is a lot of water present. Adjust liquid content accordingly by decreasing liquid in other ingredients (see page 24).

DISHARMONISERS

Honey
This so-called 'health-food' consists of 75 per cent sugar (mainly fructose and sucrose) and 20 per cent water. Although the structure is slightly different than that which is derived from sugar-cane, it still has the same reaction in the body. Honey, fruit sugar and refined white and brown sugar tend to arrest the secretion of gastric juices and therefore inhibit the stomach from moving naturally.

Molasses
Molasses is a by-product of sugar refining. It contains all the miscellaneous material remaining when sucrose is removed from sugar cane juice. There are many different kinds of molasses available, and all vary in composition. So-called sweet molasses has a fair amount of sugar left in it, whereas 'blackstrap' molasses has less sugar, but tastes stronger. It is a concentrated residue containing minerals such as iron, calcium, zinc, copper and chromium, as well as lead, pesticides and sulphur.

Essentially, molasses, whether it is sulphured or unsulphured, contains many by-products which are not necessarily mentioned on the label. It is the final residue of sugar cane, and considered inferior since it is the least wholesome of the products extracted from that plant. It is far removed from being a wholefood.

Sugar
As far as I'm concerned there is very little to say about sugar that hasn't already been said. It is quite commonly known that sugar offers us nothing in the way of nutrition and does little to raise our energy level. On the contrary it causes fatigue, depression and tooth-decay as well as robbing the body of essential B vitamins and minerals to aid in its digestion (see page 22). So called 'raw' sugar is virtually the same as refined white sugar. Raw sugar is 96 per cent sucrose

and 4 per cent water whereas white sugar is 99 per cent sucrose. You can always find another sweetener to use in place of sugar (see 'Sweetness equivalency chart' page 24).

Corn syrup

Originally made from cornstarch, it is now treated with sulphuric-acid, neutralised with sodium-carbonate and filtered through charred beef bones to give it clarity. Perhaps not the best quality sweetener to use!

Chocolate

Born and raised on chocolate, I found it was very difficult to cure my addiction! It took many years and lots of hard work. Chocolate contains considerable amounts of theobromine, an al-kaloid which is similar to caffeine but has less powerful effects on the nervous system. However, it tends to have a greater effect on the muscles, heart and kidneys. It has been used in medicine in its *pure* form to stimulate the kidneys, relax muscles and rid the body of excessive accumulations of fluid. However, most of the chocolate today is combined with sugar. To replace carob powder for chocolate see page 37.

Cornstarch

Cornstarch is another popular product used by many people today as a thickening agent. It is of no benefit to the system because it is usually treated with sulphur-dioxide. In place of corn-starch try using arrowroot flour or kuzu in equal proportions.

Baking soda and baking powder

These common leavening agents have proved to be somewhat detrimental to many people. Baking soda can cause swelling and inflammation of the stomach and intestines. Baking powders contain aluminum compounds or lime which again can cause the same 'bloated' condition as from baking soda due to excessive sodium intake. Studies now being conducted link up excessive aluminum intake with calcium deficiencies and even brain damage. Other leavening agents such as yeast or eggs can be used in place of baking powder and soda.

Vanilla essence or extract

Vanilla is a natural flavour found in the form of a bean or liquid. Most of the vanilla found in the supermarkets today is artificially produced with chemicals, and boosted with vanillin which is made from a coal derivative. There are two different vanillas available: vanilla essence and vanilla extract. These differ only in the way that they are made.

The essence is made by an extraction method that first soaks the bean in an alcohol base solution, drains off the liquid, adds caramel colouring to it (to stabilise the colour) and results in vanilla essence.

The second process involves the vanilla beans being boiled in water, and then the same colouring is added to the mixture to standardise it. This is known as vanilla extract.

If pure vanilla extract is unavailable, substitute the bean for the liquid, preparing it as follows. Soak the bean until soft in the cooking liquid. Slit the bean vertically when soft and scrape out the inside. Place everything in liquid and simmer for at least 15 minutes. (The longer the soaking or simmering, the more flavour will be added to the liquid. If you do not have the time, you may omit this step, as cooking will also help to bring out the vanilla flavour.) Remove bean and use liquid. If the mixture is to be blended and the bean is soft enough, cut it into small pieces and blend it with the other ingredients. If neither bean nor pure extract is available, substitute grated orange or lemon rind in equal proportions, or to taste.

FLOUR POWER

The most notable difference between the diet of the Western world and that of less highly developed countries concerns fibre. There seems to be a scarcity of unabsorbable fibre in a Western diet. No doubt this has caused the rapid increase in so-called 'degenerative diseases', and some medical authorities and nutritionists have now begun to establish that this decline in health is directly attributable to changes in our eating patterns.

Flour has been an important food since the end of the last ice age, when an enterprising person ground a few grains of wholewheat between two stones and presto, created the first stone-ground wholewheat flour. Today refined white flour has replaced wholewheat and become one of the world's most popular, as well as one of the most destructive foods.

In the beginning of the 20th century 'roller-milling' became the popular way of smashing the wheat between rollers and sifting it through a series of sieves which removed all the bran and germ. The bran and germ are the main repositories of the vitamins and minerals found in wheat. These two portions of the grain account for only 18 per cent of the weight, but contain 75 per cent of the eleven B-vitamins found in wheat, as well as the greatest proportion of trace minerals such as zinc, copper and iodine. Wheat germ (specifically the oil in wheat germ) is also the home of Vitamin E and the essential unsaturated fatty acids.

Up to 80 per cent of the essential nutrients are lost in the milling of flour. This refining process allows the millers to ship flour all over, and store it for months at a time. Enrichment of white flour is now the common treatment to assure the public that they are getting what they need. In actual fact a better solution would be if people decided to use wholewheat flour instead of 'unconsciously' consuming enrichment according to some state formula.

With the current interest in dietary fibre, wholewheat represents a way to get real nutrients back into foods like bread, pasta and cereals. Try using the high-gluten coarser grind for breads, helping the bread rise more and the finer, softer wholewheat flour for cakes, pies and pastries. Other whole flours suitable for natural food cooking and baking are brown rice, soy, maize, millet, oat, buckwheat and rye. Be creative ... try them all and surprise the family with wholesome and inviting creations.

FLOURS

Wheat   Staple grain, always used in bread. Summer and winter wheats have a different gluten and protein content. There is also 'soft wheat'—very fine and used in pastries. Seitan or wheat gluten is a meat substitute made from gluten, which is extracted from wholewheat high protein flour.

Brown rice flour   No gluten. It is used to give a crunchy texture. Never use only rice flour in a bread or pastry recipe.

Barley flour   This has a lot of natural sugar, and is low in gluten. Barley milk, made by squeezing out juice from cooked barley, is good for a sick stomach. It is also good in biscuits and sauces but not so good in bread due to its heaviness. Add just a little in tempura batter.

Buckwheat flour   Very heavy. Try using no more than 1/5th in whatever you are cooking. Good for buckwheat pancakes leavened with egg or yeast.

Millet flour   Good in bread, combined with wheat. It has no gluten and is high in Vitamin A and protein. Millet meal is cracked millet.

Oat flour   High in gluten, sugar, starch, fat and protein. It makes a good creamy sauce, and is good in biscuits and breakfast cereals.

Cornflour (maize)   Good in winter stews and sauces it is the hardest grain to mill. It has no gluten and a low sugar content. A little cornmeal in tempura batter helps to prevent tempura from becoming too oily.

Rye flour   Very heavy and hard to digest. A small amount in bread lends a unique flavour.

Arrowroot   Use occasionally in pastry making and for thickening wok-style vegetables. Egg and arrowroot flour makes a good tempura batter. Make a paste of arrowroot and water to seal bottom pie crusts.

Kuzu   Same as arrowroot in thickening ability, but kuzu can also be used as a medicine.

TIPS FOR THE SALT CONSCIOUS

The Roman author, Pliny once called salt 'foremost among human remedies for disease.' Today, salt (sodium chloride) is the centre of much controversy among natural-food enthusiasts. Some advocate its use whilst others would never touch salt. The more important question is knowing just how much salt our bodies need.

Besides sodium chloride, salt also contains the so-called trace minerals including zinc, manganese and magnesium. Both minerals and sodium chloride aid in the formation of bones and muscles, enable the muscles to function and the nerves to transmit messages, and help to regulate the acid/alkaline balance of the body. Not only do they affect metabolism and digestion of food, but they also maintain the volume and pressure of the circulating blood. Therefore it is critical that we do not exceed the proper proportion of salt for our body so that high blood pressure (hypertension) or the retention of too much liquid can be eliminated. It is also vital in colder weather for salt helps to contract the blood vessels and cells to keep the body warm, and a serious lack of sodium can lead to poor intestinal muscle tone and diarrhoea.

All salt is sea salt, or was at one time. However, the sea salt that is taken from the oceans today is slightly higher in trace minerals such as copper, silicon, calcium and nickel, than rock salt. The major difference is not between the sea salt and the rock salt, but more importantly, between the *refining* methods.

Refined salt is generally subjected to very intensive heat and then flash cooled, whereas sea salt is probably sun-dried. (Lima grey sea salt is sun dried thus containing a maximum amount of minerals.) In addition, refined salt is combined with potassium iodine to 'iodise' it and because of its volatile nature (it oxidises rapidly when exposed to light) dextrose, a simple sugar, is added to stabilise the iodine. This process turns the salt purple, thus a little sodium bicarbonate is mixed in to bleach the colour out. Finally the salt is coated with a compound, such as sodium silico aluminate, to make it free flowing.

Cutting down on salt alone however, which is the major source of sodium for most people, may not alone be the answer. You will have to find out which foods are high and which are low in sodium and recognise that cutting down on sodium intake is not just a case of avoiding salt. If you are a sodium-conscious consumer then you have to become aware of not only the 'salt-free' aspects, but also the other sodium compounds such as sodium citrate, sodium saccharin, monosodium glutamate (MSG), baking soda and baking powder.

We must use common sense when thinking about our needs. Look closely at climate, physical activity, water retention and diet before deciding that you need more or less salt. Be aware of all the needs of your body and be prepared to change when change is necessary.

Seasoning at the table

The necessity for cooking with salt lies in the process of ionising the salt, thus making it more digestible than if you added it to your food at the table. This way, you will feel less 'salty' after your meal with less of a desire to drink huge quantities of liquid.

There are, of course, exceptions to every rule, and one of them involves using shoyu when eating tempura. However, the shoyu should be heated and warm water or vinegar added before using. The use of grated raw radish or ginger to help neutralise the saltiness of the shoyu is advised.

The following is a chart for seasoning at the table.

Salty: Sesame salt or salt plums (umeboshi)
Spicy: Grated daikon, grated ginger or minced spring onions
Sour: Pickles, lemon juice or vinegar
Bitter: Orange or lemon rind
Sweet: Roasted sunflower or unhulled sesame seeds

Guide-lines to follow

1 For families with no infants: $\frac{1}{4}$ teaspoon sea salt to 2–3 cups raw grains. In warmer weather you may want to even reduce this amount, depending upon your activity.
2 For vegetables, the amount of salt varies according to the type of vegetables. A pinch of sea salt plus shoyu or miso at the end of cooking a wok full of green vegetables.
3 For root vegetables, the same rule would follow unless the climate is very cold. Then more salt, time and pressure is necessary.

4 If you are feeding children under three, remove vegetables before adding miso or shoyu.
5 Generally speaking, the need for salt and other tastes depends upon the age, activity, constitution and condition of each person.

SEA VEGETABLES AND VITALITY!

With the exciting and even spectacular leaps that marine science has made in the past few years, we have been given a greater understanding and knowledge of the ocean environment. Sea vegetables offer us an enormous potential food supply and believe it or not, we have been using and eating them most of our lives. They have been wisely disguised by laboratory nomenclature and thus been incorporated into cream cheese, instant puddings, sauces and salad dressings to give them body. Because of their low reactivity with other substances, they are used in cod liver oil and a whole range of beauty aids such as creams, shampoo, toothpaste and lotions.

Sea vegetables are amongst the most ancient forms of life on earth and were probably the first cellular life to exist. There is a long folk history of kelp ointments and liniments for cuts, bruises, sprains and bee stings. The use of alginates increases the rate of healing without inducing a toxic reaction or antigen response in the body. They also do not interfere with popular drugs such as penicillin or sulphur-based drugs. Sodium-alginate which is found most abundantly in agar-agar has been shown to reduce by 50–80 per cent the amount of strontium 90 absorbed by bone tissue. This was reported by L. Jacobs in 'How to Survive A Meltdown', in the *East West Journal*, 1979. It does this by binding with the radioactive substance in the intestines and other areas so that it will eliminate waste. It will also inhibit the body's absorption of cadmium up to seven-eighths the radioactive dosage received. Furthermore, agar-agar has been shown to work like pectin, and bond with toxic metals such as lead successfully carrying them out of the body.

Professor S. Kondo recently undertook a project to find out which regions of Japan sustained people to a ripe old age and how this was achieved. He discovered that the places where people lived longer and looked younger were where sea vegetables were eaten daily. The Japanese believe that if sea vegetables such as wakame, kombu, hijiki and nori are eaten daily, they will be assured of thick glossy hair, a soft, wrinkle-free skin and a clear complexion.

When we compare the composition of sea water with that of our blood it is fairly evident that they are nearly identical. Since a major part consists of minerals it is essential that we take them daily for proper health and vitality. Since we cannot ingest sea water, the next best source is sea vegetables.

One of the most popular misconceptions is that sea vegetables are only eaten in the orient. In fact natives in Ireland, Iceland, Russia, Scandinavia, Scotland, Wales, coastal sections of Europe and the South Pacific Islands all eat sea vegetables almost daily. By weight of edible portions, sea vegetables as a group rank second in containing calcium and phosphorus and first in amounts of magnesium, iron, iodine, and sodium according to D. Wollner and D. Seamens (*East West Journal*, September, 1981).

They also contain 20–30 per cent protein and are among the few complete protein sources in the vegetable kingdom. (Complete protein means that all the essential amino-acids are present, and if any are missing the protein cannot be assimilated.) They also contain Vitamins A, B1, B12, C and E as well as easily digestible carbohydrates called 'futose'.

Because of the minerals and the alkalising effect they have on the blood, sea vegetables are able to purify the blood by eliminating the acidic effects of a modern diet. Most important for vegetarians, is the fact that these vegetables contain Vitamin B12 in particular which supports the proper functioning of the neuro-musculature system, making them one of the only vegetable sources along with soy products, alfalfa, comfrey and spirulina, to contain this important vitamin. Sea vegetables have not only been supportive in giving the body what it needs, but also in proving effective in lessening the effects of cancer, nervous disorders, rheumatism, arthritis, high blood pressure, constipation, asthma, kidney, thyroid and other endocrine system malfunctions. They also help dissolve fat and mucous deposits which usually accumulate from over-indulging in dairy products, meat and rich food.

Sea vegetables can offer a variety of new flavours pleasing even to the most jaded palates. They do not taste salty, and in fact are only between 2–4 per cent salt. They can be used in soups, salads, cooked by themselves or with other vegetables and fish or beans. They shorten the cooking time when used with dried beans or peas. They can even be brewed into tea. Sea vegetables add flavour and a unique taste and texture and provide a balanced offering of nutrients.

DIFFERENT TYPES OF SEA VEGETABLES

Kelp   This versatile sea vegetable can be eaten raw, but in fact is most popular in the form of ground powder. It can be used as a condiment or flavouring in soups, salad, pickles or as an alternative to salt. Try using half the amount of kelp powder in place of salt called for in a standard recipe.

Agar-agar (kanten)   Commonly called agar-agar, it is a gelatin made from a variety of sea vegetables. These are soaked and washed to first take away the sand and sea salt. Then they are simmered overnight and when they begin to melt and the water becomes thick and soupy like, they are pressed under the weight of stones. The liquid that runs off is then pumped into shallow boxes and within one hour the liquid hardens into a gelatin. It is then taken out into the fields and dried during the night. This process is repeated over several days. After about 10 days time, it is dry and only a flaky, brittle celluloid remains.

It can be moulded in a dessert, requiring no eggs or dairy products and is ideal for those on diets because it lends bulk without calories. It also provides appreciable quantities of iron, phosphorus, calcium, and Vitamins A, B1, B6, B12, biotin, C, D and K. Just by dissolving agar-agar in apple juice or vegetable broths, adding slices of fruit or vegetables and simmering several minutes, you can make a refreshing aspic that will set at room temperature in a matter of minutes.

Kombu   This particular sea vegetable belongs to the genus Laminaria which are better known as brown algae. For many hundreds of years, the Japanese have used dishes containing kombu as a protection against high blood pressure. Another appealing quality of kombu is the fact that it aids in the process of weight loss by promoting the balanced absorption and distribution of nutrients. It also helps in much the same way to nourish the skin. Kombu is also reputed to aid digestion, cleanse the colon, relieve anaemia and aid the kidneys.

The most common usage is in the form dashi (broad flat strips) used primarily for soup stock, or placed at the bottom of a pot of rice or vegetables which will give added flavour as well as to stop food from sticking to the bottom. Strips of kombu added to a pot of beans helps them to cook faster and digest more easily.

Nori   In Ireland nori is known as 'sloke' and is served with potatoes and butter. In Scotland the word is 'laver' and the preparation involves boiling, then spreading it on a pan, covered with oatmeal and fried into cakes otherwise known as laver bread. Nori is exceptionally high in Vitamins A, C, B1 and niacin but more importantly, nori decreases cholesterol and aids digestion. The Japanese often use it with fried foods. The sheets can also be used just as they come out of the package or lightly toasted by waving them over an open flame or electric plate, then cut with scissors or crumbled over salads, stews or casseroles.

Wakame   There is a similarity between kombu and wakame. Both are a brown sea vegetable, collected in cold waters and in the spring it is sold fresh when they are tenderest. The rest of the year it can only be found dried. Wakame softens quite quickly when soaked (2–3 minutes) and does not require any special treatment. It gives soup a wonderful flavour and will enhance any salad. It can be used as a condiment by just baking it *without* soaking. A wonderful source of protein and minerals, wakame can be interchanged with kombu for soup stock anytime.

Arame   Although this particular sea vegetable takes a bit of getting used to, once eaten it may become your favourite. It can be eaten alone, or with other vegetables, in soups, salads or with grains. One quarter cup dried is enough to yield 1 cup soaked. Because of its unusual colour it makes a great conversation piece when served up at a dinner party.

THE STORY OF TEA

The first recognisable definition of tea appeared in 350 A.D. in a Chinese dictionary written by the celebrated scholar, Kuo P'o. The book defines tea as 'a beverage made from leaves by boiling.' The Chinese believed that tea was a gift bestowed by heaven and that it was a beneficial drink because it quenched the thirst, was comforting and soothing and provided stimulation. Not only was it to be indulged at every meal, but it also ranked highly amongst medicine as influencing health and longevity.

The English first stumbled upon tea drinking in the 15th century, and shortly thereafter were able to monopolise the tea trade from China. It was highly promoted at home as well as abroad and soon became known as the most popular non-alcoholic drink in England. Up until 1839 England was able to obtain tea from China, but when war broke out they lost their monopoly of the Chinese trade and had to look elsewhere to find tea. By finding wild tea bushes and transplanting Chinese bushes England soon established huge plantations in India, Ceylon and Indonesia.

Like other caffeinated drinks, tea is mostly considered a major cause of high blood pressure and excitability of the nervous system and is in some circles considered a possible carci-

Nutritional value of sea vegetables

Name	Nutrients (%)				Minerals (mg/100 g)						
	Fibre	Protein	Fat	Carbo.	Ca	I	Fe	Mg	Ph	K	Na
Agar			0.3	16.3	567	0.2	6.3		22		
Dulse	1.2	20.0–30.0	3.2	44.2	296	8.0	150.0	220	267	8060	2100
Hijiki		5.6	0.8	29.8	1400		30.0		56		
Irish moss			3.2		885		8.9		157	2844	2900
Kelp	3.0		1.1–1.8	51.9	1093	150.0	100.0	760	240	5273	3000
Kombu		7.5	1.1	51.9	800	76.2			150		
Nori-green		34.2	0.6	40.5	470		23.0		580		
-red		34.2	0.7	40.5	470		23.0		580		
Wakame	3.6	12.7	1.5	47.8	1300	7.9			260		1100
Spinach	0.6	3.2	0.3	4.3	93	0.036	3.1	88	51	470	

Name	Vitamins (mg/100 g)					
	A*	B_1	B_2	B_5	B_{12}	C
Agar						
Dulse		0.63	0.50	1.69		24–49
Hijiki	555	0.01	0.02	4.0		
Irish moss						
Kelp		0.09	0.33	5.7	0.5–1.0	13
Kombu	430	0.08	0.32	1.8	0.5–1.0	11
Nori-green	960	0.06	0.03	8.0	0.7	10
-red	6000–11000	0.12–0.25	0.20–1.24	2.0–10.0	0.7	200
Wakame	140	0.01	0.02	10.0	0.6	15
Spinach	8100	0.10	0.20	0.6		51

*Vitamin A is given in international units.

Krochmal, Connie and Arnold, *A Naturalist's Guide to Cooking with Wild Plants*; Food Heritage Health Research, *Composition and Facts About Foods*; Shufu no Tomo Sha, *Kaiso Ryori*: 1975; Muramoto Naboru, *Healing Ourselves*; US Department of Agriculture, *Composition of Foods*.

nogen. Because of the change in our lifestyles and dietary habits the effects of tea have been greatly altered. Tea was originally consumed to lightly stimulate the body from the effects of the cold, and natural lifestyles that encumbered many. Compared to the lifestyle of today, where our pace is much faster, the quickening effect of tea, rather than adding a counterpoint to our lives, contributes to the overload. Perhaps we should look more closely at the possible side effects that tea has in combination with other harmful foods, poor eating habits and bodily abuse.

Both black and green tea are made from the same plant. The difference is how the leaf is treated after it has been picked: leaves for black tea are fermented and leaves for green tea are dried in the sun or drying rooms. Caffeine is the primary ingredient in these teas. The effect of it is felt on the central nervous system, producing increased mental activity, heightened sensory interpretation and quicker thoughts. Caffeine also dominates the activity of the heart and the kidneys. It raises blood pressure and accelerates the pulse and acts as a diuretic.

Tannin, the counterpart of tea is the astringent, giving it its pungency and colour. It acts as a free acid, coagulating protein, and possibly disrupting digestion and the flow of digestive juices.

Black tea
It takes roughly three years for a tea bush to produce leaves suitable for harvest. Thereafter each shrub is productive for 25–30 years.

Choice tea is made from the two leaves nearest the bud at the very end of each stem.

Medium grade is made from the bud and first three leaves.

Coarse tea includes the fourth and fifth leaves.

The processing of black tea is done in five steps: withering, rolling, roll-breaking, fermenting and firing. Withering is drying the leaves; rolling breaks open the cells of the withered leaves and frees the concentrated juices and enzymes; roll-breaking mechanically beats the leaves to get rid of the clumps that have formed; fermenting is achieved by supplying hot air between 25–30°C for a period of between $1\frac{1}{2}$ to $4\frac{1}{2}$ hours, which determines aroma, flavour and astringency. Then the leaves are fired killing the fermenting enzymes. Black tea is then sorted according to leaf size. Orange Pekoe, Pekoe and Souchong are leaf grades. Flowery Orange Pekoe and Orange-Pekoe are rated top class and Souchong is at the bottom.

Green tea
Green tea is unfermented and the stages of processing differ slightly from that of black tea. Steaming is the first step and the major consideration behind green tea production is the retaining of the natural flavour of tea. Steaming immediately after picking destroys enzymes and prevents fermentation. Then rolling is begun where moisture is removed from the leaves and then the leaves are fired. Green tea is graded according to the age and quality of the leaf.

Oolong tea
Oolong tea combines the best qualities of green and black tea, is slightly withered, fermented, fired, rolled, refermented and refired. Most of the Oolong tea comes from Taiwan.

Twig tea (kukicha or bancha)
Both of these teas are made from the twigs of the tea plant and are therefore not legally classified as a tea because they lack the leaves. These particular teas are very low in tannin and caffeine and work as a buffer solution to the stomach, neutralising over-acidic or alkaline conditions.

Herbal teas
In recent years, many teas made from herbs and flowers have been appearing alongside caffeinated refreshments. In general they strengthen the concept that food and medicine can be one. One last reminder: all teas should be kept in an air-tight container, in a relatively dark place and should be used judiciously to invigorate oneself.

FOOD ADDITIVES

Most of what we buy in the food section of supermarkets today seems to be filled with additives: some natural and some synthetic. Natural additives are basically harmless and are mostly used for colourings: anatto (used in some margarines and butter), the spice turmeric (which adds yellow colour to curry powder) and carotene (a vegetable colouring derived from carrots and other vegetables from which the body makes Vitamin A). Some, however, are not so safe and if used in excess may prove to be harmful.

There are many people who say that if additives are allowed to be used in certain foods, they must be safe because they have been passed by government health authorities. However, we are beginning to see more and more evidence that food regulatory authorities change their minds on a number of occasions and ban certain additives that were previously considered safe.

Synthetic additive manufacture is now a thriving business. In a single year, sales of food additives in five countries of Western Europe, totalled over $200 million. The eight largest selling groups are thickeners, flavours, flavour enhancers (like monosodium glutamate), stabilisers, emulsifiers, food acids, colours, preservatives, antioxidants and sweeteners.

The common feature of additives is that they possess a property that enables the food to last longer on the shelves, look more attractive or feel different in the mouth. Some modern food products couldn't exist without additives. For example, low calories soft drinks would not be possible without an artificial sweetener, and so called 'fast' takeaway foods, which are very often kept in a warm environment for hours, can play host to certain types of bacteria.

Convenient additives make life easier and more profitable for the food business but aren't necessarily essential to the existence of the product. If you cook a pie at home would you think of adding a preservative to it? Of course not. So, preservatives aren't necessary for the pie, they are only necessary for the description detailing the time a food can be stored and still remain saleable and eatable. The longer a wholesaler can store the food, the larger the batches they can make and the bigger and fewer the loads to be delivered. The longer the food can be stored in a retail outlet the more chances there are of selling it. Also, the longer the consumer can keep it fresh at home the less likelihood of complaints of food 'going off'.

Sources in the food industry argue that the additives in food benefit the consumer by making food cheaper to distribute and produce, and by reducing wastage. In fact, the industry claims that these additives keep prices down. However, this does not appear to be the case. On the contrary, food prices keep rising in almost direct proportion to increased additives.

Flavourings: These are used to make a food product more appealing to our noses and taste buds than it would otherwise be.

Colourings: These are used to make food look better than it really is. They are not only used to intensify the existing colour of a food, but to restore colouring lost through food refining and processing for example, as with brown sugar. Colouring is also added to foods to make them look as if they contain more of a certain ingredient thereby cutting down the cost of raw materials, as is the case with soy sauce using caramel colouring.

Most children today don't know the difference between 'real orange juice' and the drink made from frozen concentrate. When given true orange juice they prefer the taste of orange juice made from frozen concentrate saying the freshly squeezed kind 'doesn't taste like real orange juice'.

Other cosmetic additives alter the look or texture of food. For example, liquid paraffin on dried fruit makes the fruit look moist and attractive.

There will never be a time when you can say, 'I'm never going to eat anything containing an additive again', unless you are a fanatic or a hermit. The answer lies in a compromise, where you choose the brands with the least amount of additives or preferably, none at all. Just think about all the foods you can enjoy that *are* additive free. Remember that less than 100 years ago we did quite nicely without additive-laden foods. Try to eat more meals at home and when dining out make sure the food is fresh, and additive free, because top-class cooking starts with the essential raw ingredients utilising no short cuts. If others can, why can't you?

Monosodium glutamate,[*] a flavour intensifier generally known by its Chinese or Japanese brand name *Vetsin* (a mixture also containing lactose and salt). 'Accent or Aji-no-moto, is a highly refined, white crystalline powder that differs in structure from natural glutamic acid. When used in more than very small quantities, it is well known to produce in some people the "Chinese restaurant syndrome" characterised by headaches, burning sensations, a feeling of pressure in the chest, and other discomforting symptoms. It is produced by hydrolysis of molasses to glucose from tapioca, cornstarch, potato starch, etc. A committee of scientists selected by the US Food and Drug Administration advises that MSG should not be given to infants under 12 months of age. United States baby and food manufacturers no longer use MSG in their products'. I strictly avoid the use of this and other so called 'flavour enhancers'.

---

[*] Excerpt taken from *The Book of Tempeh* by Shurtleff and Aoyagi, Harper and Row, New York, Hagerstown, San Francisco, London 1979.

KITCHEN HELPERS

SETTING UP YOUR KITCHEN

Just because you are considering a change in your eating habits it doesn't mean that you have to abandon your entire kitchen and start all over again. Today there are so many different cooking utensils varying in style and sophistication that the simple pot has been transformed into a complex utensil. Differing in size, shape, raw material and design, each is widely adaptable to any style of cooking and eating.

Here are some easy tips to keep in mind when purchasing cookware:

1 Make sure that the pot is light enough for you to handle but heavy enough to conduct heat evenly. Light-weight pots tend to warp easily and pots that are too heavy cannot be handled properly.
2 Choose pots with sloping sides instead of perpendicular ones so that stirring does not become awkward.
3 Covers should fit very tightly with no gaps for steam to escape.
4 Make sure that the material is suitable for your purposes. The materials most widely used today in cookware are aluminium, stainless steel, cast iron, porcelain, enamel, copper, glass and clay. Each one has its advantages as well as disadvantages.

COOKWARE

Metal pots are either drawn, forged or cast. Drawn utensils are said to be superior to cast because these utensils hold their shape better and are less likely to form hot spots which cause food to stick. Forged pots and pans are made by hammering a metal into the desired shape. This method is the most primitive, having been in use for hundreds of years. Cast pots are made by pouring molten metal into a mould. After the metal has set the irregularities are ground away and the pot is polished. Cast metals have a tendency to form tiny holes in the surface of the pot when certain foods react with the metal. This is known as pitting.

Aluminium
At the end of World War II, factories which had been producing aluminium components for the aircraft industry were able to make cheap aluminium pans, kettles and other kitchen equipment. Most people thought that these utensils were better because they were lighter to handle and less expensive, as well as easier to clean. Today, probably 90 per cent of all households cook their food and boil their coffee or tea in aluminium ware.

Aluminium is very durable, and an excellent heat conductor providing it is not spun too thin. Because it is found abundantly in the earth this makes it one of the most inexpensive materials for cooking with. You can purchase either cast or drawn aluminium pans. Cast aluminium is more expensive and pits more easily, but is heavier and more durable. The drawn utensils are thin, and they dent, burn and develop hot spots very easily.

When food is made in a factory or cooked or heated at home using aluminium ware or machinery made from aluminium, then the agitation produced by the heating process causes aluminium to be formed, which is then distributed throughout the food often entering the system. Many people believe that extensive use of aluminium cookware will eventually cause diseases of the intestines and stomach such as chronic indigestion, which will disappear once aluminium cooking utensils are abandoned. Further commentary states that if you boil water in an aluminium pot and pour it into a glass jar, aluminium particles will be visibly floating (aluminium hydroxide) in the water. These particles are said to enter the food and are absorbed by the body. Aluminium can discolour certain foods and give others an unpleasant metallic taste.

Many different parts of the body can be affected by the prolonged use of aluminium in cooking, or eating aluminium-contaminated foods. H. Tomlinson, in his book, *Aluminium Utensils and Disease* describes the following possible results: duodenal ulcers, appendicitis, diarrhoea, constipation as well as other intestinal disorders. It is possible to get aluminium contamination not only from cooking utensils, but from food as well, such as aluminium-contaminated salt, processed breakfast foods, some cakes, pastries, jams, self-raising flours, baking powders containing *alum*, flavourings, colouring-agents, sauces, pickles, meat, milk and other beverages.

Stainless steel
Stainless steel is produced by removing a percentage of carbon from carbon steel and adding chromium and nickel. As the result, an invisible oxide forms on the surface of the pot, protecting it. Some people say that if this oxide is scoured only once with an abrasive, small amounts of highly toxic metallic elements dissolve afterwards into every meal cooked. Tests made in the US have discovered small amounts of chromium and nickel in food cooked in a well-scoured stainless steel pot.

Stainless steel is also the poorest conductor of heat of all the metals used in cookware. It distributes heat unevenly and doesn't retain it well. To balance this deficiency, the manufacturers make the core with a more conductive metal such as copper, carbon steel, cast iron or aluminium. The thicker, the better for pressure cookers and utility pots; thinner stainless steel pots are best for noodles and soups.

On the whole, stainless steel is much better than aluminium, as it will not dent under normal conditions or produce tarty food. It should be used over a medium heat because high temperatures can cause it to warp.

Cast iron

Cast iron pots and pans have been made since the 11th century B.C. Ideal for long, slow, cooking, and light sautéeing, cast iron is virtually indestructable. It is one of the oldest materials used in cookware, is dark in colour, absorbs heat well and conducts and holds the heat evenly. However, avoid the use of cast iron for deep-frying, because it heats up slowly and once hot, holds heat in the pan, and thus can cause unnecessary burning. Many professional cooks say that cast iron brings out the best flavour in food. I agree.

It is best not to cook acidic foods such as tomatoes, wine, vinegar and fruit juices in cast iron because a chemical reaction will darken the colour of the food and affect its flavour. Taking food out immediately from cast iron after cooking will prevent rusting and protect the layer of seasoning.

How to season cast iron cookware:

To remove the finish (lacquer) before using:
1 Gently wash the pot with soap and water.
2 Dry and then coat the pot with oil using a soft cloth on both the inner and outer surfaces.
3 Place 2–3 tablespoons of oil in pan, and heat to thin out the oil.
4 Discard, sprinkle salt down and place in a 180°C oven for 2–3 hours.

Repeat step **3**, adding a few cups of sliced onion. Sauté till black. Wash, heat and oil.

To clean cast iron simply wipe off food, wash gently and dry on a low flame. Coat with oil when hot. Keep uncovered and well oiled at all times to prevent rusting. If food sticks scrub it thoroughly and then heat and oil.

Enamelled Cast Iron

This popular coating is used for cast iron, stainless steel and aluminium. A form of glass, it provides a non-porous cooking surface and will not rust. If it is subjected to high heat with or without food or liquid in it, it may crack or chip.

To protect enamel use only wooden utensils, low heat and careful scouring. Metal utensils can scratch and chip enamel. When staining occurs, an occasional washing with baking soda will do the job. Heavy-duty enamel pots and pans are usually imported from Europe, however prices vary according to the type of base metal used and the number of layers and degree of thickness of the porcelain coatings. These are best used for boiling, steaming and baking.

Because it holds heat, dispersing it gently thus saving fuel, it is one of the best cooking utensils to use.

Before using for the first time, wash it thoroughly. Then pour in a little cooking oil and heat until it has all evaporated. Wipe the inside with a cloth or kitchen paper.

After use   Enamelled cast iron is very easy to clean. Cool it down before washing. Soak in warm water if the food has stuck and if the pan becomes stained, boil a weak solution of bleach in it.

Carbon steel

Generally known as iron, it is most commonly fused with carbon and sometimes other elements. Most often one finds knives, woks, frying pans, crepe pans and pots made from carbon steel. Because it is rather thin, it requires constant attention over heat and warps easily at high temperatures. Woks made from carbon steel are best for quick stir-frying and tempura because they have the ability to heat up and cool down quickly, thus assuring light, crisp cooking.

Preparing a wok for use

Most of the woks around today are the rolled steel variety which have a tendency to rust. In order to stop this problem from occuring the manufacturers give it a coating of oil. Before using the wok, it is a good idea to take the following measures:

Fill wok with water. Add 2 tablespoons bicarbonate of soda and boil for 15 minutes. This softens the coating and it can be scrubbed off with a fine scourer. If not successful, then repeat instructions.

To season woks

Rinse and dry wok. Place over a gentle heat and when the metal heats up, wipe over the entire surface with a wad of absorbent kitchen paper dipped in oil. Repeat a number of times with fresh paper and oil until the wok begins to change colour. At first the paper will come away looking a rusty brown but after a few times the paper will remain clear. Cool and use.

Earthenware (sand-pot)

Usually made of clay and sand, it is known in Chinese cooking as the sand-pot. Light in colour on the outside, the inside usually has a dark brown glaze with a matching cover. This particular pot is found in Chinese shops and comes in two or three different sizes and shapes. It prevents dissipation of precious liquid during the cooking and retains heat when on the table. Because the pot is very fragile, it should not be heated over intense heat suddenly or without liquid.

Method   First sauté ingredients (if called for) in a wok or skillet and then transfer them to the sand-pot for long simmering. The bottom may crack over the years so buy one with wire around the pot to keep intact. As long as the glazed lining inside the pot is not cracked, it is still usable. Use a flame spreader for protection while simmering. To season before using, soak in water 24 hours, dry and oil outside.

Tin

A very soft metal, tin is usually used to line carbon steel or copper cookware. Being so soft and thin it is best to use over a low heat to prevent surface bubbles which can expose the base metal. Use a great deal of care with cleaning: a mild soap or baking soda is ideal, and if food sticks, soak overnight for best results. If you scour this will remove the tin and it will have to be re-tinned eventually.

Pottery (Stoneware, porcelain, china, terra-cotta, earthenware)

Before purchasing any pottery for cooking or baking, one must be sure that it is intended for use as cookware. The heavy lead glaze used on some pottery is poisonous. The best cooking vessels have an inside glaze and an unglazed outside surface for maximum heat absorption; however, a metal trivet is essential for stove top use, and all unglazed pots must be seasoned.

To season   If the pot is unglazed it should be soaked for 30 minutes before using. After adding food, place in cold oven, and then heat oven to 200°C. If you like garlic-flavoured food, rub the unfinished pot with a clove of garlic after soaking. It is best not to use soap or detergent on unglazed clay pots. Soak in warm water briefly and then scrub with a vegetable brush.

Non-stick surfaces

With the advancement of technology, science has finally invented the non-stick utensil that needs no oil. It is lined with a heat-resistant material that produces a protective coating. This type of cookware seems the least natural and desirable from a natural foods viewpoint.

Pressure cookers

I don't know what I would do without my pressure cookers. They save time, fuel and energy, and are essential for cooking easily digestible grains and beans. Like many women today, I run a business as well as keep a home and time is precious. It is wonderful to produce a full meal in a matter of minutes, not hours.

Most people are looking for appetising food at a price they can afford, which is easy to cook, quick to prepare and nutritious to eat. Over the years, scientific experiments have been carried out on the results of pressure cooking and it has been found that the food is not only delicious, but retains the maximum amount of mineral salts and vitamins.

The basic principle behind pressure cooking is quite simple. At sealevel water boils at 100°C. No matter how much heat is applied it will not reach a higher temperature. However, with contained heating as in a pressure cooker, the water temperature rises to 120°C at six kilos of pressure which is the maximum pressure for home cooking.

The ingredients and liquid in which they are cooked are enclosed in a steam-proof vessel which means that the steam which normally escapes into the air from an ordinary pan is controlled and only allowed to escape under pressure. As you seal in steam, you build up a higher pressure, which in turn produces a higher boiling point inside the cooker. This is how foods are cooked faster and more efficiently.

Method   Before using a pressure cooker make sure that the valve is not clogged and that there is no food stuck on the ring or under the rim or rubber. Do not fill more than two-thirds full with solids (because overloading can cause clogging and bubbling over from the pressure gauge), or more than half full with liquids. Always follow the instructions given by the manufacturer regarding the particular model. There should be an instruction booklet provided.

BASIC GUIDE TO SETTING UP YOUR KITCHEN

The following is a basic guide to necessary cookware and their uses.

Cookware	Useful for
2 litre saucepan with cover (enamel, stoneware or stainless steel)	heating small quantities of leftovers, boiling water or cooking sauces
4 litre saucepan with cover (enamel, stoneware, stainless steel or ceramic)	cooking sauces, vegetables, soups or boiling grains and noodles
6 litre saucepan with cover (cast iron or enamel)	slow cooking of stews, soups beans and vegetables

Cookware	Useful for	Cookware	Useful for
5–7 litre pressure cooker (enamel or stainless steel)	quick cooking	blender (electric)	creating creamy drinks, soups, sauces and dips
wok with stand (carbon steel)	stir-frying, tempura and steaming	food processor	grating, chopping, slicing, shredding, juicing, mixing, creaming and puréeing
skillet, medium size (cast iron)	frying vegetables, grains, beans, crêpés, roasting flours, seeds, frying fish and omelets	steamers (bamboo for wok*)	vegetables and fish or dumplings
large skillet (cast iron or steel)	use as above		
medium size sand-pot (Chinese) or stoneware (Japanese)	for rich stews or boiling grain and beans		
suribachi	Japanese mortar and pestle set. Ideal for grinding nuts and seeds, or mashing beans for spreads		

*Bamboo steamers are preferable as excess steam does not gather on the inside of the lid and fall back on the food, spotting them with moisture.

SUBSTITUTION AND EQUIVALENCY CHART

1 tablespoon miso (soy bean paste) $= \frac{1}{2}$ teaspoon sea salt
2 tablespoons shoyu (natural soy sauce) $=$ 1 tablespoon miso or $\frac{1}{2}$ teaspoon sea salt
1 tablespoon arrowroot $=$ 2 teaspoons kuzu
1 tablespoon mashed salted plums (umeboshi) $=$ 1 tablespoon chopped capers and $\frac{1}{2}$ teaspoon sea salt
1 tablespoon salted fermented black beans $= 1\frac{1}{2}$ tablespoons chopped olives
1 tablespoon brown rice vinegar $=$ 2 teaspoons lemon juice
$\frac{1}{4}$ teaspoon dried herbs $=$ 2 tablespoons fresh herbs
1 teaspoon concentrated garlic $=$ 2 cloves
1 bar agar-agar (kanten) $=$ 4 tablespoons agar-agar flakes
1 bar agar-agar $= 3\frac{1}{2}$ cups water
4 tablespoons darker brownish agar-agar flakes $=$ 4 cups water
4 tablespoons darker brownish agar-agar flakes $=$ 3 cups for purées or soy milk
1 teaspoon sea salt $= \frac{1}{2}$ teaspoon dried kelp powder
$\frac{1}{2}$ cup maple syrup $= \frac{1}{2}$ cup honey
$\frac{1}{2}$ cup maple syrup $= 1\frac{1}{4}$ cups barley malt, rice syrup or maltose
4 teaspoons dry yeast $=$ 30 g fresh yeast
30 g fresh yeast $=$ 15 g dried
1 cup carob powder $= 1\frac{1}{2}$ cups cocoa
$\frac{3}{4}$ tablespoon carob $=$ 1 square chocolate
1 teaspoon vanilla $= \frac{1}{2}$ teaspoon rose water
1 tablespoon mirin (cooking wine) $=$ 1 tablespoon white wine or dry sherry
$2\frac{1}{2}$ teaspoons cinnamon $=$ 1 cinnamon stick
1 tablespoon shoyu $=$ 1 tablespoon wheat-free shoyu (tamari)
1 cup wholewheat flour $=$ 1 cup ground nuts*

Equivalency measures
1 cup peanut butter $=$ 315 g
1 cup tahini $=$ 250 g**
1 cup nutmilk $=$ 1 cup hot water and $2\frac{1}{2}$ tablespoons any nut butter
4 cups chopped spinach or other leafy greens $= \frac{1}{2}$ bunch
$1\frac{1}{2}$ tablespoons lemon juice $= \frac{1}{2}$ medium size lemon
1 teaspoon dried basil and $1\frac{1}{2}$ tablespoons fresh parsley $=$ 2 tablespoons chopped fresh basil.

*To add lightness to cakes and biscuits when the amount of leavening is very little, roast and grind nuts or seeds into a meal. Substitute 1 cup ground nuts or seeds for one cup flour. It must be used in *conjunction* with wholewheat flour.
**When using tahini in recipes it may be necessary to decrease the liquid content of the recipe by $\frac{1}{4}$ cup or add a few more tablespoons of dry ingredients (carob, spices or crushed nuts) to absorb the excess liquid produced by the tahini.

WHY COOK?

In Australia I have found that there is a greater trend towards eating raw rather than cooked foods. This applies mainly to those people who, for one reason or another have decided to reduce their animal food consumption along with sugar, refined and processed foods. If we look at these people carefully, we can see a general pattern in their overall eating habits from the past. Because of an over-consumption of animals salts, an attraction to raw fruits and vegetables which helps move animal salts and excess fats (accumulated over a period of many years) out of the system is prevalent. A diet of this kind can be most welcomed by over-burdened systems. However, a word of caution—after the initial cleansing period a *change* is inevitable. Listen to your body and go with the changes.

Adaptability is the key and, just like the weather which changes from one season to another, we also must change in accordance with nature. If we want to enjoy warmth and comfort in cold weather, then we must adapt our cooking methods to provide warming foods to help us face the cold winters, and likewise, if we want to remain cool in summer then cooling foods, like salads and lightly cooked food should be consumed.

Cooking not only helps us make this transition, but also aids in the digestion of some foods. According to Dr Rudolph Ballentine in his book, *Diet and Nutrition*, 'When plant foods are cooked, the heat causes the starch inside the cell to swell. This ruptures the tough cellulose wall of the plant cell which "locks in" the nutrients, liberating the cell's contents so that they become accessible to the digestive process.'

During bread making, the conditions required for leavening—warmth and moisture—activate the enzyme, phytase which breaks up phytic acid compounds (phosphorus) and gives the body the ability to handle it. Otherwise, minerals like calcium, zinc and iron would be locked up in the intestines. So, good sour dough bread should become a staple item in every household concerned with 'getting enough' in their foods.

Dorothy C. Walker in her book, *Off the Stove* stated that, 'There is substantial evidence to indicate that the brief cooking (steaming) of sprouted legumes destroys an enzyme which, in raw legume sprouts, interferes with the activity of trypsin, an enzyme produced in the pancreas to split protein . . .' Some nutrients which are found in raw food, such as niacin and tryptoph in cornmeal, are freed when food is cooked.

It basically takes less time and energy to digest cooked foods, so we can have more energy to perform other activities. However, the best rule to follow is a balanced blend of both raw and cooked foods, using the seasons as your guide and listening to your body when change is needed.

It is by the means of food that man's body is sustained and influenced to determine one's different directions in life. Cooking therefore, is a very important skill for men as well as women, because it allows one to blend colour, shape, texture and smell into one harmonious flow which nourishes and sustains one throughout our daily life.

It's just a matter of choosing your method: grilling, sautéeing, poaching, frying, braising, steaming, boiling, pressure cooking, blanching or baking. Cooking means the transition of food from the raw to the cooked state, a phenomenon which changes its properties and outward appearance—colour, texture, flavour—releasing a surge of pleasant aromas to stir and whet the appetite.

CUTTING TECHNIQUES

When you are cutting your vegetables, try to think of the knife as being a part of your hand and then the result of the cutting will be a part of your meal. It just takes practice and perseverence to become quicker and more adept with your technique. Try to remember that each vegetable is quite unique in its shape, design and function. By choosing to cut one way or another you will directly affect how that vegetable relates to you and to those whom you are sharing it with.

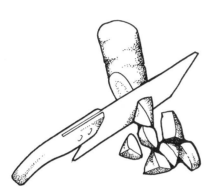

Irregular
A nice and different technique for long time stews, soups or casseroles. Make a cut on the diagonal, then turn 180° and make a diagonal cut in the same direction. Continue.

Diagonal slicing
Slice them on the diagonal so that each piece has part of the top and bottom as well as part of the inside and outside of the vegetable.

Matchsticks or Julienne
Cut the vegetables first on the diagonal, then pile them up *almost* on each other (like a fan effect) and cut lengthwise into thin strips.

Half moon
Cut the vegetable in half lengthwise. Then cut across as thick as necessary for each individual dish.

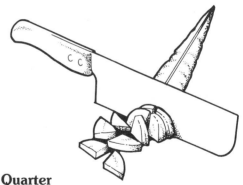

Quarter
Cut the vegetable in half lengthwise, then in half again lengthwise. Then cut across.

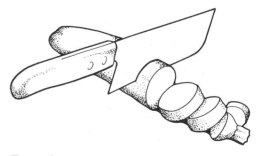

Rounds
This technique is simply cutting straight across the vegetable as thick or as thin as necessary. (The thicker the cut, the longer the cooking.)

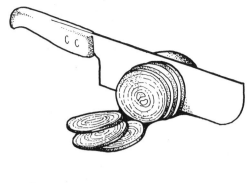

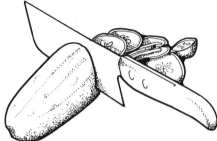

Thin slices

Good for round vegetables (onions, turnips, beets, etc). Cut lengthwise (vertically) then place each piece cut side down on cutting surface and slice vertically again as thick or as thin as you like.

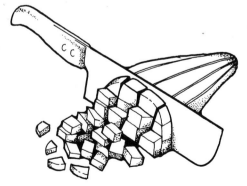

Dicing or mincing

For round vegetables, especially onions first cut the vegetable in half lengthwise. Then cutting towards the root thinly slice leaving the root intact. Then go the opposite way lengthwise as thick or as thin as you like. Finally chop across.

Decorative cutting techniques:

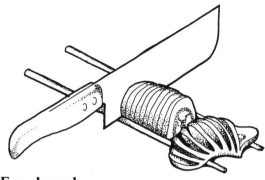

Fan shaped

Place down two chopsticks. Place cucumber inbetween and slice. Soak in ice water to open.

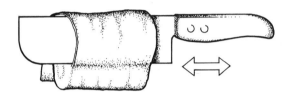

Carrot curls

Cut a 6 cm section from a carrot and peel it. Using a vegetable knife, peel a thin sheet from the carrot, turning the carrot into the blade, and gently exerting a sawing motion. Cut the sheet on the diagonal into $\frac{3}{4}$ cm wide strips. Place strips in ice water. *Not for cooking, strictly for decoration.*

COOKING METHODS

Stir-frying
This word, or technique, usually means to lightly fry vegetables in oil, over a high heat. If the vegetables all have a chance to come in contact with the oil at the bottom of the pan, the flavour is much sweeter. If the vegetables are piled up, the ones on top are just steaming.

1 Heat wok or skillet, then add several tablespoons of oil.
2 Add one vegetable at a time, starting with those that have the strongest smell, e.g. garlic, ginger, onions etc.
3 Move them quickly in the pan, coating each vegetable with oil to seal in the flavour and Vitamin C.
4 Move each vegetable aside so the next one comes in contact with oil at the bottom of skillet.
5 Add salt and shoyu at the end of cooking (if using leafy greens), otherwise the juices are released from the vegetable too soon and they will not be crisp.

Boiling
1 Salt the water or stock and bring to the boil. This is done to retain the flavour and nutrients in the vegetables.
2 Add the vegetables, cover the pot and bring the liquid and vegetables to the boil.
3 Turn the heat down and simmer until the vegetables are tender.

Boiling is not usually the best way of cooking unless the cooking water is used. *To use broth:* Thicken it with arrowroot and add shoyu to taste. Serve it as a sauce with the vegetables or utilise it as soup stock. This method of cooking can be used for any season.

Simmering
This is a method of cooking on a low heat where the vegetables are not completely covered in liquid. Bring liquid and vegetables to the boil. Lower heat, cover and simmer until tender.

Steaming
Basically a summer or spring method, food is placed in a steamer above liquid in a covered pot. The steaming liquid can be water, stock, vegetable juices or old soup. Herbs can be added to the water allowing flavour to permeate through to the steaming food. Sometimes fish or poultry can be placed in the bottom steamer and additional steamers added with the vegetables placed on top. (Always lay spinach or cabbage leaves down in steamer before placing

fish or poultry on top.) The steamer should ideally be made of bamboo, for metal can sometimes alter the taste of the food.

When steaming it is advisable to consider the following:

1 Water very often condenses on the underside of the lid causing water to drip down onto the food being steamed. To avoid this make a cloth 'cap' for your lid so that it can absorb the excess moisture that collects. Using a towel or piece of cheesecloth several centimetres larger than your lid, sew a hem around the cloth leaving four corners open. Insert elastic through this hem and tie the ends together. Place this cap over the underside of your lid. Keep very tight.
2 Secondly, if you steam on a plate which fits very snugly into the steamer, it can be difficult to fish out the hot dish. If you make a sling from a narrow strip of cloth (which is long enough to extend around the lid as well), you can place the cloth beneath your plate *before* steaming. Then, after placing the lid on the steamer, fold the ends of the cloth over the top of your lid. Secure with pin. When ready remove the lid and lift out your hot plate with the cloth.

Deep-frying
Deep-frying is done without a batter for foods like potatoes, sea vegetables, vegetable-burgers, pumpkin, sweet potatoes and yams.

Tempura (see also page 144–145)
On a cold winter's night, one of the nicest ways to warm the body is to serve tempura. Vegetables and fish can be greatly enhanced when coated with a batter and deep-fried in oil.

1 Use 30 per cent sesame oil and 70 per cent safflower or corn oil (or all safflower).
2 Fill a wok or deep fryer with oil to a depth of at least 8 cm and heat to a temperature of 180°C.
3 To test if the oil is hot enough, drop in a small amount of batter or breadcrumbs. If it falls to the bottom of the pan the oil is too cold and the tempura will be oily. If it rises faster than it goes down, the oil is too hot; if it goes down at the same speed as it came up then it is ready. When you add several pieces of vegetables or fish to the oil the temperature will fall; so each time you take out a piece of finished tempura add another *immediately.*
4 After using oil, cool and strain through muslin. Place in refrigerator.

There are many myths about deep-fried food being harmful to the system. If one uses unrefined sesame or safflower oil (which have high smoking points), one does not burn the oil, uses a dip made with shoyu (containing natural lecithin which aids in the digestion of oils), and grated radish or ginger, then there should be no harmful effects to the system.

Baking

Baking is a popular method to prepare winter-time food. Vegetables or grains can be popped into the oven and left for several hours, baking, on a low heat. Baking breads, cakes, pies and biscuits can warm a cold kitchen on any winter day.

Pressure cooking

Best to use when cooking grains and beans together, soups, stocks, fish, poultry, game, sauces, custards, cakes, puddings, cereals, and pasta.
All at 7 kg pressure:

pasta	5–6 minutes
porridge	15–20 minutes
vegetables	3–4 minutes (thinly cut)
sauce	8 minutes
chicken	5 minutes per 450 g
game	5 minutes per 450 g
fish	8–10 minutes per 450 g
vegetable soup	3–5 minutes (small pieces); 5–10 minutes (large pieces)
peas or beans	45 minutes
fruit cake (steaming)	15 minutes
custards	5 minutes
pudding (1½ kg) (steaming)	20 minutes plus 3 hours

Parboiling

Drop vegetables into boiling salted water and cook uncovered until almost tender. Add ¼ teaspoon sea salt for each 2 cups of water to help vegetables retain their colour. Then immediately plunge them into cold salted water to stop cooking. Do not let them soak too long before removing from cold water.

Blanching

Plunge food into a large quantity of boiling water and briefly cook uncovered. The purpose of this rapid cooking method is to preserve colour and texture and retain nutritional value.

Poaching

Utilising moist heat, this method cooks food in liquid just below the boiling point. At this temperature, bubbles occasionally rise to the surface of the liquid.

Braise

This method combines frying and steaming. It adds flavour to vegetables, fish and chicken. Food is first sautéed rapidly, then cooked in a small amount of liquid, in a tightly covered saucepan or skillet.

Pressing (Instant Pickles)

Salt draws liquid out of vegetables and also preserves, softens and makes them more digestible.

1 Cut up watery vegetables (lettuce, radish, cabbage, turnip, cucumber), sprinkle with salt, cover with a plate and place a heavy weight on top (or knead several minutes, squeeze out water and serve).
2 Leave one or several hours.
3 Rinse just before serving.

Cucumbers can be treated this way for only 10 or 15 minutes before serving.

Pickling

Most people do not consider pickling to be a cooking method, but it is the strongest method that employs maximum use of salt, time and pressure. See pages 122-3 for various methods.

MENU PLANNING: WHY AND HOW

Do you find yourself constantly looking for new and creative food ideas? Perhaps you have begun to think about serving a number of meatless meals to your family during the week, but don't quite know what to serve in its place! Are you sceptical about being able to provide enough of the essential 'foodstuffs'? If you have never ventured from three square, meat-centred meals a day, there is a great surprise waiting in store for you!

By simply eliminating meat, which most people consider the only 'complete' protein, a cornucopia of new and fresh foods will come your way. Fresh fish, seafood, chicken, sea and land vegetables, whole grains, seeds, nuts—all of these foods will provide more than enough protein for your daily needs. Not only do they offer more than adequate amounts of protein, they offer inspiration as well.

Freed from their supportive role, grains and vegetables provide the basis for most of our main meals, with fish, chicken and other meats, playing second fiddle! Most of us are so worried about whether we are getting 'enough' protein, that consequently we eat too much of it. According to figures presently available, we get about three times as much protein as we need. There can be a danger in consuming too much as well as too little.

A recent study conducted in America showed that vegetarians eat *twice* as much protein as they really need. Be careful not to eat too much concentrated protein food (like eggs and cheese) while moving away from meat. They can overburden the system just as much as meat, because of their high fat and cholesterol content. Thus by replacing meat, cheese and eggs with whole grains, beans, tofu, nuts, seeds, green leafy vegetables, sea vegetables, and essential fermented soy products (miso and shoyu), you can decrease your intake of saturated fats and cholesterol and *increase* your vitality and stamina!

Breakfasts

Breakfasts comprised of granola, wholemeal breads, nut butter spreads, fresh fruits and jams require very little adjustment. Once you begin to eat this way, you will walk away from the breakfast table with far more energy to start the day.

Lunches

Lunches depend very much upon where you are during the midday meal. If you are lucky enough to be at home, then preparing a light meal, such as noodles or wholemeal sandwiches, will be no problem. If you go out to work, then the solution lies in various 'wrapped snacks' accompanied with soup, fresh fruit or salad.

Dinner

This is probably the most challenging meal to plan and execute. Always vary your meals according to the season, weather and physical activity.

Primary foods

The *primary* source of food consumed should be composed of wholegrains averaging roughly about 40–50 per cent of daily intake. One quarter legumes (beans and peas) should be eaten to one quantity of grains. This grain-bean combination constitutes the 'bulk' of the meal, and provides the proper proportions of the eight essential amino-acids that are not manufactured by the body. The amount of fresh vegetables varies according to availability, but are the second largest group of foods consumed next to whole grains. Green and root vegetables should be considered the most important, nutritionally. Potatoes, eggplant, tomatoes, green and red capsicums, and cauliflower are considered by many to be inferior vegetables.

Secondary foods

A group of foods consisting of high proportions of Vitamin B12 which is sometimes absent in vegetarian diets, includes eggs, poultry, fish, mushrooms, dairy products, sea vegetables and certain *fermented* foods, such as miso, shoyu, tempeh and pickles. Vitamin B12 is only needed in very small amounts (about three micrograms daily for an average-sized person). When small portions of animal food are eaten in conjunction with other foods there is ample supply. The final group consists of raw vegetables and fruit. They should be eaten within the season which they are grown, and should be taken as an addition to the main meal.

New ingredients

Don't panic if you come across a recipe and you haven't a clue as to what some of the ingredients are! Refer to the glossary at the back and begin to frequent your nearest natural food, or wholefood shop. Don't overlook your local Asian, Chinese or Japanese food shop. If in doubt, ask the shopkeeper for assistance. Very often there are substitutes that can be used in place of one food or another!

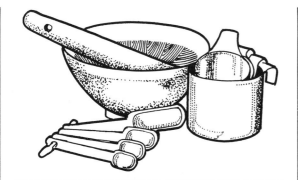

READY RECKONER

LIQUIDS
Cup Measures
1 cup = 250 ml
$4\frac{1}{2}$ cups = 1 litre
4 cups = 1 quart

Spoon Measures
1 tablespoon = 20 ml
1 teaspoon = 5 ml
4 teaspoons = 1 tablespoon

LENGTH
Metric	Imperial
5 mm	$\frac{1}{4}$ in
10 mm (1 cm)	$\frac{1}{2}$ in
20 mm (2 cm)	$\frac{3}{4}$ in
2.5 cm	1 in
5 cm	2 in
10 cm	4 in
15 cm	6 in
30 cm	12 in
45 cm	18 in

MEASURES
1 level teaspoon = 5 g
1 level tablespoon = 20 g
1 heaped tablespoon = 30 g
1 liquid pint = 600 ml
1 gallon = 8 pt
1 litre = 1000 ml
1 teaspoon liquid = 5 ml
1 tablespoon liquid = 20 ml
1 cup = 8 fluid ounces
1 T = 1 tablespoon
1 t = 1 teaspoon

All spoon and cup measures are
level unless otherwise indicated.

OVEN TEMPERATURE GUIDE
	Electric		Gas	
	F°	C°	F°	C°
Very slow	250	120	250	120
Slow	300	150	300	150
Moderately slow	350	180	325	160
Moderate	400	200	350	180
Moderately hot	425	220	375	190
Hot	450	230	400	200
Very hot	500	250	450	230

VOLUME
Metric	Standard Measures	Imperial
20 ml	1 tablespoon	$\frac{1}{2}$ fl oz
30 ml	$1\frac{1}{2}$ tablespoons	1 fl oz
40 ml	2 tablespoons	
50 ml	$2\frac{1}{2}$ tablespoons	$1\frac{1}{2}$ fl oz
60 ml	3 tablespoons	2 fl oz
65 ml	$\frac{1}{4}$ cup	
70 ml	$3\frac{1}{2}$ tablespoons	
80 ml	4 tablespoons	
85 ml	$\frac{1}{3}$ cup	
90 ml	$4\frac{1}{2}$ tablespoons	
100 ml	5 tablespoons	3 fl oz
125 ml	$\frac{1}{2}$ cup	4 fl oz
150 ml	$7\frac{1}{2}$ tablespoons	5 fl oz ($\frac{1}{4}$ pint)
170 ml	$\frac{2}{3}$ cup	
185 ml	$\frac{3}{4}$ cup	6 fl oz
250 ml	1 cup	8 fl oz
315 ml	$1\frac{1}{4}$ cups	10 fl oz ($\frac{1}{2}$ pint)
375 ml	$1\frac{1}{2}$ cups	12 fl oz
435 ml	$1\frac{3}{4}$ cups	14 fl oz
500 ml	2 cups	16 fl oz
625 ml	$2\frac{1}{2}$ cups	20 fl oz (1 pint)
1.25 litres	5 cups	40 fl oz (1 quart)
2.50 litres	10 cups	80 fl oz ($\frac{1}{2}$ gallon)
3.75 litres	15 cups	120 fl oz ($\frac{3}{4}$ gallon)
5.00 litres	20 cups	160 fl oz (1 gallon)

WEIGHTS
Gram	Ounces
15 g	$\frac{1}{2}$ oz
30 g	1 oz
60 g	2 oz
125 g	4 oz ($\frac{1}{4}$ lb)
250 g ($\frac{1}{4}$ kg)	8 oz ($\frac{1}{2}$ lb)
375 g	12 oz ($\frac{3}{4}$ lb)
500 g ($\frac{1}{2}$ kg)	16 oz (1 lb)
1000 g (1 kg)	32 oz (2 lb)

CUP MEASURES
	Metric	Imperial
1 cup flour	140 g	$4\frac{1}{2}$ oz
1 cup honey	375 g	12 oz
1 cup fresh breadcrumbs	60 g	2 oz
1 cup rice, uncooked	220 g	7 oz
1 cup mixed fruit or individual fruit such as sultanas etc	185 g	6 oz
1 cup nuts, chopped	125 g	4 oz
1 cup coconut, desiccated	90 g	3 oz

TIME SAVING STEPS

The following are some valuable tips to save time in the kitchen.

- Break apart garlic cloves and put all of them into a processor or blender. Blend until finely chopped. Put the chopped garlic and peels in a bowl filled with cold water and remove the skins that float up to the top. Do this several times changing the water as necessary until only garlic remains. Store in a jar for future use. Concentrated garlic, now available makes life a bit easier at times. Try using it when you have forgotten to make a large fresh jar of your own. 1 teaspoon = 2 cloves of fresh garlic.
- When blanching vegetables lower them into boiling water in a strainer and lift out the strainer when they are cooked.
- To skin sweet peppers, just grill them at a fairly high heat so that the skin blisters evenly. Leave to cool, covered with a damp cloth or in a paper bag. Strip off the skins and pull out the stems.
- To make a nice rich flavour for bouquet garni cut several pieces of muslin and place the parsley, thyme, celery leaves, bay leaves, dried marigold or camomile flowers on a square of the muslin, gather the edges together to make a bag and secure with string. Store in a jar for future soup stocks.
- Marinate tofu in any strong salad dressing recipe like a vinaigrette as long as you like (the longer the better). When you need a quick tasty addition to soups, grains vegetables, beans or salads, just remove from marinade, and prepare as you wish. Remember to turn over the tofu occasionally if it is not completely covered with the marinade.
- Don't forget, plain and flavoured soy milk is now available in most health food shops.
- Try using mirin (cooking wine made from rice) when you need added flavour in a hurry. Here's a simple guide to follow:

Vegetables
(cook)
shoyu 10 parts [to] mirin 8 parts

Fish
(marinate)
shoyu 10 parts [to] mirin 6 parts

Broth
shoyu 10 parts [to] mirin 4 parts

---

* These products may not be the same quality as found in the health or natural food store. Please check the label for accuracy.

SHOPPING SOURCES

All the ingredients used in this book can be purchased at one of the following retail outlets.

Natural food stores
Wholemeal flours, grains, seeds, beans, unrefined and cold pressed oils, miso, shoyu, sea-salt, kuzu, umeboshi, sea vegetables, pickles, nut butters, unsulphured dried fruits, concentrated sweeteners (honey, maltose, barley malt, maple syrup and rice honey), teas (without caffeine), grain coffees, tofu, organic fruits and vegetables and herbs and spices.

Health food shops
Basically the same selection as the natural food store with some differences. The variety may not be as great but this will depend upon the individual shop. (More vitamin and mineral supplements.)

Oriental groceries
Including Japanese, Chinese, Korean and Asian. Dried vegetables, beans, noodles, sea vegetables, some miso*, shoyu*, umeboshi*, teas dried mushrooms, dried black beans, spices, herbs, maltose and tofu.

Middle Eastern stores
Herbs, spices, couscous, dried beans, tahini, nuts, grains, seeds and unrefined olive oil.

Supermarkets
Dried beans, whole grains, wholemeal flour, nuts, seeds, fresh vegetables and fruits, nut butters and herbs and spices.

Italian delicatessens
Dried beans, nuts, seeds, unrefined olive oil, untreated olives, unprocessed cheeses, dried mushrooms, chestnut flour, freshly dried herbs and spices, pasta, etc.

Of course, not every item that you will need can be found under one roof. It will take time to familiarise yourself with where to shop, but this basic guide should help you to determine your main store. Frequent the ethnic stores in your neighbourhood, for they still carry a large variety of foods that are unprocessed, unrefined and wholesome. Local vegetables are always found by going to the nearest greengrocer and just having a good look around. You will notice unusual vegetables that come and go with the seasons. If you ask the shopkeeper how to prepare them he usually will be most eager to explain. Some of my most unusual and delicious vegetable dishes have sprung up from a quick trip to the local market.

SPRING

This is the time to bloom, to create, to bring forth. Spring is the greening season—a time for planting, sharing, re-birth, renewal and growth, both inwardly and outwardly. It is the time to clean and clear out the old and bring in the new; to restore, renovate and renew!

Goals

The key word is lightness. More sprouts, leafy greens and lighter cooking techniques. Plenty of noodles, salads, lighter soups and less animal foods, and grains. Spring is the time for planting new seeds, sowing the garden and doing more physical activity to loosen the stagnation developed over the long, hard winter. Now is the time to eat less and do more.

	DINNER	BREAKFAST	LUNCH
MONDAY	Pickled chinese cabbage Creme of water-cress soup Stir-fried green beans Gefilte fish **After dinner thought:** Soak 3 cups kidney beans		
TUESDAY	Almond biscuits Zucchini soup Boston baked beans Parsley rice Pumpkin pancakes Sesame salt condiment	Muesli Samurai soup **After breakfast thoughts:** Yeast mixture for bread Cook kidney beans	Rosemary wholewheat bread California salad/ poppyseed dressing Fresh pea potage **After lunch thoughts:** Wash sesame seeds Wash rice
WEDNESDAY	Garden vegetable soup Vegetable sauté with millet Pumpkin salad Mayonnaise	Granola parfait	Walnut balls in creme sauce Stuffed mushrooms **After lunch thought:** Wash millet
THURSDAY	Broccoli and onion tarts Onion and celery sauce Creme of rice soup Sprout salad	Buckwheat pancakes with apple sauce	Minestrone soup Parsley sauce Rolled sandwich Peanut dressing
FRIDAY	Split pea pasta Turnip pickles Apricot bars **After dinner thought:** Pam's porridge	Crepe Suzettes Apple orange filling	Millet and vegetable loaf Carrot and raisin salad Lemon-olive dressing
SATURDAY	Stuffed onions Creme of cauliflower and pea soup Prawn, sweet potato and squash cakes with garlic sauce Strawberry parfait **After dinner thoughts:** Crepe batter for Sunday	Alfalfa Sprout fritters (cucumber topping) Pam's porridge **After breakfast thoughts:** Sweet water pickles Marinate tofu	Oatmeal bread Spinach pie Steamed tofu a la vegetables
SUNDAY		BRUNCH: Broccoli salad/vinegar dressing Asparagus crepes/tarragon sauce Serve with pickled chinese cabbage from Monday	

MONDAY DINNER

PICKLED CHINESE CABBAGE (G)

$\frac{1}{4}$ cup sliced Chinese or Japanese dried mushrooms

$\frac{1}{2}$ Chinese cabbage

2 tablespoons bonita fish flakes

1 tablespoon pressed garlic

1 tablespoon minced ginger

$\frac{1}{2}$ minced chilli pepper

1 cup grated carrot

DRESSING

$\frac{1}{2}$ cup brown rice vinegar

2 tablespoons shoyu

$1\frac{1}{2}$ teaspoons sea salt

Soak mushrooms. When tender, slice finely. Separate cabbage leaves. Drop into boiling salted water for one minute. Drain and refresh under cold water. Squeeze out excess water, cut into 2 cm (1 inch) pieces and set aside. Combine the rest of the ingredients together with the cabbage. Mix dressing together and pour over cabbage. Can keep up to one week when refrigerated.

Serves: 4–6.
Time: 15 minutes.

CREME OF WATERCRESS SOUP (G)

1 bunch of watercress

1 cup chopped onion

1 tablespoon oil

$3\frac{1}{2}$ cups boiling water

bouquet garni

$\frac{1}{4}$ cup roasted brown rice or wholewheat flour

2 tablespoons oil

$\frac{1}{2}$ cup water or stock

sea salt to taste

lemon peel for garnish

Cut watercress into 2 cm (1 inch) pieces. Chop onion. Heat wok or skillet, add oil and sauté onion. Add watercress and cover with boiling water. Add garni, cover and cook 3 minutes. Meanwhile roast flour in 2 tablespoons oil (if you prefer you may dry roast the flour without using any oil) until fragrant (3–4 minutes).

Cream flour and $\frac{1}{2}$ cup hot water together until smooth. Stir into soup, season to taste and serve with garnish.

Serves: 4–6.
Time: 15 minutes.

STIR-FRIED GREEN BEANS (G)

500 g ($\frac{1}{2}$ lb) green beans

1 cup tofu

1 cup chopped onion

1–2 tablespoons oil

$\frac{1}{4}$ cup roasted unhulled sesame seeds

sea salt to taste

Slice green beans diagonally. Break up tofu or mash with fork. Chop onion. Heat wok. Add oil and sauté onion. Add tofu and lightly sauté. Add the green beans, cover and cook 2–3 minutes. Meanwhile heat skillet or saucepan and toast sesame seeds until they pop. Sprinkle in salt to taste and seeds. Serve immediately.

Serves: 4–6.
Time: 10 minutes.

GEFILTE FISH (G)

500 g (1 lb) minced snapper, bream, flathead and mullet

1–2 eggs

$\frac{1}{4}$–$\frac{1}{2}$ cup water

1 teaspoon sea salt

2 tablespoons fine Matzo meal or kuzu

FISH STOCK (G)

heads, tails and bones of minced fish

whole onions

2 bay leaves

3 slices ginger-root

2 spring onions

3 cups sliced onions

2 cups carrot chunks

8 cups water

Mix all the ingredients together for the fish. Put aside for 15 minutes. Shape into small round patties and place on an oiled plate. Set aside.

Vegetable Sauté with Millet. See page 53

Stock

Place all the ingredients for the stock in a large saucepan, cover with water and bring to the boil. Skim off any bubbles that collect on top. Lower heat and simmer gently uncovered until reduced by $\frac{1}{3}$. Strain stock, and discard fish and vegetables. Return the stock to a large pot. Bring to the boil, add fish balls, onions and carrots and simmer partially covered 20 minutes. When cooked, remove fish balls, serve warm or cold with grated white radish (daikon) or horseradish and vegetables. Save stock for sauce or soup.
Serves: 4–6.
Time: 1 hour.

After dinner thought:
Wash and soak 3 cups kidney beans in two parts volume of water. Bring to the boil and simmer uncovered for 30 minutes. Skim off residue that collects on top. Keep for Tuesday night.

TUESDAY BREAKFAST

TOASTED MUESLI

8 cups rolled oats
1 cup wheatgerm
1 cup hulled millet or buckwheat
1 cup unhulled sesame seeds
1 cup sunflower seeds
1 cup chopped apricots
1 teaspoon sea salt
$\frac{1}{2}$ cup apple juice
$\frac{1}{2}$ cup oil
1 tablespoon vanilla
1 cup sultanas

Mix first eight ingredients thoroughly. Blend the next two ingredients until creamy. Add the blended mixture to the dry one and mix until well moistened. Place on baking sheets with low sides. Preheat the oven to 150°C. Bake 1–1$\frac{1}{2}$ hours or until golden brown. Stir every 10 minutes. Add sultanas. Store in airtight container to keep fresh.

Serve with soy milk or apple juice. In summer serve with fresh fruit; peaches and strawberries blended with soy milk.
Makes: 14 cups.
Time: 1–1$\frac{1}{2}$ hours.

SAMURAI SOUP (G)

1 cup sliced onion
1 cup shredded cabbage
$\frac{1}{4}$ cup sliced carrots
$\frac{1}{4}$ cup bean sprouts
1 tablespoon sesame oil
5 cups boiling water or kombu stock (see page 147)
pinch of salt
2–3 tablespoons miso
sliced spring onions or grated ginger-root

Cut vegetables. Heat wok. Add oil and sauté vegetables in order listed above. Sprinkle with salt, cover and simmer for 10 minutes. Add enough water or stock to cover vegetables. Bring to the boil, cover and simmer 5 minutes. Add rest of stock. Remove a ladle of soup and combine with miso. Cream until smooth. Turn off heat. Return to pot and stir gently. *Do not let miso soup boil as this will destroy the valuable enzymes.* Let sit 5 minutes. Garnish with spring onions, or grated ginger-root.
Serves: 4–6.
Time: 15 minutes.

After breakfast thoughts:
While waiting for muesli to cook, set up the yeast mixture for bread. (see Lunch).

Cook kidney beans under pressure 40 minutes. Reserve for dinner and Thursday minestrone soup.

TUESDAY LUNCH

ROSEMARY WHOLEWHEAT BREAD

1 cup lukewarm water
1 tablespoon dry yeast
$\frac{1}{4}$ cup maple syrup
4$\frac{1}{2}$ cups wholewheat flour
2 teaspoons sea salt
2 teaspoons dried rosemary
1 egg
$\frac{1}{4}$ cup water

Place water in bowl. Sprinkle yeast over water and stir lightly to dissolve. Add sweetening. Cover and let rest. When yeast starts bubbling, stir in half the flour and beat. Add the salt, rosemary, remaining flour and water. Turn onto floured board and knead 10 minutes. Place back in oiled bowl, cover and set in a warm place to rise until doubled in size. Punch down, oil two warm bread tins, shape into loaves, sprinkle the bottom of each pan with maizemeal, and place in dough. Slit the top. Cover with a damp cloth, set in warm place to rise (about 30–45 minutes).

Top: Prawn, Sweet Potato and Squash Cakes.
Right: Creme of Cauliflower and Pea Soup.
Bottom: Stuffed Onions.   See page 62

Brush surface of loaf with egg wash consisting of 1 egg beaten with ¼ cup water. Bake at 180°C for 50–60 minutes (*do not preheat oven*), with a pan of water in the oven.

To test if ready—the top should be golden brown. When tapped loaf should resound with a deep hollow thump. Remove from pans after 5 minutes. Cool upside down on a rack covered with tea towel.

Makes: 2 loaves.
Time: 2 hours.

Variations

1 Mix into batter any one of the following herbs—dried basil, thyme or oregano.
2 Mix into batter ½ cup chopped sultanas and ¼ cup roasted unhulled sesame seeds.

CALIFORNIA SALAD (G)

1 whole cauliflower

POPPY SEED DRESSING

¾ cup lightly roasted poppy seeds

1 tablespoon barley malt, rice syrup or maltose

1 tablespoon prepared mustard

2 tablespoons olive oil

4 tablespoons miso

3 tablespoons lemon juice

1 tablespoon lemon rind

1 teaspoon apple cider vinegar

Steam cauliflower until tender. Roast poppy seeds. Blend all the rest of the ingredients while cauliflower is cooking.

Spoon dressing over whole cauliflower while warm. Cool to room temperature before serving. Garnish with alfalfa sprouts.

Serves: 6–8.
Time: 10 minutes.

FRESH PEA POTAGE

4 Japanese or Chinese dried mushrooms

5 cups leftover fish stock from Gefilte fish (Monday)

1 cup carrot matchsticks

½ cup fresh peas

2 teaspoons oil

1 cup thinly sliced onions

½ teaspoon sea salt

shoyu

2–3 tablespoons kuzu or arrowroot flour

orange or lemon peel

Soak mushrooms in boiling water until tender (10–15 minutes). Slice into thin strips. Reserve soaking water for another purpose (good for sauces, etc). Combine stock, carrots and peas and gently simmer uncovered until tender (5–7 minutes). Meanwhile heat skillet or wok, add oil and onions. Sauté until they are transparent. Add the soup to the onions (a wok is ideal as you can cook your soup in it), the mushrooms, salt and shoyu to taste. Bring to the boil and adjust seasoning. Dissolve the kuzu in cold water, stir into soup and continue to stir until the soup thickens and turns clear. (If too thick add more liquid or vice versa.) Garnish with lemon or orange peel before serving.
Serves: 6.
Time: 10 minutes.

After lunch thoughts:
Wash sesame seeds for dinner. Wash rice for dinner.

TUESDAY DINNER

ALMOND BISCUITS

Although fat-free biscuits made with eggs, sweetener and flour are relatively unknown here, they are traditionally served in Germany and Italy. The technique is similar to that for making sponge cakes.

2 eggs, room temperature

½ cup maple syrup or honey

1½ tablespoons ground aniseed

2 tablespoons ground almonds

1 tablespoon dry yeast

apple juice

2 cups wholewheat flour

½ teaspoon sea salt

Whip together eggs and sweetener until light and fluffy. Set over a pan of hot water (use a double boiler if possible) and whisk until thick and mousse-like. Add ground aniseed and almonds.

Combine dry yeast and 2 tablespoons apple juice together. Stir and set aside covered to rise. Combine egg and yeast mixture and beat 3 minutes. Sift the flour and salt together and fold them into the egg mixture using a wooden spoon or rubber spatula.

Turn the dough onto a lightly floured board and knead until soft. If too little flour has been added and the dough is too sticky to roll out or shape, knead in sifted flour, adding only enough to keep dough shape.

Shaping Biscuits

Form into balls 2 cm (1 inch) in diameter and arrange 5–7 cm (2–3 inches) apart on oiled baking sheets. Let stand until doubled in size. Preheat oven to 190°C and bake 15–20 minutes. During baking the balls will burst slightly. Drip warm maple syrup over them. Place on racks to cool.

Rolled Egg Fans

Prepare egg dough as directed. Roll dough into a log 2 cm (1 inch) in diameter. Slice the log into 1 cm (½ inch) rounds. Press each round into a log shape, then roll it back and forth until it is 7 cm (3 inches) long. Cut 3 short diagonal slits on one side of each log. Bend logs in a slight arch so that 'leaves' fan out. Place on oiled and floured sheet 5–7 cm (2–3 inches) apart. Allow to rise until doubled. Preheat oven to 160°C and bake 15–20 minutes or until almost browned. Brush with warm maple syrup and cool.

Variations:

1 Omit ground aniseed.
2 Reduce 2–3 tablespoons flour.
3 *Add:*
¼ teaspoon ground cloves
¼ teaspoon ground ginger
1 tablespoon cinnamon
1 tablespoon diced dried dates and sultanas
Prepare basic egg biscuits and sift dry ingredients together. Add dried fruit after dry ingredients. Knead until well blended.

Makes: 20–24.
Time: 1 hour.

ZUCCHINI SOUP (G)

5 cups soup stock (see page 147)
2 cups grated zucchini
2 cups sliced onions
¼ cup sliced mushrooms
¼ cup diced parsley
2 tablespoons oil
sea salt, to taste
fresh dill for garnish

Prepare soup stock. Grate zucchini, slice onions and mushrooms and dice parsley. Heat skillet or wok. Sauté zucchini in 1 tablespoon oil. Add 1 cup of stock, cover and simmer 10 minutes.

In a separate skillet or wok add the rest of the oil and sauté onions. When transparent add the mushrooms and parsley, lower heat, add some stock to almost cover vegetables, place lid on top and simmer 5–10 minutes.

Purée zucchini, add to the cooked vegetables, cover with remaining stock and bring to the boil. Season, and simmer 5 minutes. Serve with fresh dill. Can be served hot or cold.

Serves: 4–6.
Time: 15 minutes.

BOSTON BAKED BEANS

CRUST

1¾ cups wholewheat flour
¼ cup brown rice flour
½ teaspoon sea salt
⅓ cup safflower oil
¼ cup cold water
1 tablespoon oil
2 cups diced onions
2 tablespoons minced ginger
1 tablespoon minced garlic
3 tablespoons maltose or barley malt
3–4 tablespoons rice vinegar
3 tablespoons miso to taste
2 cups chopped parsley
1 bay leaf
2 cups cooked red beans

Crust

Combine all dry ingredients. Beat oil and water together with whisk or hand beater. Make a well in the centre of the dry ingredients and pour in. Stir until pastry begins to leave the sides of the bowl. (Adjust liquid content accordingly.) Cover and set aside.

Heat oil in skillet. Add onions, cook until clear, add garlic and ginger sautéeing until smell is sweet. Add rest of the ingredients except bay leaf. Fold into beans and place filling in oiled baking dish. Preheat oven to 190°C.

Rolling Out Pastry

On a sheet of greaseproof paper, roll out pastry dough 5 cm (2 inch) larger than the size of the baking dish, and turn upside down onto beans. Remove paper. Tuck in sides, glaze with beaten egg white and 1 tablespoon water mixed together. Bake 45–50 minutes or until crust is lightly browned.

Serves: 6–8.
Time: 1 hour.

PARSLEY RICE (G)

3 cups brown rice
(short for winter, long for summer)

$4\frac{1}{2}$ cups water or stock

pinch of sea salt

1 tablespoon oil

1 cup chopped parsley

$\frac{1}{2}$ cup chopped hazelnuts

Wash rice the night before. Place on cookie sheet in oven and dry roast until light brown. Meanwhile bring water to the boil. Add sea salt. Place rice in saucepan or baking dish, cover with liquid and bake (or simmer on top of stove) for 45 minutes. Sauté parsley. Reserve 1 cup rice. Mix into rice with nuts before serving.

Serves: 4–6.
Time: 1 hour.

PUMPKIN PANCAKES

4 cups grated pumpkin

sea salt

2 eggs, separated

$\frac{1}{2}$ cup crumbled feta cheese or pressed tofu

$\frac{1}{2}$ cup minced spring onions

3–4 tablespoons wholewheat flour

$\frac{1}{2}$ cup grated carrot

$\frac{1}{4}$ cup grated radish

shoyu

$\frac{1}{2}$ cup oil

Grate pumpkin. Place in a colander, salt it lightly and let stand 15 minutes. Meanwhile separate eggs, crumble cheese or tofu and mince spring onions. Rinse and squeeze out pumpkin. Combine the pumpkin with the yolks, cheese, onions and flour. Beat egg whites with a pinch of sea salt until they form soft peaks. Fold into pumpkin mixture. Grate carrot and radish. Set aside.

Heat skillet. Add oil and spoon mixture into skillet. Fry on both sides until golden. (Alternatively, steam for 20 minutes.) Keep warm in oven. Just before serving, add a few drops of shoyu into carrot-radish relish and serve with pancakes.

Makes: 20.
Time: 25 minutes.

SESAME SALT CONDIMENT

10 parts unhulled sesame seeds

1 part sea salt

Wash seeds after lunch. Drain well. Place in saucepan, cover with lid and toast moving the pan in a circular manner until you begin to hear the seeds pop. Roast salt lightly. Grind together in suribachi (see page 37) until seeds are cracked. (Should be done when seeds are hot.) Sprinkle on top of grains and vegetables.

Time: 10 minutes.

WEDNESDAY BREAKFAST

GRANOLA PARFAIT

$2\frac{1}{2}$ cups granola (see page 138)

2 cups fresh fruit (strawberries)

2 cups goat's milk yoghurt or tofu sour creme (see page 54)

Spoon about $\frac{1}{3}$ cup of granola into each parfait glass; top with a few spoonfuls of unflavoured yoghurt or tofu sour creme. Then spoon on mixed fresh fruit slices. Repeat layers until you get to the top of the glass. End with a sprinkle of granola.

Serves: 4.
Time: 5 minutes.

WEDNESDAY LUNCH

WALNUT BALLS IN CREME SAUCE

2 x 200 g cakes tofu

$\frac{1}{4}$ cup chopped walnuts

2 tablespoons minced onions

$\frac{1}{4}$ cup chopped parsley

1 egg (optional)

3 tablespoons wholewheat breadcrumbs

2 tablespoons brown rice, corn, barley or wholewheat flour

2 tablespoons kuzu or arrowroot flour

1 teaspoon dried basil

$\frac{1}{2}$ teaspoon dried thyme

1 teaspoon dried oregano

2 tablespoons miso or 1 teaspoon sea salt

oil for deep frying

2 cups sauce bechamel (see page 120)

Press out excess moisture from tofu and mash. Chop and mince the walnuts, onions and parsley.

Beat the egg, add the breadcrumbs, flour, kuzu, herbs and miso. Combine both mixtures and blend well. Knead several minutes for best results. Shape into little balls. Heat oil and deep fry until golden. Drain.

Preheat oven to 180°C. Place walnut balls in oiled casserole dish, cover with Sauce Bechamel and bake 15 minutes or until warmed. Sprinkle greens over casserole before serving.

Serves: 4–6.
Makes: 40.
Time: 30 minutes.

STUFFED MUSHROOMS

4–6 large mushrooms

$\frac{1}{4}$ cup chopped shallots

$\frac{1}{2}$ tablespoon minced garlic

1 tablespoon minced ginger-root

4 tablespoons chopped fish or chicken

2 teaspoons minced fennel

4 tablespoons cooked brown rice
(from Tuesday)

2 tablespoons oil

1 tablespoon minced watercress or parsley

1 tablespoon miso or $\frac{1}{2}$ teaspoon sea salt

4–6 tablespoons wholewheat breadcrumbs

1 teaspoon dried mixed herbs

2 tablespoons olive oil

Cut off stalks from mushrooms. Mince stalks finely. Set aside. Cut the rest of the ingredients and keep in separate bowls.

Heat skillet, add oil and sauté ingredients as they are listed. Stir in parsley. Cream in miso and cook filling until dry. Preheat oven to 190°C. Brush mushroom caps with oil and fill. Toss the last three ingredients together and sprinkle over each mushroom. Cover and bake 15 minutes.

Serves: 4–6.
Time: 30 minutes.

⏰ After lunch thought:
Wash and drain 1$\frac{1}{2}$ cups hulled millet for dinner.

SPRING 53

WEDNESDAY DINNER

GARDEN VEGETABLE SOUP (G)

5 cups soup stock (see page 147) or water

1 cup sliced onions

1 cup carrot matchsticks

$\frac{1}{2}$ cup sliced green beans or peas
(or broccoli stalks)

1 tablespoon oil

$\frac{1}{2}$ teaspoon sea salt

2–3 tablespoons shoyu, to taste

1 tablespoon kuzu

Bring soup stock or water to the boil. Meanwhile, cut vegetables. Heat wok, add oil and sauté onions. Cover and cook 2–3 minutes.
Add carrots, green beans, peas or broccoli stalks to stock.
Cook uncovered on a low boil until vegetables are almost tender (5–7 minutes). Add onions, salt and shoyu to stock. Bring to the boil. Dissolve kuzu in *cold* water. Stir into soup, bring to the boil, taste and adjust seasoning. Garnish with sprig of fresh mint.

Serves: 4–6.
Time: 15 minutes.

VEGETABLE SAUTE WITH MILLET (G)

1$\frac{1}{2}$ cups hulled millet

3 cups boiling water or stock

$\frac{1}{2}$ teaspoon sea salt

VEGETABLE SAUCE

8–12 broccoli flowerets (use stalks in soup)

8–12 small brussel sprouts

salted boiling water

1 tablespoon minced garlic

$\frac{1}{4}$ cup oil

1 cup button mushrooms

$\frac{1}{2}$ teaspoon sea salt

8–12 small onions

8–12 baby carrots

2 bay leaves

6 sprigs of parsley

2 teaspoons thyme

1 teaspoon cumin

1 tablespoon basil

several slices ginger-root

cheesecloth

½ cup chopped, skinned and seeded sweet red pepper (see page 90)

½–1 cup brown rice vinegar (to cover vegetables)

1 cup mirin or water

¼ cup roasted or unroasted sesame oil

2–3 tablespoons miso

Try to wash the millet after lunch.

Preheat oven to 190°C. Place millet on a flat baking sheet and roast in the oven until lightly browned (10–15 minutes). Meanwhile, bring water and salt to the boil. Add roasted millet, cover and simmer 20 minutes. Toss lightly after cooking. Remove from heat and set aside.

Cut broccoli into flowers. Bring water to the boil. Drop in broccoli and cook 3 minutes. Drain and rinse under cold running water.

Repeat with sprouts, cooking longer. Transfer both vegetables to a dish. Mince garlic. Heat wok, add oil and sauté garlic. Add mushrooms, salt, and onions and then sauté a few minutes before adding carrots. Meanwhile combine the next six ingredients and place in a wet piece of cheesecloth. Tie into a bag. Set aside. Prepare pepper.

Combine the vinegar and mirin adding enough of this mixture so that the vegetables are completely covered. Cover and simmer 20 minutes or until onions are cooked. Add the broccoli, sprouts and red pepper.

Remove several tablespoons of broth, cream together with miso, and put back in the stew along with the oil. Cover and simmer 5 minutes. Strain off the vegetables, take out the bag, pressing hard on the cheesecloth to extract all the flavours. Serve vegetables and broth over millet. Garnish with fresh parsley.

Serves: 4–6.
Time: 45–60 minutes.

Garlic, *one of the best known flavourings for food, is a member of the onion family. It has long been considered to have healing qualities and in World War I the juice was often used as an antiseptic to prevent infection when dressing wounds. It has been known to hang around the necks of some people who believe that it will prevent illness and ward off evil spirits.*

PUMPKIN SALAD (G)

2–3 cups grated pumpkin

½ cup finely chopped spring onion

lettuce cups

olives

Grate pumpkin. Finely chop spring onion. Place in a piece of muslin and rinse under cold water, kneading vegetables to extract bitterness. Squeeze out liquid, and toss with pumpkin. Rinse lettuce cups and dry well.

Place pumpkin mixture into lettuce cups and spoon dressing on top. Garnish with olives.

TOFU SOUR CREME (G)

1 x 200 g cake of tofu

¼ cup oil

4 tablespoons lemon juice

1 teaspoon sea salt

½ cup chopped parsley (optional)

Drop tofu into boiling unsalted water. Drain and combine with the rest of the dressing ingredients. Use parsley to give it a green colour. Taste and adjust seasoning. Spoon over pumpkin salad.

Serves: 4–6.
Time: 10 minutes.

THURSDAY BREAKFAST

BUCKWHEAT PANCAKES (G)

1 tablespoon dry yeast

½ cup warm apple cider or juice

2 tablespoons sourdough starter (optional) (see page 127)

½ cup buckwheat flour

1 egg (optional)

1½ cups apple cider or juice (as necessary)

1 cup buckwheat flour

½ teaspoon sea salt

oil

Dissolve yeast in warm cider or juice. Add sourdough starter and ½ cup buckwheat flour. Cover and set aside in a warm spot until it rises (10–15 minutes).

If using egg, combine it with the ½ cup cider, beating

well. *Start apple sauce.* Add the rest of the flour and salt to the first mixture after it has risen and slowly begin to stir in the egg and juice combination. Beat very well.

Adjust liquid content so that a thin batter is obtained. Cover and let it rise again.

Heat skillet or griddle. Lightly oil with a paper cloth. Ladle on batter. Wait until bubbles appear before you turn them over.

Serves: 6.
Time: 30 minutes.

APPLE SAUCE (G)

8–10 apples

2 teaspoons cinnamon

1 teaspoon cloves

2 cups apple juice

2 tablespoons shoyu or 1 tablespoon miso

1½ tablespoons kuzu

Core and cut the apples into small chunks. Place in a saucepan and add the cinnamon, cloves and juice. Bring to the boil, cover and simmer until tender. Meanwhile, combine the shoyu, 1 tablespoon juice and kuzu stirring until smooth. Remove cover from apple sauce, stir in kuzu mixture and continue stirring until sauce thickens and boils again. Spoon over pancakes.

Makes: 5–6 cups.
Time: 30 minutes.

THURSDAY LUNCH

MINESTRONE SOUP

2 cups diced potatoes and sea salt

2 tomatoes, peeled, seeded and chopped

2 cups chopped celery

1 cup sliced carrot or pumpkin

1 cup sliced zucchini

1 cup chopped onion

¼ cup olive oil

1–1½ cups cooked kidney beans leftover from Tuesday

2 teaspoons sea salt

12 cups cold water or stock (see page 147)

1 bouquet garni

100 gr wholewheat macaroni (elbow shaped)

½ cup chopped parsley or chives for garnish

PARSLEY SAUCE

1 cup fresh parsley

1½ tablespoons dried basil

½ teaspoon sea salt

2 teaspoons crushed garlic

2 tablespoons pine nuts

Dice the potatoes and sprinkle with salt. Let sit 10 minutes and drain off liquid. Blanch tomatoes. Peel and remove seeds. Chop the rest of the vegetables. Keep in separate bowls. Heat skillet. Add half the oil and the vegetables, beans, salt, water and bouquet garni. Bring to the boil, cover and simmer 40 minutes. Alternatively, pressure cook 15 minutes.

Combine all ingredients for sauce and blend until smooth. Set aside.

Add the macaroni and cook till tender (about 10 minutes). Stir in sauce, remaining oil, and serve with garnish.

Serves: 6–8.
Time: 45 minutes.

ROLLED SANDWICH

1 cup grated pumpkin or carrot

1 cup alfalfa sprouts

½ cup minced celery

1 cup shredded lettuce

¼ cup diced cucumber

8 blanched lettuce leaves or 4 flat Pita bread

PEANUT DRESSING

½ cup peanut butter

2 tablespoons warm barley malt, rice syrup or maltose

1 tablespoon miso

2 teaspoons lemon rind

Mix together all vegetables. Set aside. Combine dressing ingredients and cream until smooth. Add vegetables. Spread salad on blanched lettuce leaves or on Pita bread and roll up.

Serves: 4.
Time: 10 minutes.

THURSDAY DINNER

BROCCOLI AND ONION TARTS

| 1 cup diced onion or spring onion |
| 1 tablespoon minced ginger-root |
| 2 teaspoons chopped garlic |
| 6 cups chopped broccoli |
| 1 cup chopped parsley |
| 3 tablespoons oil |
| 1 teaspoon sea salt |
| 2 tablespoons shoyu |

CRUST

| 2 cups wholewheat flour |
| $\frac{1}{2}$ teaspoon sea salt |
| $\frac{1}{3}$ cup oil |
| $\frac{2}{3}$ cup boiling water |
| 1 egg separated |

ONION AND CELERY SAUCE

| 8 tablespoons oil |
| 8 tablespoons wholewheat flour |
| 4 cups soy milk (see page 150), soup stock (see page 147) or water |
| 1 cup sliced onion |
| 1 cup chopped celery |
| 1 cup sliced carrot |
| 1 bay leaf |
| few peppercorns |

Crust

Preheat oven to 190°C. Combine flour and salt in a mixing bowl. Bring water to the boil, beat in oil until creamy. Add oil mixture to flour combination and stir rapidly. Mix pastry until it begins to leave the sides of the bowl. Knead for 5 minutes. Cover and chill 20 minutes. Oil 20 cm (8 inch) pie shell or tart forms. Roll out half the pastry on greaseproof paper. Place in shell, prick with a fork and baste with egg white mixed with a little bit of cold water. Bake 15 minutes or until lightly browned.

Filling

Dice and chop all vegetables for filling. Heat wok or skillet. Add oil and sauté vegetables as listed. Season with salt and shoyu, lower heat, cover and cook 7–10 minutes or until *almost* tender. Remove cover and cook until there is no liquid remaining.

Sauce

Heat saucepan. Add oil and flour and roast until lightly browned. Combine the rest of the ingredients in a saucepan. Bring to the boil, cover with lid slightly ajar, and simmer 10–15 minutes. Strain off vegetables. Combine stock with roasted flour whisking together quickly so no lumps appear. Place back in saucepan, and stir over a medium heat until thick, creamy and smooth. Taste and adjust seasoning. (Make it taste fairly strong as it will lose some of its punch when combined with the vegetables.) Reserve at least half of the sauce for lunch.

Cream sauce with the vegetables, using just enough to coat. Spoon into pre-baked shell(s). Roll out top crust and cover. Add 1 teaspoon cold water to egg yolk and mix thoroughly. Brush with beaten egg yolk and bake 15–20 minutes or until golden.

Makes: 10–12 tarts (7 cm) or one 20 cm pie.

Time: 1 hour 15 minutes.

CREME OF RICE SOUP

| $\frac{1}{4}$ cup tahini |
| 4 cups vegetable or fish stock (see page 147) |
| 1 cup sliced onions |
| 1 cup cooked leftover rice |
| juice and grated rind of 1 lemon |
| 1 teaspoon sea salt or to taste |

Cream the tahini with a $\frac{1}{2}$ cup soup stock. Set aside.

Combine the onions and rice with the rest of the stock. Bring to the boil, lower heat, cover and simmer 15 minutes.

Add tahini combination, grated lemon rind and juice. Heat but *do not boil.* Season to taste and garnish with spring onion.

Serves: 4.
Time: 20 minutes.

SPROUT SALAD

| 500 g (1 lb) mung bean sprouts |

MAYONNAISE (G)

| 2 egg yolks (room temperature) |
| 1 tablespoon prepared mustard |
| $\frac{3}{4}$–$1\frac{1}{2}$ cups olive oil |
| 1–2 teaspoons brown rice vinegar or lemon juice |

½–1 teaspoon sea salt

1½ tablespoons fresh minced chives, or spring onions

Place the yolks and mustard in a warm bowl and whisk. Then put the bowl over boiling water (double boiler is best) and continue to beat for 10 seconds to slightly heat. It should feel slightly thicker. Remove from heat, and begin to drip in the oil, beating continuously. When the mixture starts to become creamy and ¾ of the oil is used, add 1½–2 tablespoons of hot vinegar, or lemon juice.

As the mayonnaise starts to become clearer and creamier, add the remaining oil, beating constantly. Season with salt, chives or spring onions. Drop sprouts into boiling water. Bring to the boil again and drain. Squeeze out all excess moisture and toss with dressing *just* before serving.

Time: 10 minutes.

FRIDAY BREAKFAST

CREPE SUZETTES

1 cup corn flour
2 cups wholewheat flour (finely milled)
7–9 cups water
1 tablespoon oil
2 teaspoons sea salt

APPLE ORANGE FILLING (G)

5 large apples
2 tablespoons oil
1 tablespoon orange rind
1 tablespoon lemon juice
1 teaspoon cinnamon
½ cup roasted chopped almonds
1 cup sultanas
½ teaspoon sea salt
1 teaspoon vanilla
1 tablespoon barley malt, rice honey or maltose (optional)
strawberries for garnish

Mix ingredients. Let stand 1 hour or if you wish to begin cooking the crepes at once, beat in an electric mixer, blender or processor.
Heat crepe pan well. Oil it with a piece of paper towel or brush. Lower heat. Pour the batter into a ladle and as you pour turn the pan clockwise to spread the batter

evenly. Cook several minutes or until edges begin to turn up. Detach the crepe carefully with a very flat spatula and then turn. Cook 30 seconds.

Peel, core and cut apples into 1 cm (1 inch) thick slices. Heat skillet. Add oil, apple slices, rind, juice, cinnamon sultanas and sea salt. Cook on a low heat until apples begin to soften and look translucent. Add sweetener, and reduce until thick and creamy.

To Assemble
Crepes and filling should be at room temperature. Spoon 3 tablespoons of filling across lower third of each crepe, turn sides in and roll to enclose.
Place filled crepes seam side down in a lightly oiled dish. Preheat oven to 180°C. Spoon remaining filling over top, cover and bake 15 minutes or until crepes are heated through. Garnish with strawberries.
Stuff crepes with any leftover vegetable filling. Mash or cut up filling into tiny pieces. For a quick filling: grate carrots and squash. Slice an onion. Heat skillet, add oil and lightly sauté together for 1–2 minutes. Fill crepe.

Serves: 4–6.
Time: 15–20 minutes.

FRIDAY LUNCH

MILLET AND VEGETABLE LOAF

1 cup diced onion
1 cup chopped spring onion
½ cup sliced mushrooms
½ cup chopped cauliflower
½ cup chopped celery
½ cup grated apple
½ cup grated carrot or pumpkin
2–3 tablespoons oil
1 teaspoon garam masala or curry
1 teaspoon coriander
1 cup roasted, ground sunflower seeds
1 cup roasted ground almonds
2 bars agar-agar
1 cup vegetable soup (leftover) or soup stock (see page 147)

| 1 cup wholewheat breadcrumbs |
| 2 cups cooked millet (leftover) |
| 2 tablespoons miso |
| 1 eggplant |
| 1 tablespoon oil |
| sea salt to taste |

Dice, chop, slice and grate all the vegetables and apples. Heat a wok or skillet, add oil and stir fry the vegetables as they are listed. Add the spices and cover and simmer 5 minutes (add a small amount of liquid if wok is very dry). Meanwhile roast the seeds and almonds on separate baking sheets in the oven till lightly browned (5–10 minutes).

Rinse agar-agar under cold running water. Squeeze dry, add to vegetable soup and bring to the boil. Simmer until agar-agar dissolves.

Go back to the vegetables, add the breadcrumbs and cooked millet. Cover and warm. Stir in miso, taste and adjust seasoning. Stir agar-agar mixture into vegetables, add roasted nuts and seeds. Set aside. Cut eggplant into thin slices. Heat skillet, add oil and sauté until lightly browned. Oil a casserole dish, place eggplant into a decorative pattern, spoon over millet and vegetable mixture and press down firmly. Set aside to gel. If desired, serve with yoghurt or tofu sour creme.

Serves: 4–6.
Time: 1 hour.

CARROT AND RAISIN SALAD (G)

| 3 cups grated carrots |
| ½ cup chopped raisins |
| ¼ cup roasted slivered almonds |
| ¼ cup diced parsley |
| ¼ cup diced celery |
| ¼ cup diced spring onion |

LEMON-OLIVE DRESSING (G)

| 6 tablespoons olive oil |
| 2 tablespoons lemon juice |
| 1 teaspoon maple syrup |
| 1 teaspoon prepared mustard |

Combine carrots, raisins, almonds, parsley, celery and spring onion.
Combine all the salad dressing ingredients and whisk until creamy. Add the carrot salad and toss.

Serves: 4–6.
Time: 5 minutes.

FRIDAY DINNER

SPLIT PEA PASTA

| 2 cups yellow split peas |
| 2 tablespoons oil |
| ½ teaspoon mustard seeds |
| 1 teaspoon assorted chilli pepper |
| 2 cups chopped onion |
| ½ teaspoon tumeric powder |
| 1 teaspoon pepper |
| 1 teaspoon cinnamon |
| 4 crushed garlic cloves |
| 2 cardomon pods, crushed |
| 1 tablespoon lemon juice |
| miso or sea salt to taste |

WHOLEWHEAT PASTA

| 250 g wholewheat noodles |

Sauce
Boil the peas for 30 minutes without a lid and skim off any residue that floats on top. Add more water if necessary to cover peas, bring to the boil, cover with lid ajar and simmer till soft (40–50 minutes). Heat skillet, add the oil and fry the mustard seeds till they splatter. Add the assorted chilli pepper and onion and sauté till the onion lightly browns. Stir in the tumeric, pepper, cinnamon, cloves and cardomon. Fry for 3 minutes and stir this into the cooked peas. Add lemon juice and miso to taste. Heat until flavours are well combined.

Pasta
Bring a pot of water to the boil. Add noodles separately (see page 58 for technique). Bring back to the boil, and add cold 'shock' water to stop it from boiling. Repeat this three times. Simmer several minutes longer until *al-dente*. Rinse immediately under cold water until the noodles feel cold. Set aside. When the dahl is ready, dip the noodles into a pot of boiling water to reheat, and serve under dahl. Garnish with fresh coriander, cress or sprouts.

Serves: 4–6.
Time: 1½ hours.

TURNIP PICKLES (G)

4–6 small turnips

1 carrot

1 teaspoon sea salt

3 tablespoons brown rice vinegar

2 tablespoons maltose, rice syrup or barley malt

$\frac{1}{3}$ cup water

15 cm (6 inch) strip of kombu (optional)

Cut turnips and carrot into thin slices. Salt and leave 10 minutes. Boil the remaining ingredients. Pour over turnips and leave to marinate until serving.

Serves: 4–6.
Time: 20 minutes.

APRICOT BAR

$\frac{1}{2}$ cup chopped sun dried apricots

$\frac{1}{2}$ cup apple cider

1 tablespoon lemon or orange rind

2 teaspoons grated ginger

$\frac{1}{4}$ cup chopped almonds

$\frac{1}{2}$ cup barley malt, rice honey or maltose

$\frac{1}{3}$ cup oil

1 egg (room temperature)

1 cup wholewheat flour

1 teaspoon cinnamon

$\frac{1}{4}$ teaspoon sea salt

TOPPING

$\frac{1}{2}$ cup apple juice

2 tablespoons maple syrup

$\frac{1}{2}$ cup sliced strawberries

2 teaspoons grated orange rind

$\frac{1}{2}$ teaspoon sea salt

3 teaspoons arrowroot

Base
Combine first four ingredients together and set aside. Preheat oven to 180°C. Roast chopped almonds until lightly browned.

Heat sweetener, and immediately blend with oil until light and fluffy. (A food processor is excellent for this step.) Continue beating and add egg. Stir the first mixture into this egg mix and beat well. Sift the last three ingredients and add almonds. Fold into egg batter. Oil baking sheet (15 cm x 20 cm x 2 cm) (6 inch x 8 inch x $\frac{3}{4}$ inch), spoon onto sheet and bake 30–35 minutes, or until skewer comes out clean when inserted into middle of mixture.

Topping
Combine all ingredients except arrowroot in a saucepan. Cover and cook for 3 minutes on medium heat. Dissolve arrowroot in 1–2 tablespoons cold juice, stir into saucepan and bring to a boil constantly stirring. Spoon on top of bar 5 minutes before removing from oven. Cool and cut.

Makes: 16 slices.
Time: 1 hour.

 After dinner thought:

PAM'S PORRIDGE

Due to a shortage of time, Pam devised this wonderful way of cooking porridge without having to be there. Great for busy mothers or for travelling. (You will need a wide mouth thermos for this.)

2 cups boiling water

1 cup mixed rolled oats and barley

$\frac{1}{2}$ teaspoon sea salt

4 cups boiling water

This recipe is for a $4\frac{1}{4}$ cup-wide thermos, but if yours is smaller just divide the recipe accordingly.

Bring water to the boil. Put the cereal in the thermos. Add the boiling water and stir briefly. Pour off the hot water, place the grain back into the thermos, add the 4 cups of boiling water and salt, cover and set aside. It will be ready in 4 or 5 hours or leave it overnight for a great breakfast cereal.

Serves: 4.
Time: 5 hours or overnight.

SATURDAY BREAKFAST

ALFALFA SPROUT FRITTERS

FRITTERS

1 cup chopped onion
1½ cups breadcrumbs
1 cup chopped sunflower seeds or walnuts
½ cup alfalfa sprouts
½ teaspoon sea salt
½ teaspoon Japanese lemon pepper
4 tablespoons wholewheat flour
4 tablespoons arrowroot flour
water to bind

CUCUMBER TOPPING

1 large cucumber or 2 small ones
½ cup chopped cress
goat's milk yoghurt (about ½ cup)
1 tablespoon tahini

Fritters

Chop onion. Place onion, breadcrumbs and sunflower seeds in blender or processor and chop finely. Add sprouts, salt and pepper and mix again. Stir in flours, add water to bind if necessary.

Shape into patties. Heat oil and pan fry until golden.

Makes: 16 fritters.
Time: 20 minutes.

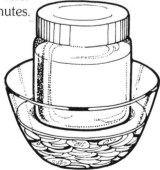

Topping

Remove the ends of the cucumber. Place the tips in salt and rub into the cucumber ends until they begin to get foamy. Discard the ends. Seed and skin the cucumber leaving a small amount of skin for effect. Cut in half and then lengthwise into strips. Sprinkle with salt and press to drain. Chop parsley. Squeeze out cucumber, toss with parsley and spoon yoghurt mixed with tahini over vegetables. Serve this on top of the fritters!

Serves: 4.
Time: 10 minutes.

After breakfast thoughts:
Marinate tofu for dinner (see page 61).

SWEET WATER PICKLES (G)

tops of 1 bunch of daikon (white radish), turnips, or mustard greens
½ cup shoyu
1 teaspoon barley malt, maltose or rice honey
1 tablespoon grated ginger
1 tablespoon tahini
1 teaspoon dry mustard powder (optional)

Cut greens into 2 cm (1 inch) strips. Place in jar and pack firmly. Combine shoyu and sweetener in saucepan and heat until sweetener dissolves. Combine the rest of the ingredients with first mixture and pour over vegetables. Cover and refrigerate at least 24 hours. Will keep 3–4 weeks.

Time: 10 minutes.

SATURDAY LUNCH

OATMEAL BREAD

1 cup rolled oats
1 cup boiling water or apple juice
2 tablespoons oil
1 teaspoon sea salt
1 tablespoon dry yeast
½ cup lukewarm apple juice
1 cup wholewheat flour
4 tablespoons chopped almonds
2¼ cups wholewheat flour
2 tablespoons rolled oats
1 egg white and 1 tablespoon water for glaze

Cook oats in boiling water or apple juice in the top of a double boiler for 15 minutes. Place in mixing bowl and add oil and salt. Set aside. In a small bowl combine yeast and warm apple juice. Set aside covered until it appears to be frothy. Add it to the oatmeal mixture and stir well. Add 1 cup wholewheat flour and nuts to this yeast mixture. Add the rest of the flour and cooked oatmeal. Knead on a floured surface adding more flour or liquid as necessary to make a soft but not sticky dough. Shape the dough into a ball, place it in an oiled bowl and turn to coat it. Cover and let the dough rise in a warm spot until almost doubled in size. Punch down and knead again several minutes. Shape into loaf, oil bread tin sprinkle with cornmeal and place in tin. Cover and let rise again until almost double. Preheat the oven to 190°C. Brush the loaf with the glaze and sprinkle rolled oats on top. Bake 40–50 minutes or until loaf sounds hollow when the bottom is tapped. Cool on rack several minutes and then *remove from pan.* Cover with towel and cool.

Time: 2 hours.

SPINACH PIE (G)

PASTRY

5 cups wholewheat flour

1 teaspoon sea salt

6 tablespoons olive oil

1½–2 cups lukewarm water

corn or olive oil

SPINACH FILLING

1 kg (2 lb) spinach

1 cup chopped onion

½ cup olive oil

½ cup chopped parsley

2 teaspoons minced dill

1 cup crumbled feta cheese or crumbled tofu

2–3 eggs, lightly beaten (use three if small)

sea salt

Pastry

Combine flour and salt in large mixing bowl. Stir in oil and as much water as needed to form a soft dough. Knead on a flat surface until dough is smooth and blisters begin to appear under surface (10–15 minutes). Brush surface of dough lightly with oil, invert warm bowl over dough and let stand 30 minutes.

Filling

Wash spinach and cut off coarse stems. Chop coarsely and put in a large pan. Cover and cook 10 minutes or until spinach wilts and the juice starts to run out of it. Drain well, discarding any juice, and rinse under cold water pressing or squeezing out remaining water. Set aside. Heat oil in skillet. Add onion and sauté until transparent. Add parsley and dill. Cover and simmer 3 minutes. Place spinach in mixing bowl, add onion mixture, cheese and eggs. Stir in salt to taste.

Oil a 20 x 30 cm (8 x 12 inch) baking dish.

Rolling out the Pastry

Roll out pastry into a log. Divide into 5. Cover. Roll logs out on cloth into a rectangle as thin as possible, but slightly larger than the size of the baking dish. (Layer

each sheet on top of previous one with wax or greaseproof paper in between, until ready to use.) Brush each sheet with oil. Place 2 rectangles in the bottom of baking dish. Spread filling in pastry-lined dish and top with remaining three sheets. Reserve extra pastry.

Trim edges if necessary and tuck pastry in on all sides. Brush top with oil and score top layer of pastry lightly into squares. (If served as a party snack, score top layers of pastry with a razor blade into diamonds before baking.)

Preheat oven to 190°C.

Bake 45–50 minutes until lightly browned and slightly puffed. Cool 10 minutes before cutting.

Serves: 6–8.
Time: 1 hour.

Shape Variation

Cut each rectangular sheet of pastry dough into three strips about 8 x 30 cm (3 x 12 inches) in size. Stack on a cloth and cover with another folded, dry cloth.

Take a strip of pastry dough and brush with oil. Place a tablespoon of the spinach mixture towards the bottom edge of the strip and fold end of strip diagonally over filling, forming a triangle. Oil. Fold up once, oil, then fold again diagonally to opposite side. Continue oiling and folding until the end of the pastry. Tuck in end. Repeat with remaining dough and filling. Place on oiled sheet and brush lightly with oil. Bake 20 minutes or until slightly puffy and lightly browned.

STEAMED TOFU A LA VEGETABLES (G)

500 g (1 lb) tofu

MARINADE

½ cup shoyu

2 tablespoons orange or lemon rind

2 tablespoons corn oil

2 tablespoons brown rice vinegar

1 tablespoon grated ginger

1 teaspoon grated garlic

2 tablespoons bonita flakes

1 cup brown rice flour

1 teaspoon Japanese lemon pepper

STIR FRIED VEGETABLE SAUCE

3 tablespoons sesame oil
1 cup onion wedges
½ cup sliced shallots
¼ cup sliced celery
½ cup washed bean sprouts
½ cup matchstick carrots
1–1½ cups stock
marinade juice
2–3 teaspoons kuzu

Press tofu if necessary. Bring marinade ingredients to a boil. Cut tofu into cubes. Add to marinade. Set aside at least 30 minutes or better still, overnight. Make sure that the marinade covers all the tofu. Turn occasionally.

Roast flour. Lightly roast pepper and combine the two. Drain off marinade from tofu, roll in brown rice flour mixture, place on spinach or cabbage leaves and steam 15–20 minutes.

Meanwhile, cut vegetables for sauce. Heat wok, add oil and sauté onions until clear. Add shallots and sauté until strong smell disappears. Add the remaining vegetables in order listed, and sauté. Pour in marinade and 1 cup stock. Cover and simmer 5 minutes.

Dilute kuzu in a few tablespoons cold stock. Stir into vegetables and keep stirring until sauce thickens, turns clear and boils. (Adjust liquid content accordingly.)

Remove tofu from steamer, place on serving platter and spoon vegetable sauce on top. Garnish with chives, grated egg yolk or spring onions.

Serves: 4–6.
Time: 1 hour.

SATURDAY DINNER

STUFFED ONIONS

1 cup breadcrumbs or leftover grain
¾ cup water or soy milk (see page 150)
4–6 large onions
boiling water
1 cup sliced mushrooms
2 tablespoons oil
2 tablespoons chopped almonds
½ teaspoon dried thyme
¼ cup chopped green pepper
1–2 tablespoons miso
sea salt
1 cup stock (see page 147)
parsley for garnish

Soak breadcrumbs in water or soy milk. If using leftover grain *do not soak*. Scoop out the centre of onions with melon baller. Chop the centres.

Bring water to the boil and blanch onions for 1 minute. Turn upside down to drain.

Slice mushrooms. Heat skillet, add oil and sauté mushrooms and almonds. Add thyme and green pepper.

Squeeze liquid out of breadcrumbs and crumble into onions. Cover and simmer several minutes. Add miso and mix well.

Season onion shells with salt and spoon filling in.

Preheat oven to 180°C. Oil casserole dish, place onions upright in dish and pack very closely together so that they cannot move. Pour stock around, cover and bake 10 minutes. Remove cover, baste and bake until tender. Sprinkle with parsley before serving.

If there is any liquid left after baking, thicken with arrowroot or kuzu: 1 teaspoon kuzu to 1½ cups liquid. Spoon over onions.

Serves: 4–6.
Time: 30 minutes.

CREME OF CAULIFLOWER AND PEA SOUP (G)

2 cups chopped cauliflower
3 cups shelled peas
8 cups soup stock (see page 147) or water
1 cup sliced onion
1 tablespoon oil
1 bay leaf
1 tablespoon arrowroot flour
¼ cup cold water
sea salt, to taste
4 cups liquid from boiling peas
sea salt, to taste

Chop cauliflower. Shell peas and set aside. Prepare soup stock. Slice onion. Heat wok, add oil and onion.

Sauté until onion is transparent. Add cauliflower and lightly sauté. Add some stock to cover vegetables, and the bay leaf. Cover and simmer 10 minutes. Remove bay leaf, and blend soup until creamy. Add more stock if necessary. Dissolve arrowroot in cold stock, add sea salt to soup. Stir arrowroot into soup and bring it to the boil. Pour into bowls.

Bring peas to the boil in 4 cups stock. Cook 5 minutes. Blend in a small amount of the cooking water till creamy. Add the rest of the cooking water to measure 4 cups or until desired consistency is reached. Pour into a saucepan and heat until boiling. Slowly pour into one side of the serving bowl already containing califlower mixture. Using a spoon, coax the peas in. (See photo.)

Serves: 4–6.
Time: 30 minutes.

PRAWN, SWEET POTATO AND SQUASH CAKES

2 cups water
12 prawns (1 cup cooked and chopped)
1 teaspoon sea salt
$\frac{1}{3}$–$\frac{1}{2}$ cup wholewheat flour
4 tablespoons arrowroot flour
1 cup grated sweet potato
2 cups grated squash or pumpkin
$\frac{1}{2}$ cup chopped coriander
safflower oil for deep-frying

GARLIC DIP

2 tablespoons pressed garlic
2 tablespoons warm shoyu
$1\frac{1}{2}$ cups brown rice vinegar

Bring water to the boil. Drop prawns in and cook until pink.

Drain and rinse in cold water. Remove heads, shells and de-vein. Chop to yield 1 cup. Set aside.

Mix the salt and flours together. Grate the vegetables.

Combine all the ingredients and mix very well. Knead several minutes. Chop the coriander. Crush the garlic and mix with shoyu and vinegar set aside. Heat oil. Meanwhile shape the cakes. Place on oiled plate. Set up draining paper. Deep fry several at a time.

Serve with warm dip.

Makes: 24 cakes.
Time: 25 minutes.

After dinner thoughts:
Prepare crepe batter for Sunday brunch.

STRAWBERRY PARFAIT (G)

3 cups apple juice
$1\frac{1}{2}$ bars agar-agar
1 tablespoon orange rind
4 tablespoons maple syrup
1 cup strawberries
1 tablespoon tahini or almond butter
crushed nuts or granola (see page 138)

Place apple juice in a saucepan and begin to heat. Meanwhile wash agar-agar under cold running water. Squeeze dry, shred into juice and bring to the boil. Add rind, syrup. Lower heat and simmer until agar-agar dissolves.

Meanwhile wash 1 cup strawberries. Blend 2 cups cooked mixture with 1 tablespoon tahini. Set. Blend the other cup with the strawberries. Set.

When almost set, blend them again, separately. Layer them into a parfait glass sprinkling nuts or granola in between layers. Top with whole strawberry.

Serves: 4–6.
Time: 1 hour.

SUNDAY BRUNCH

BROCCOLI SALAD (G)

1 kg (2 lb) broccoli
large pot of boiling water
sea salt

VINEGAR DRESSING

$\frac{1}{2}$ cup fresh lemon juice or $\frac{1}{2}$ cup brown rice vinegar
1 teaspoon dry mustard powder
$\frac{1}{2}$ teaspoon sea salt
1 cup olive oil
$\frac{1}{4}$ cup sliced green olives
2 tablespoons minced parsley

Trim broccoli and remove leaves. Peel the stems if skin is not completely tender (save the heavy stem for soups). Add a tablespoon sea salt to pot of boiling water and drop in the broccoli. (It is best if the broccoli is tied in bunches.) Stand up and cook stems first then slide in flowers and boil till just tender-crisp.
DO NOT OVER COOK
Drain and rinse with cold water until broccoli is very cold (this stops the cooking and sets the colour).

Salad Dressing
Pour lemon juice into a bowl and then whisk in the mustard and salt. Add the oil, beating until emulsified (drip in for best results). Stir in last two ingredients. Toss broccoli with dressing.

Serves: 4–6.
Time: 15 minutes.

ASPARAGUS CREPES

CREPE

2 eggs, room temperature

2 tablespoons oil

1½ cups soy milk, nut milk or water (see page 150)

1 cup wholewheat flour

½ teaspoon sea salt

FILLING

¼–½ kg (½–1 lb) asparagus

sea salt

miso to taste

TARRAGON SAUCE

1 cup sliced spring onion

2 tablespoons oil

4 tablespoons mirin (optional)

1 tablespoon brown rice vinegar

2 tablespoons oil

3 tablespoons brown rice or barley flour

2⅓–3 cups water

1 tablespoon tarragon

shoyu to taste

sprouts for garnish

CREPE BATTER

Blender method
Place all of the ingredients in a blender in the order listed above. Cover and blend at high speed for 30 seconds or beat with a hand beater until smooth and frothy. Refrigerate for best results. If it thickens while standing, thin to right consistency. The batter should be thin enough to run freely around the bottom of the crepe pan when it is tilted.

Mixer method
Beat eggs, soy milk and oil with hand beater or electric mixer until smooth and frothy. Gradually add dry ingredients and beat continuously. Refrigerate while preparing filling.

Filling
Tie stalks together. Boil water and salt in tea kettle and place stalks downwards in the kettle. Cook on low boil until stalks are tender. Slide in tips and cook until tender.

Rinse under cold water and drain. Cut into diagonal pieces and cream with miso. Set aside.

TARRAGON SAUCE

Cut spring onion into slices. Heat skillet, add oil and sauté onion till tender. Stir in cooking wine and vinegar. Simmer liquid until reduced by half.

In another skillet heat oil, add flour and cream together. Slowly add warm water stirring continuously until thickened and boiling. (Adjust liquid content.) Add tarragon, lower heat, cover and simmer 10 minutes. Add shoyu to taste, bring to the boil. Stir in onion mixture.

Putting it all Together
Heat crepe pan or skillet. The temperature is correct when the batter sizzles slightly when ladled into pan. Ladle in the batter and quickly tilt the pan so the batter covers the bottom entirely with a thin coating. Pour the excess back in the bowl. Cook on one side for 1–2 minutes or until holes appear. Turn over and cook slightly on the other side. Remove to warm plate.

Combine asparagus with hot sauce (1–2 tablespoons to warm asparagus). Place vegetables in crepe, roll up crepe and cover with sauce. Garnish with grated carrot before serving. Serve with pickled Chinese cabbage from Monday.

Serves: 4–6.
Makes: 12–14.
Time: 35 minutes.

Strawberry Kiwi Cheesecake.   See page 71

🪢 FORGET ME KNOTS

1 When boiling or steaming vegetables re-use the cooking water that is leftover (except from bitter greens).

2 Many vitamins and minerals are contained in the skin of a fruit or vegetable. Never peel organically grown ones. Save the peels of oranges and lemons. Dry and use as rind for flavouring.

3 Keep all vegetables as cool as possible because nutrients are lost more rapidly when the food is left in a warm spot.

4 Always look for the freshest vegetables in season because old wilted vegetables have lost a considerable amount of Vitamin C.

5 Avoid frozen and canned vegetables whenever possible.

6 When washing vegetables don't soak them, just wash root vegetables under cold running water and leafy greens in a bowl with cold water. Move greens around quickly to remove dirt clinging to the leaves.

7 Salt in cooking helps vitamins and minerals to remain in the food longer.

8 Cooking vegetables with oil helps to seal in vitamins and minerals.

9 To remove skin from capsicums, roast over open flame until black, or bake in oven until skin is soft. *Immediately* place in paper bag and cool. When cool, rinse under cold water, remove skin and discard seeds.

10 Scoop out vegetables for stuffing with melon baller.

11 Most vegetables are rich in vitamins. Although vitamins do not provide energy, they regulate its release and use by the body.

12 Cut vegetables just before cooking.

13 Leftover vegetables that have been cooked may also be used very successfully as filling for omlettes, crepes, spreads for sandwiches and cream soups.

14 Pureé leftover vegetables that have been steamed or boiled as a base for a soup.

15 Leftover cooked pureéd root vegetables make a great meal when mixed with any type of cooked pasta and baked. Layer greens inbetween.

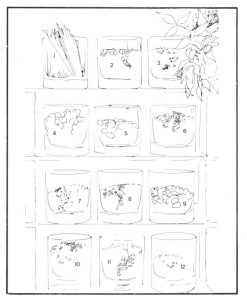

1 wholewheat noodles (udon)
2 brown lentils
3 wholewheat berries
4 garbanzos (chickpeas)
5 red kidney beans
6 mung beans (for sprouting)
7 hulled millet
8 red lentils
9 small lima beans
10 brown rice
11 Chinese barley
12 roasted buckwheat

SUMMER

Summer's energy usually makes us feel like being more active, perhaps doing some travelling, going on picnics, playing sports, or just laying on the beach and soaking up the sun. It's the season of growth and maturity when everything and everybody is coming into full bloom and fruition. Full of her bounty, nature produces an excessive amount of moist, cooling foods to be enjoyed without much, if any, preparation.

A special day, summer solstice marks the longest day of the year, occurring as a reminder that autumn is not far away. Barbecues, basil, mint, fresh greens and cooling drinks all tell the joyful song of summertime when the living is easy.

Goals

At this time of the year, your diet should reflect the hot weather and light, moist cooling elements represented by salads, sprouts, more leafy greens, noodles, lightly steamed fish, tofu and cooling soups and desserts. Too much heat-producing foods such as alcohol, animal protein, fatty, fried foods and grain should be avoided.

If you are fortunate enough to have a garden, pick the wild greens, like dandelion that make an appearance ever so often, and combine her bitter taste with the other sweet flavours of summertime.

	DINNER	BREAKFAST	LUNCH
MONDAY	Gramma pumpkin potage Brownies/strawberry topping Steamed fillet of sole Olive and orange salad Noodles in sesame hot sauce Pickled mushrooms **After dinner thought:** Soak chickpeas		
TUESDAY	Vegetable curry pie Watercress and bean salad Tofu stroganoff Portuguese bridal cookies	Gingered mangoes Egg and tomato	Vegetable strudel Green bean salad/lemon garlic dressing Strawberry kiwi cheesecake **After lunch thoughts:** Pressure cook chickpeas Marinate 200 g tofu for dinner Summer sardines
WEDNESDAY	Steamed chicken in melon soup Onion and tomato pizza Orange and onion salad with vinaigrette dressing **After dinner thoughts:** Soak 1 cup lentils Cook beetroots Tomato sauce	Fresh fruit salad Almond-peach butter	Sweet and sour dumplings **After lunch thought:** Impromptu chicken stock for dinner
THURSDAY	Bulghur pilaf with onion and raisin sauce Lentil and silverbeet soup	Blintzes with cherry sauce Cheese filling	Borscht (beetroot soup) Strawberry tahini custard Zucchini pasta
FRIDAY	Scalloped noodles Apricot yoghurt slice Mustard pickles from lunchtime	Vegetable pancakes Lemon coriander sauce	Pocket bread surprise alfalfa-almond filling or sunflower-date filling Ginger beans **After lunch thought:** Mustard pickles
SATURDAY	Pea and mushroom aspic Steamed buns Black bean sauce Sesame carrot	Waffles Orange-almond topping Strawberry melon	Bulghur patties Mint sauce **After lunch thought:** Soak 2 cups split peas for dinner
SUNDAY		BRUNCH: Zucchini piroshki Basil and garlic sauce Steamed date cake Green salad	

MONDAY DINNER

GRAMMA PUMPKIN POTAGE

6 cups sliced pumpkin

$\frac{1}{2}$ cup dried Chinese or Japanese mushrooms

$2\frac{1}{2}$ cups water or stock

1 cup orange juice

2 tablespoons oil

1 tablespoon chopped ginger-root

$\frac{1}{2}$ cup chopped onion or spring onion

$\frac{1}{2}$ teaspoon ground cumin

$\frac{1}{2}$ teaspoon ground coriander

$\frac{1}{2}$ teaspoon cinnamon

$\frac{1}{4}$ teaspoon mustard powder

$1\frac{1}{2}$–2 teaspoons sea salt

few pinches chilli pepper

croûtons

chopped parsley

Cut the squash lengthwise and either bake face down in an oiled tray at 190°C for 30–45 minutes or until tender or steam under pressure 10 minutes. Cool and scoop out the insides. Reserve some for following day. Soak mushrooms in warm water until tender (10–15 minutes). Slice into thin strips and soak in shoyu. (Use soaking liquid in soup.)

Heat the water or stock and purée with the squash until smooth. Add the juice and set aside.

Heat a deep skillet or wok. Add the oil and sauté the ginger and onion. Squeeze out mushrooms and sauté with onions. Add the next four spices and salt, cover and cook until onions and mushrooms are soft.

Combine the squash with the vegetables and spices and heat together. Taste and adjust seasoning and liquid.
Prepare croûtons. Chop parsley. Serve warm or cool.

Serves: 4–6.
Time: 1 hour.

BROWNIES

$\frac{1}{2}$ cup maple syrup

$\frac{1}{4}$ cup oil

$\frac{1}{2}$ cup apple juice

1 teaspoon vanilla

1 tablespoon instant grain coffee

$\frac{1}{2}$ cup wholewheat flour

2 cups rolled oats

$\frac{1}{2}$ teaspoon sea salt

$\frac{1}{2}$ cup carob powder

1–2 tablespoons orange rind

1 cup currants

$\frac{3}{4}$ cup chopped walnuts, almonds or sunflower seeds

Preheat oven to 180°C. Oil sheet.

Heat sweetener. Combine with the rest of the liquid ingredients and mix till smooth.

Add all the other ingredients. Fold into liquid batter just until well combined. Pour into oiled sheet.

Bake 20 minutes or until centre is firm to the touch or cake tester comes out clean when inserted. Cut and cool.

Makes: 16–20 slices.
Time: 45 minutes.

STRAWBERRY TOPPING (G)

1 cup maltose, barley malt or rice syrup

1 cup fresh strawberries

1 teaspoon grated ginger

$2\frac{1}{2}$ tablespoons arrowroot

few tablespoons cold water

Combine first three ingredients in saucepan. Bring to the boil, stirring occasionally. Dissolve arrowroot in cold water, and stir into strawberry mixture. Spoon over each individual serving. Garnish with crushed nuts.

STEAMED FILLET OF SOLE (G)

1 sole fillet per person (125 g)

sea salt

Japanese lemon pepper (optional)

2 cups water

$\frac{1}{2}$ lemon shell

3 slices ginger-root

½ cup sliced shallots

pinch of sea salt

2 teaspoons shoyu and ¼ cup mirin (optional)

1–2 teaspoons kuzu or arrowroot

fresh mint

Sprinkle fillets with salt and lemon pepper and fold in half crosswise. In a steamer set over simmering water seasoned with the remaining ingredients except kuzu, arrange fillets in one layer and steam them covered 3–5 minutes. Remove lemon shell and ginger from water. Reduce stock by one-third. Dissolve kuzu in cold water. Stir kuzu into steaming liquid and bring to the boil. Add shallots. Season to taste. Transfer the fish to platter and spoon sauce over. Garnish with mint.

Serves: 4–6.
Time: 15 minutes.

OLIVE AND ORANGE SALAD (G)

½ head bib lettuce

3 oranges

⅓ cup olives

¼ cup apple juice

2 tablespoons tahini

1 tablespoon lemon juice

1 tablespoon shoyu

Separate leaves. Wash and drain.

Skin and slice oranges. De-pit olives. Layer oranges and olives on lettuce leaves.

Combine the remaining ingredients and purée until creamy. Spoon over each individual salad.

Serves: 4–6.
Time: 10 minutes.

NOODLES IN SESAME HOT SAUCE

250 g (8 oz) Chinese or Japanese clear noodles (made from rice, bean or potato starch)

1½ teaspoons roasted sesame oil

3 tablespoons brewed tea

2 tablespoons shoyu

2 tablespoons tahini

1 tablespoon oil

2 teaspoons brown rice vinegar

1 tablespoon black bean chilli sauce

1 cm (¾ inch) pared crushed ginger or 1 teaspoon grated ginger-root juice

2 tablespoons chopped shallots

Cook noodles in boiling water according to instructions, until al-dente (medium-hard). Rinse under cold water, drain well. Toss noodles in sesame oil. Cover and chill. Just before serving mix remaining ingredients together except shallots. Pour over noodles. Toss and garnish with shallots.

If black bean chilli sauce is unavailable, use 1–2 teaspoons miso mixed with 1 teaspoon oil, ¼ teaspoon chilli pepper and 1 crushed garlic clove.

Serves: 4.
Time: 20 minutes.

PICKLED MUSHROOMS (G)

500 g (1 lb) button mushrooms

1 cup finely chopped onion

1 teaspoon finely chopped garlic

2 tablespoons chopped parsley

1 teaspoon sea salt or 2 tablespoons miso

¼ teaspoon tarragon

½ cup mirin

¼ cup brown rice vinegar

2 tablespoons oil

2 tablespoons lemon juice (optional)

Wash mushrooms and trim stems. Combine remaining ingredients in saucepan. Add mushrooms and bring to the boil. Reduce heat and simmer covered 8–10 minutes or until mushrooms are tender. Cool and place in glass jar. Cover. Refrigerate overnight. Serve on top of greens, grains or noodles.

Serves: 4–6.
Time: 10 minutes.

After dinner thought:
Soak 2 cups chick peas. Bring to a boil and simmer 30 minutes.

Noodles *are said to have been discovered by Marco Polo around the 13th century in China. He was credited with bringing them to Europe where they became known as spaghetti and macaroni. Noodles to the Chinese, however, are a symbol of longevity and are very often served at a birthday party in the manner of a birthday cake.*

TUESDAY BREAKFAST

GINGERED MANGOES (G)

2 large or 4 small ripe mangoes

2–3 cm (1 inch) piece ginger-root, peeled and grated

1 lemon or lime

4 teaspoons maple syrup

Peel the mangoes, and cut into small, bite size pieces. Grate ginger and squeeze out ginger juice over mangoes. Remove the skin from the lemon or lime, and cut it into very thin strips. Squeeze out the juice over the fruit. Spoon syrup over the fruit, sprinkle with thin strips of rind and set aside to marinate for 30 minutes before serving.

Serves: 4.
Time: 40 minutes.

EGG AND TOMATO (G)

500 g (1 lb) tomatoes, peeled, and pitted

2 teaspoons chopped garlic

2 cups thinly sliced onions

1 cup thinly sliced green pepper

2 tablespoons oil

4 eggs

3 tablespoons fresh basil or thyme or 1 teaspoon dried

sea salt to taste

Drop tomatoes into boiling water. Bring to the boil and drain. Rinse under cold water, remove skin and seeds. Chop.

Chop and slice other vegetables. Heat oil. Sauté vegetables as listed. Sprinkle in salt, cover and simmer 30 minutes. With the back of a spoon make 4 depressions into vegetables. Carefully break open an egg and drop into each hole. Cover pan and steam until egg whites have set. Sprinkle with fresh basil before serving.

Serves: 4.
Time: 45 minutes.

> **Kiwi fruit** *actually originated in China, but was renamed by some enterprising New Zealanders.*

TUESDAY LUNCH

VEGETABLE STRUDEL

2 cups chopped shallots

1 tablespoon chopped garlic

1 cup bean sprouts

1 cup chopped parsley

1 cup grated carrot

1 cup grated zucchini

2 tablespoons oil

3 tablespoons tahini

1 tablespoon miso

1 tablespoon shoyu

HOT WATER PASTRY

2 cups whole wheat flour

$\frac{1}{2}$ teaspoon sea salt

$\frac{2}{3}$ cup boiling water

$\frac{1}{3}$ cup oil

Pastry
Sift flour and salt into a mixing bowl. Boil water and beat in oil until creamy. Stir hot liquid into dry mixture all at once and mix together until smooth. (Adjust liquid content if too wet or too dry.) Knead several minutes. Cover and chill 30 minutes.

Filling
Chop and grate all vegetables. Place each vegetable in a separate bowl. Heat wok, add oil and sauté vegetables as listed. Cover, adding a small amount of liquid if wok is very dry. Combine all the remaining ingredients. Stir into vegetables. Remove and cool on a plate.

Putting it all together
Roll dough into a log. Divide in half, keeping the other half covered. Roll out into a thin rectangle and spread with cool filling. Roll up into tight strudel. Prepare steamer. Place cabbage or spinach leaves on steamer. Cover with strudel. Place lid on steamer and cook 40 minutes. Repeat process with remaining dough.

Alternatively
Bake in a preheated 180°C oven 40–45 minutes. Before baking, brush with egg yolk and 1 tablespoon water beaten together. Sprinkle with unhulled sesame seeds or poppy seeds before placing it in the oven.

Serves: 4–6.
Time: 1 hour.

GREEN BEAN SALAD (G)

4 cups sliced green beans

2 cups pickled mushrooms from Monday

½ cup diced spring onions

1½ cup minced parsley

LEMON GARLIC DRESSING

1 teaspoon crushed garlic

3 tablespoons lemon juice

2 tablespoons tahini

1 teaspoon sea salt or kelp powder

Steam beans until bright green, but crisp. Drop beans into cold salted water immediately to stop cooking. Remove quickly. Dice pickled vegetables, mince parsley. Add to beans and mix through.

Garlic dressing
Whisk together next 4 ingredients and mix through salad. Chill in refrigerator until ready to serve.

Serves: 4.
Time: 10 minutes.

STRAWBERRY KIWI CHEESECAKE

NUT CRUST

½ cup almonds or almond meal

1½ cups rolled oats

½ cup wholewheat flour

½ teaspoon sea salt

¼ cup safflower oil

few tablespoons apple juice to bind

FILLING

3 eggs separated

½–¾ cup maple syrup

4 x 200 gram cakes tofu

2 tablespoons lemon rind

juice of 1 lemon

½ teaspoon sea salt

2 teaspoons vanilla

2 tablespoons arrowroot flour

¼ cup carob powder

TOPPING

1–2 kiwi fruits

250 grams fresh strawberries

1 cup roasted chopped walnuts

Roast almonds till lightly browned then grind until very fine. Add the rolled oats and blend together until oats are mealy. Then add the flour and salt; oil and blend quickly. Slowly drip in apple juice until mixture just begins to bind together.

Preheat the oven to 190°C. Oil a 20 cm (8 inch) spring form pan, and press or roll crust on the bottom only. Bake 20 minutes or until firm.

Meanwhile separate eggs. Add yolks and syrup to blender or processor and whip till creamy.

Bring a pot of water to the boil, add tofu and bring to the boil again. Drain. Add tofu to the first mixture, beating well. Then add the rest of the ingredients except the arrowroot.

Divide the mixture in half. Stir in the carob powder to half. Then stir in the arrowroot to each half and set aside.

Beat the whites till peaked, and divide between the two mixtures. Fold into each half gently. Spoon the plain mixture into the pie shell, alternating with the carob flavoured one. Bake 30–40 minutes or until cake is ALMOST firm to the touch. Turn off oven and leave cake in to cool with oven door slightly ajar.

Press crush nuts around the sides. Slice fruit, and arrange the kiwi in the centre around fresh strawberries. Then cut open the remaining strawberries, and position them around the edge of the cake. Serve quickly to preserve the look of the fresh fruit.

Serves: 8.
Time: 1½ hours.

After lunch thoughts:
Pressure cook chick peas 1 hour or boil until soft. Reserve for dinner.
Marinate 200 g tofu for dinner.

SUMMER SARDINES (G)

1 kg (2 lbs) fresh sardines

sea salt

arrowroot flour

⅔ cup olive oil

6 garlic cloves

1 tablespoon minced red chilli pepper

1½ tablespoons ground cumin

3 tablespoons brown rice vinegar

minced shallots for garnish

Rinse sardines, clean and salt. Allow to stand 10

minutes. Rinse and drain. Pat dry, dust them in arrowroot flour shaking off any excess. Heat skillet, add oil and fry sardines over medium heat, 1–2 minutes on each side, or until they are golden. Drain off excess oil by placing them on cooking rack with tray underneath to catch excess oil. When fish are finished add the next three ingredients cooking over low heat and constantly stirring for 2–3 minutes. Add the vinegar and more salt if desired and pour the mixture over the sardines. Let the fish cool and chill it covered overnight. Serve for lunch the next day or save for when uninvited guests arrive.

Serves: 4–6.
Time: 15 minutes.

TUESDAY DINNER

VEGETABLE CURRY PIE

CHICKPEA PASTRY

1½ cups wholewheat pastry flour

1 teaspoon sea salt

2 cups diced spring onions

½ cup puréed cooked chickpeas

⅔ cup oil

4 tablespoons water

FILLING (G)

2 tablespoons oil

½ teaspoon ground coriander

2 cups diced onions

1 teaspoon diced garlic

2 cups chopped sweet potatoes

1 cup grated carrots

4 teaspoons curry powder

¼ cup chicken stock (page 147) or water

1½ teaspoons sea salt

2 tablespoons peanut butter

2 tablespoons plain yoghurt (optional)

Pastry

Mix flour, salt and coriander in medium size bowl. Rub in chickpea purée with fingertips until mixture is flaky. Heat oil and water in saucepan. Slowly pour into flour mixture tossing with fork until well mixed. Knead briefly on light-floured surface. Roll out dough ½ cm (¼ inch) thick. Cut pastry 2 cm (1 inch) larger all around than top of casserole, just before filling is cooked.

Filling

Heat oil in large skillet. Add spring onions, onions and garlic. Sauté until onions are transparent. Add the rest of the vegetables. Add curry powder, stock or water and simmer until vegetables are tender (10–15 minutes). Remove from heat, stir in peanut butter and yoghurt, then allow to cool if not using immediately. Preheat oven to 190°C. Oil 4 cup casserole dish. Place filling in dish, roll out pastry and place over casserole. Press overhanging pastry against the sides of the casserole to seal. Then slit top of pastry for steam to escape. Bake until pastry is lightly browned, about 25 minutes.

Serves: 4–6.
Time: 1 hour.

WATERCRESS AND BEAN SALAD (G)

4 cups mung bean sprouts

1 bunch watercress

4 tablespoons roasted unhulled sesame seeds

3 tablespoons shoyu

3 tablespoons brown rice vinegar

carrot or beetroot for garnish

Bring a pot of salted water to the boil. Drop in sprouts and blanch 30 seconds. Drain and rinse in cold water. Drain. Repeat with watercress using *fresh* salted water. Squeeze out both the sprouts and watercress so that they are not watery. Cut watercress into 1 cm (2 inch) pieces. Set vegetables aside.

Roast sesame seeds in a dry skillet until they begin to pop. Crack *immediately* while they are still hot in a blender or processor. Then add the shoyu and vinegar, blend, and spoon over watercress and sprouts. Garnish with carrot or beetroot.

Serves: 4.
Time: 10 minutes.

TOFU STROGANOFF (G)

200 g tofu (marinated)

¼ cup oil

1 cup chopped onion or shallots

250 g (½ lb) fresh mushrooms (4 cups) quartered or 2 cups dried

1 teaspoon dried oregano or 2 tablespoons fresh

1 cup sliced green beans

¼ cup mirin

1 cup yoghurt

MARINADE

$\frac{1}{2}$ cup shoyu
$\frac{1}{2}$ teaspoon garlic
1 teaspoon cumin or 5 spice powder
$\frac{1}{4}$ teaspoon pepper
$\frac{1}{4}$ cup water to cover

Marinate tofu after cutting into $1\frac{1}{4}$ x $2\frac{1}{2}$ cu ($\frac{1}{2}$ x 1 inch) pieces for at least 30 minutes or at lunch. Meanwhile prepare vegetables.

Heat skillet. Add oil and sauté onion 2–3 minutes or until transparent. Add mushrooms and lightly sauté.

Add tofu and the oregano. Cover and cook 5 minutes. Meanwhile blanch the green beans in salted water. Drain and rinse in cold water. When mushrooms are tender, add mirin and yoghurt.

Serves: 4–6.
Time: 20 minutes.

PORTUGUESE BRIDAL COOKIES

30 blanched almonds
$\frac{1}{3}$ cup oil (room temperature)
1 tablespoon maple syrup
$\frac{1}{2}$ teaspoon rose-water or 1 teaspoon vanilla
1 cup wholewheat flour
$\frac{1}{4}$ teaspoon sea salt
$\frac{1}{2}$ cup roasted, crushed almonds

Preheat oven to 180°C.

Drop almonds into boiling water. Rinse and remove skins. Spread on baking sheet and bake at 180°C until lightly browned.

Heat oil and sweetener together until warm. Remove from heat and add rose-water or vanilla. Sift flour and salt together and stir into oil mixture. It may be necessary to add several tablespoons water. Gather dough into a ball. Raise oven temperature to 200°C after almonds are roasted. Roll dough into a log, cut into 30 pieces. Flatten a piece in the palm of your hand. Place 1 toasted almond in centre, wrap dough around almond, into an oval shape.

Place on oiled baking sheet. Repeat with remaining dough and almonds. Bake until bottoms are lightly browned, about 15 minutes. Cool on wire racks, but before they get very cool, brush with warmed maple syrup or honey. Roll in crushed almonds.

Makes: 30 cookies.
Time: 30 minutes.

WEDNESDAY BREAKFAST

FRESH FRUIT SALAD (G)

3 oranges, peeled
4 cups chopped peaches
4 cups chopped sultanas
1 cup chopped dates
2 cups chopped apricots
4 tablespoons roasted unhulled sesame seeds

TOPPING (G)

$\frac{1}{2}$ cup goat's milk yoghurt
1 teaspoon miso
3 teaspoons tahini
1–2 teaspoons lemon juice

Chop fruits and combine. Roast sesame seeds. Blend all topping ingredients together. Spoon over salad 15 minutes before serving. Sprinkle sesame seeds on top.

Serves: 4.
Time: 20 minutes.

ALMOND PEACH BUTTER

6 peaches
1 cup blanched almonds
$\frac{1}{2}$ cup apple juice
1 teaspoon cinnamon
$\frac{1}{2}$ teaspoon ginger juice
pinch of sea salt

Boil water in a medium saucepan. Drop in peaches for 1–2 minutes, then drain and rinse under cold water. Remove skins and pit. Set aside. Bring water to the boil and drop in almonds. Remove and drain. Rinse under cold water, then remove skins. Place blanched almonds in blender or processor with apple juice and blend until reduced to liquid paste. Add peaches and remaining ingredients and blend once again. Spread thickly on wholemeal toast or rice wafers.

Serves: 4–6.
Time: 10 minutes.

WEDNESDAY LUNCH

SWEET AND SOUR DUMPLINGS (G)

500 g (1 lb) tofu

1 egg, lightly beaten

1 teaspoon sea salt

1 tablespoon pressed garlic

1 tablespoon grated ginger-root or orange rind

3 tablespoons minced parsley

$\frac{1}{2}$ teaspoon dried oregano

3 cups soup stock (see page 147)

SWEET AND SOUR SAUCE (G)

$\frac{1}{2}$ cup fresh peas

3 tablespoons oil

4 tablespoons brown rice or wholewheat flour

$\frac{1}{2}$ cup leftover cooking stock from boiled dumplings

$\frac{1}{2}$ cup brown rice vinegar

$\frac{1}{2}$ cup barley malt, rice syrup or maltose

$\frac{1}{2}$ teaspoon ginger-root juice

2–3 tablespoons shoyu (to taste)

2 teaspoons caraway seeds (crushed)

Press out tofu (see page 85). Mash all the dumpling ingredients with the tofu and egg. Shape into balls, about 2 cm (1 inch) in diameter. Bring 3 cups of stock to the boil, add salt and drop in dumplings. Return to the boil and add cold water to stop the boil. Repeat three times. When they rise to the surface, scoop out and drain.

Sauce
Drop peas into boiling, dumpling stock. Bring to the boil, and cook uncovered 5 minutes, drain and reserve cooking water. Rinse peas in cold water. Set aside. Heat skillet. Add oil and roast flour, until fragrant. Heat stock and whisk a small amount into flour-oil combination gradually stirring in more liquid until smooth and creamy.
Combine the rest of the ingredients, and add to the flour mixture. Bring to the boil, lower heat, cover and simmer 10 minutes. Add peas. Serve over dumplings and garnish with spring onions or shallots.

Sardines (G)
Serve prepared sardines (see page 71).

After lunch thought:
Impromptu chicken stock (see page 147).

WEDNESDAY DINNER

STEAMED CHICKEN IN MELON SOUP (G)

10 dried Chinese or Japanese mushrooms

1 broiler-fryer chicken (1 kg)

3 spring onions

3 slices pared ginger-root

4 cups boiling water

$\frac{1}{4}$ cup mirin

$1\frac{1}{2}$ teaspoons sea salt

1 large melon (2 kg)

Soak mushrooms in boiling water to cover until soft (15 minutes). Drain reserve soaking liquid. Discard stems, and cut caps in half. Remove backbone from chicken. Cut chicken into 2–3 cm (1–2 inch) pieces. Blanch chicken in boiling water to cover for 1 minute. Rinse under cold running water. Drain.

Smash spring onions and ginger-root with the side of a cleaver. Place all the ingredients in a large heat-proof bowl, and cover tightly with a lid that fits inside the bowl. Cover with aluminium foil. Place bowl on large bamboo steamer over large pot or wok and fill vessel with boiling water. Cover and steam $1\frac{1}{2}$ hours, replacing water in pot or wok if necessary.

While chicken is cooking prepare melon. Cut thin slice from the bottom so that the melon can stand upright securely. Cut off top quarter of melon, rinse and reserve top. Remove and discard seeds, scoop out flesh leaving 1 cm ($\frac{1}{2}$ inch) of shell all around. Reserve flesh for another day.

When chicken is cooked, place melon in large heatproof bowl, and ladle chicken mixture into melon. Cover melon with top, place bowl on steamer. Steam covered about 10 minutes. Serve soup from melon at the table.

Serves: 6.
Time: 2 hours.

Brown rice *is more nutritious than white rice. It contains Vitamin B which is necessary for the digestion of all carbohydrates whether they come from rice, bread, pasta or potatoes. Most carbohydrate foods contain traces of vitamins but not enough per weight for the digestion of the food. Thus they take Vitamin B from the body for digestion. Brown rice contains more than enough Vitamin B for its own digestion and so it leaves extra Vitamin B behind. Brown rice is also valuable for its protein content and provides cellulose and roughage, as well as having a wonderful, chewy, nutty flavour that compliments any meal.*

ONION AND TOMATO PIZZA

CRUST (Double recipe to keep for buns or piroshki)

$\frac{1}{2}$ cup tepid water

1 tablespoon dry yeast

$\frac{1}{2}$ cup wholewheat flour

1 teaspoon sea salt

$2\frac{1}{2}$ cups wholewheat flour

water to form dough

cornmeal for base of pizza

TOPPING

3 tablespoons diced ginger-root

4 cups sliced onions

$\frac{1}{2}$ cup shoyu (to taste)

24 quartered tomatoes (6 cups)

3 tablespoons olive oil

2 tablespoons chopped garlic

1 cup water

pickled mushrooms (from page 69)

2 x 200 g cakes tofu or $\frac{1}{2}$ cup grated cheese

sea salt to taste

olives for garnish

minced parsley

1–2 tablespoons sea salt

2 tablespoons oil

2 tablespoons oregano

1 tablespoon dry basil or 10 tablespoons
fresh basil

Crust

Combine the first two ingredients. Stir until smooth. Stir in the $\frac{1}{2}$ cup flour, cover and set aside in a warm place until mixture bubbles (5–10 minutes). Beat down, add the rest of the ingredients and only enough water to form a smooth elastic dough. Knead several minutes.

Preheat the oven to 190°C. Warm oiled pizza tray and sprinkle cornmeal over the oiled tray. Divide the dough in half and wrap one half and refrigerate for buns or piroshki (see page 83). Shape the remaining half into a circle with your hands. Place pizza on tray, oil fingers and press fingers into the dough, shaping it into a large circle to fit the tray. Cover and set aside till the dough doubles in size. Bake 20–25 minutes.

Topping

Place ginger in pan, cover with onions, water and shoyu. Bring to the boil, cover and simmer 5 minutes. Remove cover, reduce until dry.

Meanwhile, place tomatoes in a large pot, and bring to the boil. Add a pinch of salt, lower heat and simmer covered till tender (10–15 minutes). Strain off juice, and press through a sieve. Set aside, discarding the skin and seeds. Heat skillet, add oil and sauté garlic. Then add herbs, tomatoes and salt and bring to the boil. Cook without a lid until reduced by one-third or desired consistency is reached. Slice mushrooms.

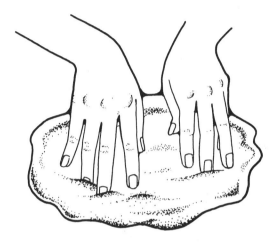

Break tofu into pieces or mash with a fork. Heat skillet, add oil and sauté tofu sprinkling with salt to taste.

Remove crust from oven, place onions on top alternating with tomato sauce. Cover with pickled mushrooms and tofu. Sprinkle with parsley and place olives around the edges. Reheat in oven just before serving.

Serves: 4.
Time: 1 hour.

ORANGE AND ONION SALAD

1 head bib lettuce

1 red onion

2 oranges

1 green pepper

parsley for garnish

Wash lettuce. Dry well. Separate into leaves and line plate. Slice the onion in rings and peel the oranges so that no white is visible. Cut the green pepper horizontally. Arrange the salad decoratively on the plate over the lettuce leaves.

VINAIGRETTE DRESSING

$\frac{1}{2}$ cup oil

2 tablespoons brown rice vinegar

1 tablespoon shoyu

1 tablespoon roasted sesame oil

$\frac{1}{2}$ teaspoon Japanese lemon pepper or assorted chilli pepper

1 teaspoon grated ginger-root juice

sea salt to taste

Combine all the dressing ingredients and blend till creamy and smooth. Spoon over salad just before serving.
Makes: $\frac{3}{4}$ cup.
Serves: 4.
Time: 10 minutes.

After dinner thoughts:
Wash and soak 1 cup lentils for Thursday night. Pressure cook 4 beetroots for 40 minutes. Cool.

THURSDAY BREAKFAST

BLINTZES WITH CHERRY SAUCE

3 eggs

$\frac{1}{2}$ teaspoon sea salt

$\frac{1}{2}$ cup soy milk or nut milk (see page 150)

2 tablespoons oil

CHEESE FILLING

2 cups chopped onion

1 tablespoon oil

4 cups goat's milk cheese (feta is best)

CHERRY SAUCE

2–3 cups pitted cherries

$\frac{1}{2}$ cup barley malt, maltose or rice syrup

$\frac{1}{4}$ cup apple juice

1 tablespoon kuzu or arrowroot flour

Blintzes
Beat the eggs, salt and milk together. Heat 15 cm (6 inch) skillet. Pour about 2–3 tablespoons of the batter into it using a ladle. Tilt the pan quickly to coat the bottom. (Use just enough batter to make a very thin pancake.) Let the bottom lightly brown. Then carefully turn out onto a towel brown side up. Continue with the rest of the batter.

Filling
Chop onion. Heat skillet, add oil and sauté onions until golden brown. Transfer onions to mixing bowl, add cheese and beat until smoothly blended.

Sauce
Pit cherries. Combine sweetener and cherries in a saucepan. Bring to the boil. Dissolve kuzu or arrowroot in apple juice and stir into cherries. Keep stirring until mixture begins to thicken and turn clear. Remove from heat and set aside.

Putting it all together
Spread 1 heaped tablespoon of filling along one side of the blintze. Turn opposite side in and roll up. Spoon over cherry topping and warm in oven or fry in oil before spooning over topping.

Serves: 4–6.
Time: 45 minutes.

THURSDAY LUNCH

BORSCHT

4 beetroots

3–4 cups chicken stock (prepared on Wednesday)

2 tablespoons brown rice or apple cider vinegar

2 tablespoons finely chopped parsley

2 tablespoons finely chopped dill

several tablespoons tofu sour-creme (see page 54)

Peel beetroots if not already done. Slice and combine with hot stock. Bring to the boil, cover and simmer 10 minutes. Purée with vinegar. Put back in saucepan, add herbs and warm. Taste and adjust seasoning. Serve with sour cream in centre of soup, hot or cool.

Serves: 4–6.
Time: 15 minutes.

STRAWBERRY TAHINI CUSTARD (G)

$1\frac{1}{2}$ bars agar-agar

3 cups apple juice

1 cup apple juice

2 tablespoons tahini

2 cups chopped strawberries (250 g) ($\frac{1}{2}$ lb)

3 tablespoons arrowroot or kuzu

1 tablespoon vanilla

1 teaspoon ginger juice (optional)

Rinse agar-agar under cold water. Squeeze out excess liquid, shred into 2 cups juice and bring to the boil. Lower heat and simmer until agar-agar dissolves. Blend 1 cup juice and tahini until creamy. Add to agar-agar mixture. Stir in strawberries. Dissolve arrowroot in remaining cup of juice. Stir into custard until mixture boils. Remove from heat, add vanilla. Blend half of the mixture, and spoon into parfait glasses. Add ginger juice to other half and when cool, spoon over blended custard. Top with strawberries.

Serves: 4–6.
Time: 20 minutes.

ZUCCHINI PASTA

1 dry hot red pepper, seeded

6 tablespoons olive oil

2 cloves garlic

4 cups sliced zucchini

sea salt to taste

1 cup minced flat leafed Italian parsley

250 g wholewheat pasta

water for boiling pasta

Seed and slice pepper into two strips. Heat skillet. Add oil, garlic and pepper. Continue cooking until the garlic is golden and the pepper is dark. Remove skillet from heat and discard the garlic and pepper.

Slice zucchini into thin circles. Heat oil that was used for the garlic, pepper add zucchini. Stir fry several minutes or until tender. Season to taste with salt and parsley.

Meanwhile, bring water to the boil. Add noodles and bring to the boil. Add shock water three times to stop it from boiling each time. Cook until al-dente (medium firm). Drain thoroughly and place in bowls. (If not using immediately rinse under cold water and re-heat when ready to serve.) Dress with zucchini parsley sauce.

Serves: 4–6.
Time: 35 minutes.

THURSDAY DINNER

BULGHUR PILAF WITH ONION SAUCE

5 cups soup stock (see page 147) or water

2 tablespoons oil

12 very thin wholewheat noodles or bean threads (broken into 5 cm (2 inch) pieces)

2 cups bulghur wheat

$\frac{1}{2}$ teaspoon sea salt

Prepare soup stock. Heat skillet. Add oil and sauté noodles. Remove from pan and set aside. Add bulghur and lightly sauté. Add noodles. Pour boiling soup stock over grain and noodles, add salt, cover and simmer 10 minutes. Remove from heat and set aside. Reserve leftover bulghur for patties on Saturday.

Serves: 4–6.
Time: 20 minutes.

ONION AND RAISIN SAUCE (G)

2 tablespoons oil

6 cups sliced onions

10 threads saffron

hot water or stock

3 teaspoons grated ginger-root

1 teaspoon dry cumin

$\frac{1}{2}$ teaspoon dry coriander

1 teaspoon cinnamon

1 teaspoon sea salt to taste

2 cups soup stock (see page 147)

$\frac{1}{2}$ cup raisins

Heat deep skillet. Add oil and sauté onions. Meanwhile, dissolve saffron in hot water or stock. Add the rest of the spices, salt and saffron, cover with soup stock and add raisins. Simmer 30–40 minutes. Remove cover and reduce until creamy. Serve over bulghur.

Serves: 4–6.
Time: 50 minutes.

LENTIL AND SILVERBEET SOUP (G)

1 cup lentils (soak overnight for faster cooking)

6 or more cups water or stock (see page 147)

6–8 leaves, silverbeet

$\frac{1}{4}$ cup olive oil

1 cup finely chopped onion

$1\frac{1}{2}$ tablespoons finely chopped garlic

$\frac{1}{4}$ cup chopped coriander leaves

sea salt to taste

$\frac{1}{4}$ cup lemon juice

lemon wedges

Wash lentils and place in heavy saucepan with water. Bring to the boil, and simmer without a lid 30 minutes.

Skim off grey matter on top, add more liquid if necessary, cover and simmer until tender (30–40 minutes) or pressure cook 15 minutes.

Wash silverbeet and cut off stems. Reserve. Slit leaves and shred. Heat oil, add onion and garlic and sauté until onion is transparent. Add silverbeet and cook till wilted.

Combine onion-silverbeet mixture with lentils, add coriander, salt to taste along with the lemon juice. Cover and simmer 15 minutes. Serve with lemon wedges.

Serves: 4–6.
Time: 1 hour.

FRIDAY BREAKFAST

VEGETABLE PANCAKES (G)

1 cup rolled barley
1 cup wholewheat flour
$\frac{2}{3}$ cup water
1 egg (optional)
$\frac{1}{2}$ teaspoon sea salt
4 tablespoons green peas (boiled for 5 minutes)
4 tablespoons oil
$\frac{1}{2}$ cup leftover grain
$\frac{1}{2}$ cup diced spring onion
$\frac{1}{2}$ cup shredded cabbage
$\frac{1}{2}$ cup bean sprouts
$\frac{1}{2}$ cup grated carrots
shoyu to taste
oil for frying

LEMON-CORIANDER SAUCE

2 bunches fresh coriander
juice of 1 lemon
sea salt or miso to taste

Pancakes

Combine first five ingredients and blend until smooth and creamy. Set aside 30 minutes. Boil green peas.

Heat skillet. Add oil and sauté vegetables in order listed, allowing spring onions to lose their harsh smell before adding the next vegetable. Lightly cook 2–3 minutes. Add shoyu to taste. Cool on plate.

Combine batter and vegetables together. Adjust consistency. Batter should be thick, but pourable. Heat skillet or crepe pan. Add oil and ladle out small pancakes, turning over when holes appear. Repeat. Serve with sauce. Garnish with spring onions or parsley.

Sauce

Drop coriander into boiling salted water. Drain and blend with lemon juice and salt or miso to taste. Serve on top of pancakes.

Serves: 4–6.
Time: 30 minutes.

FRIDAY LUNCH

POCKET BREAD SURPRISE

ALFALFA-ALMOND FILLING

2 x 200 g cakes tofu or 1 cup grated cheese
4 tablespoons miso
4 tablespoons almond butter
1 tablespoon grated orange rind
2 teaspoons mustard
1 cup alfalfa sprouts
1 cup grated carrot
$\frac{1}{4}$ cup grated cabbage
pocket bread or flat pita bread

SUNFLOWER-DATE FILLING

1 cup finely chopped dates
2 tablespoons maple syrup (optional)
1 cup almond butter or tahini
4 tablespoons lemon juice or orange
$\frac{1}{2}$ cup roasted, chopped sunflower seeds
2 tablespoons shoyu to taste

Alfalfa-Almond Filling

Drop tofu into boiling water. Drain. Meanwhile cream the next four ingredients together. Mix in the sprouts, carrot and cabbage. Cut open bread and stuff with filling.

Sunflower-Date Filling

Simmer first three ingredients in a covered saucepan for 5–10 minutes. Add lemon juice, seeds and shoyu to taste. Mix, cool and spread on bread with sprouts.

Serves: 4.
Time: 10 minutes.

GINGER BEANS (G)

| $\frac{3}{4}$ kg (1$\frac{1}{2}$ lbs) green beans |
| 1 cup sliced onion rings |
| 1 cm ($\frac{1}{2}$ inch) piece of ginger-root, peeled |
| $\frac{1}{4}$ cup water |
| 1 tablespoon oil |
| $\frac{1}{2}$ teaspoon sea salt |
| $\frac{1}{4}$ teaspoon fennel seed or fresh dill |

Wash and drain the beans. Cut into 1 cm ($\frac{1}{2}$ inch) diagonal pieces. Slice onion into thin rings. Cut ginger into thin slices, then into julienne strips. Boil the water, stir in remaining ingredients. Add vegetables, cover and cook 3 minutes. Remove cover and cook until all of the moisture is evaporated.

Serves: 4–6.
Time: 10 minutes.

After lunch thought:
Prepare mustard pickles for dinner.

MUSTARD PICKLES (G)

| 3–4 cucumbers (small pickling ones) |
| 1$\frac{1}{2}$ teaspoons sea salt |
| 1 tablespoon dried horseradish or whole grain prepared mustard |
| 1 tablespoon oil |
| 2–3 tablespoons rice honey, barley malt or maltose |
| 2 tablespoons brown rice vinegar |

Salt, skin and seed cucumbers. Slice into thin pieces. Meanwhile, combine all the rest of the ingredients in a saucepan. Warm. Place cucumbers in a jar, pour over marinade and cool. Can keep up to several weeks refrigerated. Serve with dinner. (Make sure pickles are completely covered with brine.)

Serves: 4–6.
Time: 10 minutes.

FRIDAY DINNER

SCALLOPED NOODLES (G)

| 2 tablespoons mirin |
| 2 slices ginger-root |
| 1 teaspoon sea salt |
| $\frac{1}{2}$ kg (1 lb) scallops |
| 6 dried Chinese or Japanese mushrooms |
| 12 prawns |
| 2 squid |
| 1 bunch Chinese broccoli |
| 150 g bifun (brown rice noodles) |
| 2 tablespoons soup stock (see page 147) |
| 1$\frac{1}{2}$ tablespoons shoyu |
| 1 teaspoon arrowroot or kuzu |
| 1 teaspoon roasted sesame oil |
| 1 teaspoon sea salt |
| 2 tablespoons sliced spring onion |
| 1 tablespoon peeled and minced ginger-root |
| 6 cups chicken stock or other stock (see page 147) |
| 1 tablespoon mirin |
| 1$\frac{1}{2}$ teaspoons sea salt |
| 2 tablespoons oil |
| 6 boiled pea pods |

Combine the first three ingredients in a bowl. Cut the scallops in half and toss them to coat with the mixture. Let them marinate 20 minutes. In another bowl soak mushrooms in hot water until they are soft and spongy. Drain and reserve the liquid. Cut into bite size pieces discarding the stems. Shell and de-vein prawns. Drop into boiling salted water and cook until colour changes. Drain and cool. Set aside. Diagonally cross score the outside (shiny, smooth side) of the squid to a depth of about 6 mm intervals. Cut into 1 cm ($\frac{1}{2}$ inch) strips.

In a large saucepan, blanch the broccoli in boiling salted water to cover 3–4 minutes. Drain and refresh under cold running water. Cut into 2 cm (1 inch) pieces. Bring several litres of water to the boil, add noodles and cook until al-dente. Drain and rinse under cold running water. Divide the noodles among 6 bowls.

Combine the next five ingredients in a bowl.

Remove and discard the ginger from the scallops marinade. Drain off liquid.

Slice mushrooms and mince spring onion and ginger-root. Set aside. Heat wok. Add oil and lightly stir fry the scallops, prawns and squid. Remove them to a plate. Add the spring onion and ginger-root and stir fry about 30 seconds. Add the shoyu mixture and stir until thickened. Add the broccoli, seafood, mushrooms and toss them to coat with the sauce. Remove. Bring broth to the boil, ladle it over the noodles, top with seafood, vegetables and pea pods.

Serve with mustard pickles from lunchtime preparation.

Serves: 6.
Time: 45 minutes.

APRICOT YOGHURT SLICE (G)

ALMOND CRUST

$\frac{1}{2}$ cup almonds, blanched
$\frac{1}{2}$ cup walnuts
$\frac{1}{4}$ cup coconut
$\frac{1}{4}$ cup currants
$1\frac{1}{2}$ teaspoons cinnamon
$\frac{1}{2}$ teaspoon cardomon
$\frac{1}{2}$ teaspoon sea salt
2 tablespoons warm maple syrup
$\frac{1}{4}$ cup almond butter

FILLING

125 g (4 oz) dried apricots
boiling water to almost cover apricots
$\frac{1}{2}$ teaspoon sea salt
$\frac{1}{2}$ bar agar-agar
$\frac{3}{4}$ cup water or apple juice
3 tablespoons arrowroot
3 tablespoons water
2 x 200 g plain yoghurt
2 eggs, separated
2–4 tablespoons maple syrup
$\frac{1}{4}$ teaspoon sea salt

Crust

Roast and grind nuts separately. Combine all ingredients into mixing bowl except nut butter and sweetener. Warm sweetener, mix with tahini and stir into nut-spice mixture. Knead for several minutes. Press onto oiled pie dish. Cool in the refrigerator to set.

This crust tends to be less firm when cutting. You may use another if you want it to be very firm.

Filling

Combine first three ingredients together. Bring to the boil and simmer until tender, reducing excess liquid. Wash agar-agar and shred into water. Bring to the boil, cover and simmer until dissolved. Dilute arrowroot in water. Combine agar-agar, arrowroot and yoghurt together. Beat egg yolks and sweetener together and add yoghurt mixture to this. Beat egg whites and salt until peaked. Gently fold into mix and place on crust. Bake at 180°C for 20 minutes or until set. Cool on rack several hours before cutting.

Serves: 4–6.
Makes: 8 slices.
Time: 45 minutes.

Variation

Try using crust as a sweet. Roll into logs or balls and roll in coconut or sesame seeds.

SATURDAY BREAKFAST

WAFFLES

$2\frac{1}{2}$ cups wholewheat flour (finely milled)
1 teaspoon sea salt
1 tablespoon oil
2 cups apple juice

ORANGE-ALMOND TOPPING (G)

2 cups apple juice
2 tablespoons almond butter
1 tablespoon arrowroot flour
1 tablespoon orange rind
1 teaspoon ginger juice
pinch of sea salt

Blend flour and salt. Rub oil into mixture, then add juice. Beat with an electric mixer or processor at least 3 minutes. This beating will incorporate air into the batter and excludes the need for baking powder or other forms of leavening.

Heat waffle iron. Oil top and bottom of griddle with a brush. Wait until iron is hot enough then pour in batter. Cook approximately 5 minutes or until golden brown.

Onion and Tomato Pizza.   See page 75

Topping

Cream a little juice and almond butter together. Then mix ingredients together. Pour into saucepan, stirring continuously. Bring to the boil and simmer 1 minute. Cool and serve over waffles. For variation, add 1 cup strawberries and increase arrowroot by 1 tablespoon.
Serves: 4.
Time: 15 minutes.

STRAWBERRY MELON (G)

1 ripe honeydew melon

1 punnet of fresh strawberries

Carefully cut out wedges from the honeydew melon, leaving the little round section at the top and bottom. Scoop out the seeds from inside the melon. Stand it in the centre of a plate and arrange the cut slices to radiate out like a flower. Fill the hollow centre of the melon with fresh strawberries and let them spill out over the slices.
Serves: 4.
Time: 10 minutes.

SATURDAY LUNCH

BULGHUR PATTIES (G)

2 cups leftover bulghur from Thursday

¼ cup chopped parsley

½ cup chopped spring onions

¼–1 cup wholewheat flour

2 tablespoons miso

oil for frying

MINT SAUCE

1 kg (2.2 lb) onion wedges

4 tablespoons diced ginger

3 tablespoons sesame oil

4 tablespoons fresh mint

4 cups leftover stock plus 2 teaspoons sea salt

2–3 tablespoons shoyu

Patties

Combine cooked grain, parsley and onions together. Add enough flour and a little water creamed with miso, so that it sticks together.

Roll into balls, flatten and pan fry in shallow oil until crisp on both sides. Cut in half horizontally and sandwich together with mustard pickles from Friday or prepared mustard.

Sauce

Heat skillet, add oil and sauté onions and ginger until sweet. Add mint. Combine 3–4 cups stock, sea salt and 1 tablespoon shoyu and pour over onions. Bring to the boil, lower and simmer on a medium heat reducing the liquid. Add more stock mixture with shoyu and again bring to the boil following the same procedure. When there is no more liquid left, and the onions are creamy, remove from skillet. Purée and reheat. Adjust seasoning. Serve with patties. (Reserve leftover for spread on bread.)

Serves: 4–6.
Time: 30 minutes.

After lunch thought:
Soak 2 cups split peas in water for dinner.

SATURDAY DINNER

PEA AND MUSHROOM ASPIC (G)

6 cups water

2 cups split peas

1 x 15 cm (8 inch) strip kombu sea vegetable

½ cup dried Chinese or Japanese mushrooms

2 bars agar-agar

1–2 teaspoons sea salt to taste

2 tablespoons grated ginger or garlic

1 cup grated carrot

1 tablespoon oil

shoyu to taste

fresh coriander

Bring peas and water to the boil, and simmer 30 minutes without a lid. Skim off residue on top. (Add more water if necessary to cover peas 2 cm (1 inch).) Add kombu, cover and simmer with lid slightly off the pot until tender (30–40 minutes). Alternatively, pressure cook 15 minutes. Soak the mushrooms. When soft, slice. Reserve soaking water.

Scalloped Noodles.   *See page 79*

Rinse agar-agar under cold running water. Squeeze out dry. Shred and combine with 1 cup soaking water in saucepan. Bring to the boil, and simmer until dissolved. Add the salt, ginger or garlic to peas. Grate carrot. Add oil to wok, sauté carrot, add mushrooms and season with shoyu. Stir the agar-agar mixture into the peas. Rinse mould. Sprinkle on carrots and mushrooms, and slowly pour or ladle the peas into the mould. Do not choose a deep mould, otherwise the jelly will take hours to set.

When the aspic is set, run a knife around the edge and place in hot water if difficult to remove. Turn out and decorate with coriander.

Serves: 6.
Time: 1½ hours.

STEAMED BUNS

1 cup soaked vermicelli (Chinese green bean threads)
250 g (½ lb) raw shelled prawns
1 tablespoon roasted sesame oil
1 tablespoon diced ginger-root
1 teaspoon chopped garlic
½ cup chopped parsley
½ cup diced celery
1 teaspoon sea salt to taste
shoyu to taste

SKIN

use leftover yeasted pastry from pizza (see page 75) or ½ cup boiling water
2 cups wholewheat flour
¼ teaspoon sea salt
¼ cup cold water
1 tablespoon oil

OPTIONAL FILLING

2 cups butternut pumpkin
½ cup crushed roasted almonds

Soak bean threads in boiling water until soft. Cut up. Discard soaking liquid. Rinse, peel and de-vein prawns. Cut into bite-size pieces. Heat wok, add oil and sauté ginger and garlic until smell is sweet. Add parsley prawns and celery. Sprinkle in cut noodles and lightly stir-fry. Season to taste. Remove to plate to cool.

Skin

Add boiling water and salt to flour and mix. Add cold water and oil. Knead into a smooth dough. Roll out into a log and cut into 24 or 48 pieces.

Shaping and Filling

Using a rolling pin roll each section into a thin circle. Place 1 spoonful of filling in the centre of each circle, gather opposite edges together and pinch at midpoint. Repeat for opposite side. Place filled dumplings on green leaf or oiled greaseproof paper. Cover and steam 20–30 minutes over medium heat.

Makes: 48.
Time: 45 minutes.

Optional filling

Bake pumpkin or steam under pressure. Mash with crushed roasted almonds and add sea salt to taste.

BLACK BEAN SAUCE (G)

2 tablespoons salted dry black beans
½ cup rice honey, barley malt or maltose
¼ cup brown rice vinegar
1 cup chopped spring onion
1 tablespoon pressed garlic
1 tablespoon minced ginger
2 tablespoons kuzu or arrowroot flour
1 cup water

Rinse black beans in water several times. Drain and chop. Combine the rest of the ingredients in saucepan except ½ cup water and kuzu. Bring to the boil. Simmer 3–4 minutes. Dissolve kuzu in cold water, stir into sauce and bring to the boil. Season to taste. Serve over dumplings.

Time: 10 minutes.

Long before forks were introduced, the pie was a convenient way to eat meat, gravy and vegetables with your fingers. Pies originated in England and their name is said to have been derived from magpie, which suggests the collection of many things all together in a nest.

Pies in the past were elaborate creations. A great deal of effort was put into the decoration of their casings. By the end of the 19th century the popularity of pies declined partly due to the general acceptance of the potato which took the place of the pastry.

SESAME CARROT (G)

3 cups carrot matchsticks

2 teaspoons oil

1 teaspoon sea salt

1–2 teaspoons shoyu

1 cup orange juice

1–2 tablespoons rice syrup, barley malt, or maltose

3 tablespoons roasted unhulled black sesame seeds

Cut carrots. Combine all the rest of the ingredients in a saucepan except the sesame seeds. Bring to the boil. Cover and simmer 5 minutes. Meanwhile, roast the sesame seeds until they begin to pop. Remove cover and reduce liquid until dry. Toss with seeds and serve.

Serves: 4–6.
Time: 15 minutes.

SUNDAY BRUNCH

ZUCCHINI PIROSHKI

2 cups chopped onions

4 cups grated zucchini

2 tablespoons oil

1 teaspoon sea salt

BASIL AND GARLIC SAUCE

2 cups of basil leaves

2 cloves garlic, peeled

4 tablespoons pine nuts

1 teaspoon sea salt

4 tablespoons olive oil

2 tablespoons grated parmesan cheese (optional)

PASTRY DOUGH

$\frac{2}{3}$ cup hot water

$\frac{1}{3}$ cup oil

2 cups wholewheat flour

$\frac{1}{2}$ teaspoon sea salt

egg yolk and 1 teaspoon water

Filling
Chop onions. Grate zucchini just before using. Heat skillet or wok, add oil, sauté onions until they are transparent. Add zucchini and stir-fry rapidly to avoid water from leaching out. Cook several minutes till tender, add salt. Set aside.

Basil and Garlic sauce
Put the basil, garlic, pine nuts, salt and olive oil into a blender and mix until smooth. Transfer to a mixing bowl and stir in the grated cheese. Combine just enough sauce with the zucchini mixture to bind. Reserve extra sauce for topping.

Pastry
Bring water to the boil. Whisk in oil until fully emulsified and cloudy in appearance. Combine flour and salt in a mixing bowl, make a well and add the hot mixture *all at once*, with a wooden spoon until dough begins to leave the sides of the bowl. (Adjust liquid content if necessary.) Knead several minutes until smooth. Cover with a damp cloth and chill at least 15 minutes.

Putting it all together
Roll out the dough into a log and cut into 12 pieces. Keep the remaining pieces covered while you roll. Flatten to a small circle and roll out. Put a few teaspoons of filling on each, pinch the edges together firmly to seal and place on an oiled baking sheet. Preheat the oven to 190°C. Brush with beaten egg yolk and water and bake 15 minutes or until golden. You may make them smaller if you wish and have double the quantity.

Serves: 6–8.
Time: 1 hour.

According to Timothy Hall, author of How Did Things Start, it seems that the damper's inventor was William Bond, a member of the First Fleet and Australia's first baker, who set up shop in Pitt Street, Sydney.

Since baking facilities were quite primitive William Bond decided to bake round loaves of unleavened bread made from flour and water and baked them in ashes. Sometime later it was discovered that a handful of white wood ash thrown into the dough would substitute for baking powder. When bore water was used, the damper would rise even more. The name came about, according to Mr Hall, from the custom of 'damping down' or covering the fire with ashes 'to preserve the red coals till morning', a procedure closely followed in the baking of the 'bushman's bread'.

STEAMED DATE CAKE (G)

1 tablespoon dried shrimp or 3 tablespoons bonita flakes
2 tablespoons mirin
2 tablespoons minced dried Chinese dates
2 cups grated yams
$\frac{2}{3}$ cup water or leftover soup stock
$\frac{2}{3}$ cup brown rice flour
2 teaspoons tahini or almond butter
2 teaspoons oil
$\frac{3}{4}$ cup minced shallots
$\frac{1}{2}$ cup chopped mushrooms
$\frac{1}{2}$ cup chopped parsley
2 teaspoons barley malt, rice syrup or maltose
1 teaspoon sea salt
1 tablespoon minced coriander leaves
2 tablespoons unhulled sesame seeds

Soak shrimp in mirin 15 minutes. Mince. If using bonita flakes *do not soak*. Soak dried dates in boiling water 15 minutes or until tender. Pit and chop finely.

Grate yams. Mix with water or stock and simmer covered until soft. Mix in the flour, tahini or almond butter.

Heat wok. Add oil and sauté shallots, mushrooms, parsley and shrimp 3–4 minutes on medium heat. Add the yam mixture, sweetener and salt. Prepare steamer. (See page 41 for steamer preparation.) Roast sesame seeds in dry skillet. Place mixture in oiled dish. Sprinkle on coriander and sesame seeds. Place covered dish on steaming rack, and steam covered 45 minutes. Serve warm or cool.

Variation
Cool overnight. Cut into 1 cm ($\frac{1}{2}$ inch) squares or diamond shapes. Deep fry until golden. Serve warm or cool.

Serves: 4.
Time: 1 hour.

TOSSED GREEN SALAD (G)

1 head of cos lettuce
1 head of romaine lettuce
1 clove of garlic

DRESSING
1 tablespoon apple cider vinegar
sea salt to taste
4 tablespoons olive oil
1 tablespoon freshly chopped mint

Wash, drain and dry lettuce. Tear into bite size pieces, and pile them into a salad bowl that has been rubbed with garlic.

Place vinegar in a small bowl with salt. Gradually whisk in oil until thick and then add herbs.

Serves: 6.
Time: 10 minutes.

FORGET ME KNOTS

1 The skin and seeds of a tomato can easily be removed by dropping the tomato in boiling water for 60 seconds. Rinse under cold water, peel and remove the seeds before using.

2 To remove the bitter flavour from cucumbers cut off the ends 1 cm (½ inch). Dip the end pieces into sea salt and rub into the exposed ends of the cucumbers until it begins to foam. Rinse, discard the end pieces and use. The salt neutralises any bitter taste.

3 To dry out orange or lemon peel, cut the skin in a continuous piece. Hang it up to dry 2–3 days. Cut up or blend when dry enough and store in paper bag.

4 Store herbs, miso, shoyu and oils in dark glass containers in a cool place. Heat and light destroys nutritional quality.

5 Combine fresh chopped fruit and fruit juice. Place in ice-cube trays for summer drinks or insert in popsicle forms and freeze them for children's treats.

6 Tofu should be kept in a glass or ceramic container and covered with cold water. Keep refrigerated and change the water every other day. This will assure freshness for at least one week.

7 When using raw garlic in salad dressings or whatever, peel and press on brown paper bag with salt until moist and creamy. This helps remove pungent oil from cloves. Use garlic and remaining salt.

Preparing and Pressing Tofu

To preserve the form and structure of tofu, so that it may be cut into slices and picked up without falling apart, here are some handy hints:

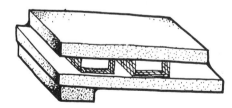

• Wrap tofu in a cotton towel and place on wooden board. Cover with another board and slant the board slightly for better drainage.

• Cut crosswise into thin slices, arrange on towels and place on slanted cutting boards. Cover as described above and press. Good method for use in deep-frying or tempura.

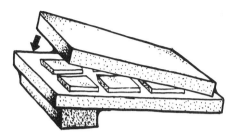

• For a mashed texture that resembles 'cottage cheese' press tofu in towel or cloth, then twist closed and squeeze firmly. Knead it several minutes to expel as much water as possible. (Use a tightly woven towel or muslin.)

The pressing time will vary according to the dish being prepared: lightly pressing tofu preserves the softness and is good for salads or light stir-frying with vegetables. Longer pressing gives a firmer, drier texture good for tempura, deep-frying, salad dressings, 'cheese-cakes' or sour cream. Because the process of pressing and deep-frying greatly reduces the water content, it will stay fresher longer without refrigeration.

To add to the versatility of tofu, it can be frozen, thawed, squeezed dry and crumbled. (The consistency somewhat resembles that of ground meat and it can be used in this way.) It is best to freeze it anywhere from 4–7 days. After freezing leave to thaw at room temperature only until soft, then return to the refrigerator if not using immediately.

—LATE SUMMER—

The shortest 'season' of the year, 'late summer' is a very special time when summer is almost over and autumn has not yet begun. The provisions of nature are most abundantly displayed in the form of apples, corn, and young pumpkins. For most of us it means returning to work or school or putting new plans into action. Earth, the element associated with this season means harmonising in thoughts, actions, opinions and vision, laying the foundation for strong will and good memory.

Goals

Now is the time to consider what lies ahead in the coming months and what you will need for yourself to make that vision a reality. First off a change in eating habits is necessary—more warming foods, more protein, fats, whole grains (such as corn), dried beans and a little salad, seeds, nuts and sweet tastes. Too many ice creams could have brought about congestion, so radishes can help to dissolve mucous. Think about cooking at home more and eating out less.

Strength and vitality may be lacking because the intestines seem a bit sluggish. Eat vegetables with lots of cellulose and fibre to help brush the walls of the intestines as well as whole grains for roughage. Eat smaller amounts of fruit, so that the body can begin to make the transition from warmer to cooler weather more gracefully.

	DINNER	BREAKFAST	LUNCH
MONDAY	Almond bar with a carob coating Celery and French bean salad with orange onion dressing Cous-cous with eggplant and garlic sauce **After dinner thought:** Soak lentils		
TUESDAY	Late summer fish stew Hot sauce Plenty of pasta Walnut and apple salad **After dinner thought:** Corn relish	Corn fritters with Russian sauce **After breakfast thought:** Wash and soak Chinese barley	Barley, rice sesame Coriander-lentils **After lunch thought:** Bake yams for dinner
WEDNESDAY	Vegetables in lemon creme over bulghur wheat Sweet nut rolls Egg drop soup	Tiered pancakes Pumpkin-apple jam	Green beans in walnut and dill sauce Silverbeet and basil soup Salad in a basket
THURSDAY	Pear pie Mexican beans Mexican rice Herb roasted corn Mexican tomato sauce	Puffed wheat, rice or corn cereal with nut or soy milk **After breakfast thought:** Wash and soak kidney beans for dinner Wash rice for dinner Wash millet for lunch	Carrot slice Prawns in black bean sauce Peas in a pod Fluffy millet **After lunch thought:** Cook kidney beans for dinner
FRIDAY	Caraway onion soup Cucumber pickles Buckwheat noodle salad Grilled peaches with pecans **After dinner thought:** Dill pickles	Oat cakes Almond-peach spread	Almond mushroom sauce Bulghur wheat Stir-fried vegetables
SATURDAY	Spinach lasagne rolls Country style fish with teriyaki sauce Date wontons	Corn pones Apple delight	Sprout and bean medley Herb vinaigrette sauce Treasure triangles Mayonnaise curry corn relish **After lunch thoughts:** Pea pâte Zucchini and almond loaf
SUNDAY		BRUNCH: Nut burgers Spring onion salad Sweet and sour turnips	

MONDAY DINNER

ALMOND BAR (G)

½ cup roasted, chopped almonds

1 cup almond meal

½ cup tahini

½–¾ cup barley malt, rice syrup or maltose

1 teaspoon vanilla or ½ teaspoon rose-water

2 tablespoons carob powder

2 teaspoons dried coriander

½ cup grated coconut (optional)

CAROB COATING (G)

½ cup maple syrup

½ cup carob powder

¼ cup tahini

¼ teaspoon sea salt

2 teaspoons vanilla

Roast almonds in oven until lightly browned. Chop. Combine the first seven ingredients kneading until well mixed. (Liquid may need to be added at this stage or some dried chopped fruit. This will depend upon the sweetener that you choose.) Place on greaseproof paper and shape into bars.

Meanwhile, while bars take shape, heat syrup in heavy saucepan until just warm. Stir in carob powder (sift if lumpy) and continue to cook, stirring constantly until just under the boil. Stir in the next two ingredients. Remove from heat and stir in vanilla. Spoon glaze over immediately otherwise the glaze will harden into fudge.

Serves: 6–8.
Time: 15 minutes.

CELERY AND FRENCH BEAN SALAD

½ cup roasted almond slivers

6 cups sliced green beans

4 cups sliced celery

ORANGE ONION DRESSING

½ cup orange juice

1 tablespoon orange rind

¼ cup grated onion

2 tablespoons umeboshi paste or capers

2 tablespoons tahini

Roast almonds until golden brown. Sliver if not already done so. Trim and slice green beans on the diagonal. Bring a pot of salted water to the boil. Add beans and cook 2–3 minutes uncovered. Drain and refresh in cold water. Drain. Set aside.

Wash and trim celery. Cut into diagonal thin strips. Place in same boiling water 2–3 minutes. Drain and refresh in cold water. Drain well. Mix together with beans. Set aside.

Meanwhile, blend all of the dressing ingredients, taste and adjust seasoning. Spoon over salad and sprinkle almonds on top.

Serves: 4–6.
Time: 15 minutes.

COUS-COUS WITH EGGPLANT AND GARLIC SAUCE (G)

3 cups cous-cous

1 tablespoon olive oil

3½ cups soup stock (see page 147)

¾ teaspoon sea salt

EGGPLANT AND GARLIC SAUCE

4 cups chopped eggplant

1 cup oil

1 cup cold water

½ cup shoyu

4 tablespoons mirin

2 tablespoons maple syrup

3 tablespoons roasted sesame oil

3 tablespoons brown rice vinegar

15 cloves crushed garlic

4 tablespoons miso

2 cups chopped shallots or spring onions

Cous-Cous
Place cous-cous in a bowl, add oil and rub between your hands. Bring stock to the boil, season with salt and pour over the cous-cous. Cover and set aside.

Sauce
Chop eggplant into 1 cm. (½ inch) pieces. Sprinkle with salt and set aside to drain in a colander. Pat dry. Heat oil and fry eggplant till lightly golden. Remove eggplant, and all but one tablespoon of oil. Add eggplant and all the rest of the ingredients except garlic, miso and shallots. Cover and cook 3 minutes. Remove cover, and reduce excess liquid by half. Combine crushed garlic, miso and shallots. Add to eggplant and bring to the boil. Toss cous-cous and spoon sauce on top.

Serves: 4–6.
Time: 15 minutes.

TUESDAY BREAKFAST

CORN FRITTERS (G)

1 cup stock, water or soy milk (see page 150)

1 cup wholewheat flour or 1 egg and ½ cup wholewheat flour (decrease liquid content)

2 cups fresh corn kernels (crushed)

1 cup minced onion

½ cup minced parsley

½ teaspoon sea salt

RUSSIAN SAUCE (G)

1 x 200 g cake tofu

2 tablespoons tahini or 1 tablespoon sesame oil

2 tablespoons lemon juice

1 tablespoon brown rice vinegar

1 teaspoon sea salt to taste

1 teaspoon hot mustard or grated garlic

1 hard boiled egg (optional)

3 tablespoons diced onions

1 cup minced olives

3 tablespoons minced parsley

Fritters
Combine first two ingredients. Mix to form a paste. Stir in remaining ingredients. Heat oil and drop by spoonfuls into oil. Fry until lightly brown.

Sauce
Drop tofu into boiling water. Bring to the boil. Drain and combine with the next six ingredients. Blend until creamy and smooth. Mix in olives and parsley. Serve over fritters.
Serves: 6–8.
Time: 15 minutes.

After breakfast thought:
Rinse 3 cups chinese barley. Combine with 6 cups water and bring to the boil. Simmer 30 minutes. Remove from heat and let sit until ready to cook rice (for lunchtime).

TUESDAY LUNCH

BARLEY RICE SESAME (G)

1½ cups brown rice

3 cups chinese barley (regular barley may be used instead)

6 cups water (include the soaking water from the barley)

2 tablespoons shoyu

1 bay leaf

1 cup toasted unhulled sesame seeds

Rinse rice until water is clear. Combine the barley and rice in a heavy saucepan or pressure cooker. Add the water, shoyu and bay leaf. Cover and bring to the boil. Simmer 45 minutes or pressure cook* for same time. Remove from heat and let sit at least 5 minutes before mixing in sesame seeds. (If consistency is too wet use less water, or too dry use more.)

Serves: 4–6.
Time: 1 hour.

CORIANDER LENTILS (G)

2 cups lentils (picked over and rinsed)

5–6 cups water

½ teaspoon turmeric (optional)

2 large cloves pressed garlic

2 teaspoons sea salt

5 tablespoons lemon juice

1 teaspoon garam masala

1 cup minced coriander (Chinese parsley)

3 tablespoons oil

1½ teaspoons black mustard seeds

Bring lentils to the boil. Add tumeric and garlic to the lentils. Bring to the boil, cover and simmer 20–25 minutes or until soft.

Remove cover, add the next four ingredients. Cover and simmer 5 minutes. Heat the oil. Put in mustard seeds. When they begin to pop pour over lentils and serve.

Serves: 4–6.
Time: 1 hour 10 minutes.

After lunch thought:
Bake 4–5 yams for dinner.

*Use less water if pressure cooking.

TUESDAY DINNER

LATE SUMMER FISH STEW (G)

STOCK

3 kg (6 lbs) fresh fish bones, heads and tails with gills removed

6 litres water

1 leek, halved and cut into 2.5 cm (1 inch) pieces

1 stalk celery, cut into 2.5 cm (1 inch) pieces

4 cloves unpeeled garlic, halved

½ bay leaf

3 sprigs parsley

2 slices ginger root

1 cup sliced carrot

½ cup chopped onion

SOUP (G)

½ cup chopped onions

1 cup sliced leeks

1 tablespoon diced garlic

1 cup sliced, peeled and seeded tomatoes

2 tablespoons olive oil

pinch of saffron diluted in warm water

5 cm (2 inch) piece of orange peel (optional)

sea salt to taste

FISH FOR SOUP (G)

250 g (8 oz) tuna or steamed mullet

125 g (4 oz) crab or lobster or yabbies

250 g (8 oz) clams or mussels (washed)

250 g scallops

HOT SAUCE (G)

1 large red pepper

5 cm (2 inches) piece fresh hot red pepper

2 large garlic cloves

1 piece stale wholemeal bread or 1 cooked potato

1–2 cups stock or water

2 tablespoons oil

Stock

Wash the fish trimmings under cold running water until the water runs clear. Place them with water in a large pot. Bring to the boil and skim off residue. Add the remaining ingredients, lower heat, half cover and cook 25 minutes. Keep skimming if necessary. Strain the stock, return to pot and cook uncovered until two-thirds the volume remains. Can be refrigerated.

Soup

Cut vegetables. Dice garlic. Drop tomatoes into boiling water and blanch. Rinse under cold water, peel and remove seeds. Heat skillet. Add onions, leeks and garlic. Sauté until smell is sweet. Add chopped tomatoes, saffron, orange peel and salt. Cover mixture with stock (just enough to cover) and simmer on a low heat uncovered for 15 minutes.

Fish

Steam tuna or mullet and break into flakes. Add to vegetable pot. Sprinkle in crab or lobster and clams and simmer 5 minutes. After 3 minutes, add scallops and season to taste. Stir in the rest of the stock and bring to the boil.

Sauce

Roast pepper over gas or electric burner until charcoal. Place in paper bag for a few minutes. Remove skin and rinse under cold water. Simmer chopped red pepper in salted water until tender. Boil red hot pepper until tender. Crush garlic in salt. Crush all ingredients together to form a sticky paste.

Soak bread in some stock until soft. Squeeze out excess liquid or mash potato. Cream together with stock and cook on a low heat until thick and creamy with the red pepper paste. Just before serving soup, add 1 tablespoon of sauce to each bowl. Garnish with spring onions or parsley. Serve with garlic bread.

Serves: 4–6.
Time: 1 hour.

PLENTY OF PASTA

500 g wholewheat pasta

½ cup green beans

½ cup carrots julienne

1 cup broccoli florets

½ cup bean sprouts

2 cups fresh basil leaves

2 cloves peeled garlic

4 tablespoons pine nuts

1 teaspoon sea salt or 2 tablespoons miso

4 tablespoons warm olive oil

Bring a pot of water to the boil. Drop in noodles, a few at a time so that they do not stick together. Bring to the boil, stirring occasionally. Add just enough water to stop the boil. Do this three times. Then simmer until al-dente (firm but cooked). Drain and reserve the cooking water. Rinse in cold water. Bring salted water to the boil. Drop in beans for 2–3 minutes. Drain and rinse in cold salted water. Repeat with other vegetables.

Combine the rest of the ingredients except the oil. Blend well. Slowly drip in the oil and keep beating until smooth. Serve on top of pasta with vegetables.

Note This sauce can be used on top of grilled fish, added to soup or on top of grains or vegetables. Keeps well in the refrigerator.

Serves: 6.
Time: 30 minutes.

WALNUT AND APPLE SALAD (G)

6 cups chopped endive
1 cup walnut pieces
1 cup chopped apples
$\frac{1}{4}$ cup diced celery

DRESSING (G)

2 tablespoons tahini
$\frac{1}{2}$ cup oil
1 teaspoon prepared mustard, to taste
$\frac{1}{4}$ cup brown rice vinegar
1 teaspoon sea salt or 2 tablespoons miso
grated carrot or pumpkin

Wash endive. Shake out excess water by wrapping endive in a towel and shaking hard. Shred or chop. Chop walnuts, apples and dice celery. Combine all the dressing ingredients and whisk. Combine all the salad ingredients, pour over dressing *just* before serving. Garnish with grated carrot or pumpkin.

Serves: 4–6.
Time: 10 minutes.

After dinner thoughts:

CORN RELISH (G)

4–6 fresh ears yellow sweet corn
$\frac{1}{2}$ cup apple cider or brown rice vinegar
$\frac{3}{4}$ cup barley malt, rice syrup or maltose
$\frac{1}{2}$ cup chopped onion
$\frac{1}{2}$ cup chopped cabbage
$\frac{1}{4}$ cup diced green pepper
$\frac{1}{4}$ cup diced red pepper

$\frac{1}{4}$ cup celery
1 tablespoon sea salt
2 teaspoons mustard powder
$\frac{1}{2}$ teaspoon turmeric (optional)
pinch of pepper

Blanch the corn in a saucepan of boiling water for 5 minutes. Drain. Reserve cooking water for another day. When corn is cool enough to handle, slice off kernels. Place remaining ingredients with corn in a saucepan. Bring to a boil over medium heat. Cover partially and simmer 20 minutes, stirring occasionally. Place in glass jar, cover and store in the refrigerator. Can be kept 3–4 weeks before serving to achieve a richer flavour.

To store Heat mixture to boiling. Ladle boiling relish into hot sterilised jars, leaving 1 cm headspace at the top of the jar. Apply lids, process jars 15 minutes in boiling water bath. Transfer the jars to a wire rack, and cool to room temperature. (This process is for storage over the winter months.)

Time: 50–60 minutes.

WEDNESDAY BREAKFAST

TIERED PANCAKES

BATTER

$\frac{1}{2}$ cup wholewheat pastry flour
$\frac{1}{4}$ teaspoon sea salt
1 egg*
1 cup soy milk (see page 150)**

PUMPKIN-APPLE JAM (G)

6 cups chopped apples
6 cups chopped pumpkin
1 cup currants
1 teaspoon cinnamon
apple juice to cover
kuzu or arrowroot to thicken (1 tablespoon per every 2 cups jam)
grated ginger-root to taste
miso or sea salt to taste

* For a richer mixture use 2 eggs.
** For a lighter batter use one-third icewater and two-thirds soy milk.

Sift flour and salt together into a bowl. Beat egg and combine with flour. Gradually beat in enough liquid to make stiff, smooth batter. Be sure there are no lumps.

To prevent sticking add a little oil to batter.

Allow to stand for a few minutes then beat the rest of the liquid into batter. For a lighter batter use one-third ice water and two-thirds soy milk. Allow to stand in the refrigerator for at least 30 minutes. Whisk before using.

Jam

Wash and chop fruit and pumpkin. Combine fresh and dried fruit and pumpkin in saucepan with cinnamon. Cover with juice. Bring to the boil and simmer until tender. Dissolve kuzu in a little cold juice, add grated ginger, miso and stir into fruit mixture, until boiling. Remove from heat and serve over pancakes reserving leftovers for another day.

Method for pancakes

Heat oil in the bottom of a frying pan or crepé pan. Pour in batter when oil is hot. Fry on both sides then turn out onto greaseproof paper. Keep warm. Spread a spoonful of filling in between each layer. Keep the pile hot in a moderate oven and build up layer by layer. Top the last pancake with crushed nuts and serve hot, cutting into wedges as you would a cake.

Serves: 4–6.
Time: 45 minutes.

WEDNESDAY LUNCH

GREEN BEANS IN WALNUT AND DILL SAUCE (G)

$\frac{3}{4}$ kg (1$\frac{1}{2}$ lb) green beans, trimmed

1 cup minced spring onion

$\frac{1}{4}$ cup brown rice vinegar

$\frac{1}{2}$ cup minced fresh dill

$\frac{1}{4}$ cup minced parsley

3 tablespoons lightly roasted walnuts

2 tablespoons olive oil

$\frac{1}{2}$ teaspoon sea salt or 1 tablespoon miso

grated red radishes

Drop beans into boiling salted water. Bring to the boil, lower heat and simmer uncovered until *almost* tender. Drain well and immediately run under cold water. Drain again. Place in salad bowl.

Combine the remaining ingredients and purée until smooth and creamy. Toss with beans. Garnish with grated red radishes.

Serves: 6–8.
Time: 15 minutes.

SILVER BEET AND BASIL SOUP (G)

5 cups soup stock (see page 147)

2 tablespoons pine nuts

1 cup peeled and thinly sliced stalks from silverbeet

1 tablespoon minced garlic

2 tablespoons minced shallots

2 tablespoons oil

4 cups chopped silverbeet leaves

1 cup chopped fresh basil*

1–1$\frac{1}{2}$ tablespoons miso or $\frac{1}{2}$–1 teaspoon sea salt

2–3 tablespoons tahini or almond butter (optional)

croûtons for garnish

Prepare soup stock or use leftover fish soup or corn-water for stock. Meanwhile, toast the pine nuts in oven or dry skillet until lightly golden. Set aside for garnish. Cut all vegetables. Bring a pot of water to the boil. Add salt. Meanwhile heat skillet, or wok, add oil and sauté garlic and shallots. *Do not let the garlic burn.* Drop the silverbeet leaves into the boiling water. Bring to a boil and remove immediately. Drain. Repeat with chopped stalks. Add the chopped basil to the garlic and onion mixture, then the silverbeet. Add just enough soup stock to almost cover. Cover and simmer 5 minutes. Meanwhile combine the miso and tahini with some stock, mixing until creamy. Blend the soup mixture, adjusting liquid content with the rest of the stock. Add the stalks, stir in the miso combination. Chill. Serve garnished with pine nuts and croûtons.

*When fresh basil is unavailable, substitute 1 teaspoon dried basil with 1$\frac{1}{2}$ tablespoons fresh parsley to equal 2 tablespoons chopped fresh basil.

Serves: 6–8.
Time: 45 minutes.

SALAD IN A BASKET

1 unsliced wheat sandwich loaf (one day old)

several garlic cloves with skins removed

oil

endive

cos lettuce

carrot strips

brown rice vinegar

Remove the end crusts and slice through the loaf every 10 cm (4 inches). Remove the crusts and carefully cut out the middle section to form a square basket. Bruise garlic and rub the bread with it. Deep fry in oil one at a time. Drain thoroughly and cool.

Wash vegetables for salad. Tear. Toss salad with vinegar *immediately* before serving. Sprinkle with sliced shallots for garnish.

Serves: 4.
Time: 15 minutes.

WEDNESDAY DINNER

VEGETABLES IN LEMON CREME (G)

| 4 tablespoons roasted sesame or olive oil |
| 1 tablespoon brown rice vinegar |
| 3 tablespoons lemon juice |
| $\frac{1}{2}$ cup mirin |
| 2–3 teaspoons sea salt (to taste) |
| 2–3 peppercorns |
| 1 bay leaf |
| $\frac{1}{2}$ cup minced parsley |
| $\frac{1}{2}$ cup minced celery or fennel |
| 1 clove garlic, smashed |
| water to almost cover the vegetables |
| 1 onion per person |
| $\frac{1}{2}$ zucchini per person |
| 1 cup diced carrots |
| 1 cup diced turnips or swedes |
| $\frac{1}{2}$ cup chopped celery |
| 1 brussel sprout per person |
| 2–3 teaspoons kuzu or arrowroot flour |

Place first five ingredients in a saucepan and bring to the boil. Add the remaining five. Cover and simmer 10 minutes. Add the water, and the rest of the vegetables, except sprouts. Cover and simmer 20 minutes or until vegetables are *almost* tender. Parboil sprouts in salted water 3–5 minutes or until almost tender. Strain off vegetables, dissolve kuzu or arrowroot in cold water and stir into broth. Bring to the boil. Add sprouts and more liquid if necessary and seasoning to taste. Serve over bulghur.

Serves: 4–6.
Time: 1 hour.

BULGHUR WHEAT

| $2\frac{1}{2}$ cups bulghur wheat |
| 2 tablespoons oil |
| $4\frac{1}{2}$ cups water or stock (see page 147) |
| $\frac{1}{2}$ teaspoon sea salt |

Roast bulghur lightly in oil. Add boiling water or stock, salt, cover and simmer 10 minutes. Remove from heat and set aside another 10 minutes. Serve under marinade and vegetables. Reserve extra for Friday lunch.

Serves: 4–6.
Time: 20 minutes.

SWEET NUT ROLLS (G)

| $\frac{1}{2}$ cup roasted ground sunflower seeds |
| 1 cup minced dates |
| 1 teaspoon cinnamon |
| $\frac{1}{2}$ teaspoon ground coriander |
| $\frac{1}{4}$ cup tahini or peanut butter |
| 1–2 teaspoons miso or $\frac{1}{4}$ teaspoon sea salt |
| 1 tablespoon lemon or orange rind |
| 1 teaspoon ginger juice |
| $\frac{1}{4}$ cup coconut |

Knead or blend all ingredients together except coconut. Shape into rolls and cover with coconut.

Makes: 20.
Time: 10 minutes.

EGG DROP SOUP (G)

| 5 cups soup stock or water (see page 147) |
| $\frac{1}{2}$ cup sliced mushrooms |
| $\frac{1}{2}$ cup chopped Chinese broccoli or regular broccoli |
| 3–4 slices ginger-root (very thin) |
| 2 teaspoons minced garlic |
| 3 tablespoons shoyu |
| $\frac{1}{2}$ teaspoon Japanese lemon pepper |
| 2 tablespoons kuzu or arrowroot |
| $\frac{1}{4}$ cup mirin |
| 1 egg, lightly beaten |
| 1 tablespoon roasted sesame oil |

2–3 cups bean sprouts

1 cup chopped shallots

Bring stock or water to the boil. Meanwhile slice, chop and mince all the vegetables. Add the vegetables, garlic, shoyu and pepper, cover and simmer 15 minutes.

Dissolve kuzu in mirin and stir into soup. Bring to the boil. Remove from heat. Beat egg, and pour in slowly, stirring gently with a fork until egg forms light strands. Stir in sesame oil. Divide sprouts and shallots among soup bowls and ladle in hot soup.

Serves: 4–6.
Time: 25 minutes.

THURSDAY BREAKFAST

PUFFED WHEAT, RICE OR CORN CEREAL

4 cups nut or soy milk (see page 150)

5 cups puffed whole grain cereal

maple syrup to taste

Prepare nut or soy milk. Pour over cereal to taste. Add maple syrup while blending milk if you have a very sweet tooth.

Serves: 4.
Time: 5 minutes.

After breakfast thoughts:

Wash 2 cups kidney beans. Place in pot, add 6 cups cold water and bring to the boil. Simmer on a low boil 30 minutes. Skim off any residue that may have collected on top. If you have the time, add a strip of kombu sea vegetable, cover and simmer until tender (1–2 hours). If not, just leave until you can cook.

Wash 1½ cups of long grain rice. Drain. (For dinner.)
Wash 3 cups millet. Drain. (For lunch.)

THURSDAY LUNCH

CARROT SLICE

½ cup oil

2 cups carrot pulp or grated carrots

1 cup date purée (see page 140)

2 eggs

¼ cup tahini or sesame butter

2 cups wholewheat pastry flour

1 teaspoon cinnamon

½ teaspoon cloves

½ teaspoon sea salt

2 cups sultanas

2 cups roasted chopped sunflower seeds

juice and grated rind of ½ orange

Heat skillet. Add oil and sauté pulp or grated carrots on a medium heat for 5 minutes. Set aside.

Beat together date purée and eggs until light and fluffy. Slowly drip in tahini beating continuously until thick and creamy. Set aside.

Combine all dry ingredients. Toss in sultanas and sunflower seeds. Add juice and grated rind.

Fold in flour mixture into egg combination gently and mix until flour mixture is incorporated. (Adjust liquid here—batter should be thick enough to cling to a wooden spoon when inverted.)

Preheat oven to 190°C. Oil a shallow baking tray (no more than 5 cm (2 inch) high, and spoon batter into pan.

Bake 30–40 minutes or until firm, and slice pulls away from the sides of the pan. Cool on cake rack before cutting.

Serves: 6–8.
Time: 1 hour.

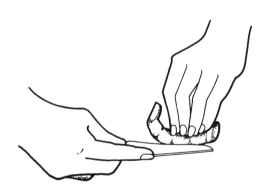

PRAWNS IN BLACK BEAN SAUCE (G)

½ kg green or mung bean threads

15 green prawns

½ teaspoon sea salt

1 tablespoon dark sesame oil

2 large cloves garlic, finely chopped

2 tablespoons finely chopped ginger-root

1 cup finely chopped spring onion

2 tablespoons salted black beans, rinsed and chopped

2 tablespoons shoyu
2 tablespoons mirin
2 teaspoons maple syrup
1 tablespoon arrowroot or kuzu dissolved in $\frac{3}{4}$ cup cold water
2 tablespoons sesame oil

Bring water to a boil. Drop bean threads into boiling water and bring to the boil. Remove from heat and set aside to swell. After 10 minutes, drain and chop. Toss in oil. Set aside.

Shell the prawns and make a slit along the outer curve. Remove the vein and rinse. Sprinkle salt on the prawns and toss in sesame oil. Set aside 10 minutes. Chop.

Prepare garlic, ginger, onions and black beans.

Combine the next 3 ingredients and set aside 20 minutes. Dissolve arrowroot in separate bowl.

Heat skillet or wok. Add oil. Sauté garlic, ginger, spring onions, beans and prawns, cover and steam until prawns turn white. Combine liquid ingredients with arrowroot and stir into prawns. Cook until clear, thick and boiling. Serve over noodles.

Serves: 4.
Time: 45 minutes.

PEAS IN A POD (G)

outside leaves from a lettuce
1 kg (2 lb) shelled peas
2 tablespoons grated onion
2 tablespoons fresh thyme or pinch of dried
4 tablespoons oil
1 teaspoon sea salt

Wash leaves, dry and place in bottom of heavy skillet. Spread fresh peas on top of lettuce. Sprinkle with onion and thyme. Pour over oil. Cover and simmer until almost tender. Season with salt and cook until tender.

Serves: 4.
Time: 15 minutes.

There are several known stories about the origins of **rice**. *One tells of the time when man lived by hunting the rice plant's ears. The goddess Kuan Yin saw how hard life was and she went secretly to the rice fields and squeezed milk from her breasts into the ears of the rice plants. In order to have enough to complete her task the final ears were filled with a mixture of milk and blood and this accounts for the two kinds of rice: white and red.*

FLUFFY MILLET

3 cups hulled millet
$4\frac{1}{2}$ cups water
$\frac{1}{2}$ teaspoon sea salt

Preheat oven to 190°C. Place washed millet on a baking sheet with low sides, and bake till lightly browned. Meanwhile bring water to the boil. Add salt, millet and bring to the boil. Cover and simmer 20 minutes. Mix gently before serving. Spoon prawns in black bean sauce over millet. Save leftover millet for another day.

Serves: 6–8.
Time: 50 minutes.

After lunch thought:
If the 2 cups of kidney beans have not been cooked, try cooking them now. You can pressure cook them much faster (50–60 minutes). If there is still no time, cook them this evening.

THURSDAY DINNER

PEAR PIE (G)

FILLING

3 cups chopped pears
1 bar agar-agar
1 cup raisins
$2\frac{1}{2}$ cups apple juice
1 teaspoon cinnamon
1 teaspoon ginger juice
$\frac{1}{4}$ teaspoon sea salt
2 tablespoons kuzu dissolved in $\frac{1}{2}$ cup apple juice

NUT CRUST

2 cups rolled oats
$\frac{1}{4}$ cup wholewheat flour
$\frac{1}{2}$ cup chopped nuts
$\frac{1}{2}$ teaspoon cinnamon
$\frac{1}{2}$ teaspoon sea salt
4 tablespoons warm maple syrup
5 tablespoons oil
1 teaspoon vanilla

Filling

Chop pears and shred into saucepan. Rinse agar-agar. Combine all ingredients *except* kuzu in saucepan. Bring to the boil. Simmer 5 minutes. Dissolve kuzu in cold juice, stir into saucepan and cook till thick. Set aside.

Crust

Combine first five ingredients in mixing bowl. Whisk next three ingredients together until well blended. Stir into dry ingredients. (Add warm water or apple juice to *lightly* bind crust together.)

Preheat oven to 190°C. Oil pie dish, press three-quarters of the crust into the *bottom* of the dish. Bake 10–15 minutes. Sprinkle remaining crust onto oiled baking sheet. Bake until crisp and lightly browned. Place cooked pears in crust. Sprinkle crumb topping over pears and set.

Serves: 6–8.
Time: 1 hour.

MEXICAN BEANS (G)

| 2 cups kidney beans |
| 2 pieces kombu sea vegetable (optional) |
| 1 x 5 cm (2 inch) piece ginger root |
| 2 cups chopped onions |
| 2 large tomatoes, peeled, seeded and chopped |
| 1 tablespoon crushed garlic |
| 4 tablespoons oil |
| 4 tablespoons corn flour |
| 2–3 tablespoons miso or 1 teaspoon sea salt |

Boil beans for 30 minutes and remove residue from top. (If already done this is not necessary to repeat.) Add more water if necessary so that water level is at least 5 cm (2 inches) above beans. Add kombu (to cook more quickly and add flavour and minerals). Cover and pressure cook 30 minutes or boil until tender. Meanwhile, blanch tomatoes in boiling water 1 minute. Drain and rinse in cold water. Peel, seed and chop. Crush garlic.

Heat skillet. Add oil, garlic and the flour stirring continuously until it browns lightly. When the beans are cooked, drain off excess liquid, and reserve for soup or sauce. Mash the beans and add them to the skillet stirring in the flour. Cook until fairly dry. Sprinkle in salt or add miso as you are cooking. Mould the beans into a long roll and place on a heated serving platter with tortillas, tacos, salad and rice.

Serves: 4–6.
Time: 1–2 hours.

MEXICAN RICE (G)

| 1½ cups long grain brown rice |
| 1 cup chopped onion |
| 2 teaspoons minced garlic |
| 1 sliced green chilli, seeds removed |
| 1 cup chopped green pepper |
| 1 tomato, skinned and seeded |
| 1 teaspoon sea salt |
| 1¾ cups boiling water or chicken stock |
| ½ cup chopped chives |
| olives |

Wash rice, if not done in the morning. Chop, mince vegetables. Bring a pot of water to the boil. Blanch tomato for 1 minute. Remove, drain and rinse in cold water. Skin and seed. Chop finely. Bring stock or water to the boil.

Meanwhile, heat skillet or wok. Add oil and sauté onions and garlic, until harsh smell disappears. Add the green chilli, pepper and tomato. Cook 1–2 minutes. Then add rice. Remove chilli and cover with boiling stock or water. Sprinkle in salt and bring to the boil. Cover and simmer 40 minutes. Use olives and parsley or chives for garnish.

Serves: 4–6.
Time: 50 minutes.

HERB ROASTED CORN (G)

| ⅓ cup oil |
| 1 teaspoon minced garlic |
| 1 tablespoon fresh chopped basil |
| ½ teaspoon oregano |
| ½ teaspoon sea salt |
| 4 ears fresh corn with husks |
| ½ cup grated parmesan cheese (optional) |

Heat saucepan. Add oil, stir in the next four ingredients. Brush this mixture over the ears of corn. Cover the corn back up with the husks. (Only pull back the husks do not take them off.) Allow to marinate 30 minutes. Preheat oven to 180°C and bake 30 minutes or steam under pressure 10 minutes.

Serves: 4–6.
Time: 40 minutes or 1 hour.

Steamed Buns.   See page 82

MEXICAN TOMATO SAUCE (G)

½ kg (1 lb) skinned and seeded tomatoes
2 cups diced onion
2 tablespoons minced garlic
3 tablespoons minced ginger-root
1 tablespoon minced chilli pepper or 1 teaspoon Japanese chilli pepper
1 teaspoon oregano
1 teaspoon ground cumin
1 teaspoon ground coriander
1 cup chopped celery
½ cup diced carrot pumpkin
2 tablespoons olive oil or corn oil
1–2 teaspoons brown rice vinegar or apple cider vinegar
sea salt to taste

Bring a pot of water to the boil. Drop in tomatoes and blanch 1 minute. Drain and rinse in cold water. Skin, seed and chop. Set aside to drain. Chop, mince other vegetables. Heat skillet or wok. Add oil and onions, garlic and ginger. Cook until harsh smell disappears. Add the next four ingredients and stir lightly. Then add the vegetables, cover and simmer 10 minutes. Add the vinegar and salt and cover and simmer again 20 minutes. For a better flavour, simmer several hours. Remove cover and reduce by one-third. Can store until ready to use. Will keep at least one week.

Serves: 4–6.
Time: 40–50 minutes.

FRIDAY BREAKFAST

OAT CAKES

12 Chinese pitted dates soaked in 1 cup water or apple juice
½ cup oil
½ teaspoon sea salt
1 tablespoon orange rind
1 teaspoon grated ginger-root
4 cups rolled oats, wheat or rice
½ cup wholewheat or brown rice flour
¼ cup sunflower seeds, roasted and ground

Soak dates until soft. Pit and reserve soaking water or juice. Blend dates, soaking water (1 cup) and oil

together. Mix the remaining ingredients together. Combine the two mixtures. Roll out on greaseproof paper. Preheat oven to 190°C.

Cut into 5–6 cm (2–2½ inch) circles. Place on oiled baking sheet. Bake for 15 minutes, turn over and bake another 15 minutes.

Makes: 36.
Time: 40 minutes.

ALMOND-PEACH SPREAD

3 parts almond butter
1 part miso
few tablespoons boiling peach juice

Blend all ingredients together until smooth. Spread on oat cakes.

FRIDAY LUNCH

ALMOND MUSHROOM SAUCE (G)

½ cup chopped onion
1 teaspoon chopped garlic
4 cups chopped mushrooms
2 tablespoons oil
¼ teaspoon crushed tarragon or basil
1 tablespoon miso or ½ teaspoon sea salt to taste
½ cup chopped parsley
½ cup chopped almonds

Chop vegetables. Heat wok, add oil and sauté onion and garlic until harsh smell disappears. Add mushrooms and tarragon. Cook, stirring occasionally until most of the liquid has evaporated. Blend mushroom mixture with miso, parsley and almonds. (Add *hot* liquid to adjust consistency.) This recipe can also be used as a pâté by cooking until dry and blended without adding extra liquid.

Serves: 4.
Time: 15 minutes.

Bulghur Wheat
Steam leftover bulghur wheat from Wednesday's dinner for 10 minutes or until heated through. Serve mushroom sauce over wheat.

Corn Fritters with Russian Sauce.   See page 89

STIR-FRIED VEGETABLES (G)

1 cup onion wedges

1 tablespoon diced ginger

1 cup diagonally sliced green beans or green pepper

½ cup chopped Chinese cabbage

½ cup matchstick carrots

2 tablespoons oil

¼ cup chicken, fish or vegetable stock (see page 147)

¼ teaspoon sea salt

1 teaspoon kuzu

1 tablespoon cold stock or water

1–2 tablespoons shoyu to taste

Cut onions, dice ginger, slice beans or pepper. Cut cabbage, and carrots. Heat wok, add oil and sauté vegetables in order listed above, stirring constantly so that water does not leach out from vegetables. Add stock, salt and simmer 2–3 minutes. Dissolve kuzu in stock or water stirring rapidly into vegetables and cook till thickened. Season with shoyu. Serve with bulghur.

Serves: 4.
Time: 10 minutes.

FRIDAY DINNER

CARAWAY ONION SOUP (G)

4 cups kombu stock (see page 147)

1 tablespoon sesame or safflower oil

1 cup sliced onion

½ cup sliced cabbage

1 cup sliced carrot

1 tablespoon caraway seeds

1 x 200 g cake tofu cut into 1.2 cm (½ inch) cubes

2–3 teaspoons miso to taste

garnish with spring onions or grated ginger

Bring stock to boil. Heat wok, add oil and lightly sauté onion. Then add cabbage, lightly sauté, and add carrot, and lightly sauté. Cover with boiling stock, cover and simmer 5–10 minutes. Remove several tablespoons of stock and cream with miso. Add seeds and tofu. Add back to soup, remove from heat and let sit 2–3 minutes. Garnish with spring onions or add grated ginger.

Serves: 4–6.
Time: 20 minutes.

CUCUMBER PICKLES (G)

2–3 cucumbers (medium size)

1½ teaspoons sea salt

1 tablespoon wasabi (horseradish)* or mustard powder

1 teaspoon tumeric

2–3 tablespoons maple syrup

2–3 tablespoons brown rice vinegar

Cut cucumbers in half lengthwise, remove seeds and slice into thin pieces. Combine the rest of the ingredients together. Add cucumber, cover. Will keep if refrigerated several weeks.

Serves: 4–6.
Time: 10 minutes.
*Found in oriental food stores.

BUCKWHEAT NOODLE SALAD (G)

6 large Japanese or Chinese dried mushrooms

1 x 200 g cake tofu

2 tablespoons brown rice vinegar

2 tablespoons lemon juice or orange

½–1 teaspoon sea salt

4–6 tablespoons oil

minced onions (optional)

minced parsley or basil (optional)

2 teaspoons prepared mustard (optional)

2 cups quartered zucchini cut into 2 cm (1 inch) lengths

2 cups carrot flowers

1 cup shelled peas

1 cup minced spring onions

½ cup water or stock (use soaking water from mushrooms)

1 tablespoon shoyu

2 tablespoon mirin

250 g buckwheat noodles

Place mushrooms in bowl. Boil water and pour over mushrooms. Soak till tender. Discard stems and slice finely. Set aside. Keep soaking liquid.
Boil water. Drop tofu in. Bring to the boil. Simmer 1–2 minutes. Drain and combine with next three ingredients, blending till creamy. Slowly drip in oil. Add optional ingredients here. Chill.
Cut vegetables. Steam or blanch 2–3 minutes in salted

water. Drain and rinse. Place chopped spring onions in cloth (cheesecloth or muslin) and rinse under cold running water 2–3 minutes. Squeeze dry.

Combine the next three ingredients, add sliced mushrooms and boil uncovered until almost dry. Cook noodles in boiling water until al-dente, 8–9 minutes. Drain and rinse under cold running water to cool. Pour dressing over salad after arranging salad on plates. Garnish with spring onions.

Serves: 4–6.
Time: 45 minutes.

GRILLED PEACHES WITH PECANS (G)

6 small nectarines or peaches, halved and pitted

1 tablespoon mirin (optional)

½ cup chopped pecans

2–3 tablespoons chopped sultanas or currants

2–3 tablespoons almond or sesame butter

1–2 teaspoons breadcrumbs

1 teaspoon coriander (dry)

1 teaspoon miso

Arrange fruit cut side up on baking sheet, sprinkle with mirin. Combine the rest of the ingredients, blending until well mixed. Spoon filling into fruit. Grill 3–4 minutes.
Serves: 6.
Time: 15 minutes.

DILL PICKLES (G)

2 kg (4 lb) pickling cucumbers

¼ cup sea salt

8 cups water

3 tablespoons chopped garlic

2 tablespoons mixed pickling spices

fresh dill or other herbs

1 slice day old sour dough bread

Wash cucumbers. Arrange cucumbers in large glass jar or stoneware container. Bring salt and water to the boil. Add garlic and spices. When water has cooled slightly, pour over pickles. Lay herbs on top. Add rye bread, cover with plate that fits inside the jar. Fill plastic bag with water, tie securely and sit on top of plate.

Let stand at room temperature 3–5 days. When pickles smell sour and turn a darker shade of green, taste them. If they are to your liking remove weight, and cover with lid. Refrigerate to keep fresh.

Makes: 4 litres.
Time: 30 minutes.

SATURDAY BREAKFAST

CORN PONES (G)

1⅓ cups water

2 cups cornmeal

1 teaspoon sea salt

3 tablespoons oil

Heat the water to boiling point. Put cornmeal and salt into a mixing bowl. Add the boiling water and oil. Mix quickly and allow to stand covered 15–20 minutes. Form the mixture into little cakes with your hands. (Moisten your hands with oil to prevent sticking.) Preheat oven to 190°C and bake on oiled skillet 35–40 minutes. Top with Apple Delight.

Serves: 4–6.
Time: 30 minutes.

APPLE DELIGHT (G)

4 apples

½ cup chopped dates

1 tablespoon fresh lemon juice or orange

1 tablespoon maple syrup or 3 tablespoons barley malt, maltose or rice honey

1 cup yoghurt

½ tablespoon miso

½ teaspoon ginger juice

chopped roasted nuts or seeds

Chop apples finely. Combine with dates. Set aside. Blend together juice sweetener, yoghurt, miso and ginger juice. Fold mixture into fruit and top with roasted nuts or seeds.

Serves: 4.
Time: 5 minutes.

SATURDAY LUNCH

SPROUT AND BEAN MEDLEY (G)

½ Chinese cabbage, finely shredded

2 cups shredded Chinese broccoli tops or
broccoli leaves

3 cups bean sprouts

2 cups snake beans

2 cups carrot matchsticks

Bring a pot of salted water to the boil. Meanwhile, shred cabbage and broccoli leaves. Wash sprouts and drain. Cut beans into 2 cm (1 inch) lengths. Cut carrots into matchsticks. Blanch each vegetable separately 3–5 minutes or until tender but still crisp. Blanch sprouts only 1 minute. Set aside.

Serves: 4–6.
Time: 15 minutes.

HERB VINAIGRETTE SAUCE (G)

1 cup parsley leaves

2 tablespoons chopped chives or spring
onions

1 teaspoon dried basil

1 medium clove garlic, peeled

¾ cup oil

¼ cup water

3 tablespoons brown rice vinegar

1 teaspoon dried tarragon

1½ teaspoons prepared mustard

½ teaspoon sea salt

Mince parsley. Chop chives. Blend the remaining ingredients until smooth then add the parsley and continue to blend adjusting liquid content if necessary. Can be kept refrigerated for several weeks. Spoon over salad before serving.

Makes: 1⅓ cups.
Time: 5 minutes.

Salt, *a desirable condiment, is used frequently on or off the dinner table. A ready source of salt in some coastal regions of Australia is the river mangrove. This small shrub takes up salt through its roots and excretes it through glands on the upper leaf surface. Here the solution evaporates, leaving behind deposits of salt crystals.*

TREASURE TRIANGLES (G)

4 x 200 g cakes tofu

arrowroot flour or breadcrumbs

oil for deep frying

SALAD FILLING (G)

2 cups thinly sliced radishes

⅓ cup olives, pitted and cut lengthwise into
thin strips

1 tablespoon tahini

4 tablespoons spring onions

4–6 lettuce leaves

MAYONNAISE CURRY (G)

leftover tofu after making pockets

3 tablespoons lemon juice

4 tablespoons oil

¼ cup brown rice vinegar

1 teaspoon curry powder or tumeric

½ teaspoon sea salt

4 tablespoons minced parsley

4 tablespoons minced carrots or red pepper

corn relish (see page 91)

Press tofu 15 minutes with a heavy weight. Cut diagonally into triangles. Roll in arrowroot or breadcrumbs. Heat oil. Deep fry until lightly browned. Drain. When cool, scoop out centres with melon baller after cutting initially with knife. (Save tofu for mayonnaise.)

Mayonnaise Curry
Blend the dressing ingredients except carrots and parsley until smooth and creamy. Mix in carrots and parsley. Cut the radishes, pit the olives and cut. Chop the spring onions and tear the lettuce leaves. Toss together with dressing. Stuff into triangles. Spoon relish over triangles before serving.

CORN RELISH

2 teaspoons kuzu for every 1 cup relish

cold water to dissolve kuzu

Dissolve kuzu. Bring relish to the boil. Stir in dissolved kuzu and bring to the boil again. Remove from heat immediately, and spoon over triangles.

Serves: 4–6.
Time: 30 minutes.

⊛ **After lunch thoughts:**

PEA PÂTE (G)

2 cups split peas

1 x 15 cm (6 inch) piece kombu (optional)

2 cloves crushed garlic

2 cups chopped onions

1 tablespoon crushed garlic

½ cup minced parsley

2 tablespoons oil

½ tablespoon thyme

½ tablespoon sea salt

1 tablespoon miso

Bring peas to the boil. Skim off grey residue that collects on top. Simmer 30 minutes. Add kombu and garlic, cover and pressure cook 15 minutes or simmer 45 until tender. Meanwhile crush, chop and mince vegetables. Heat skillet, add oil and sauté onions till golden brown. Add garlic and parsley. Strain off excess liquid from peas, add peas to vegetables and cook 2–3 minutes. Remove from heat, mould in bread tin, and cool. Serve with crackers or raw vegetables, or with zucchini and almond loaf.

Serves: 4–6.
Time: 60 minutes.

ZUCCHINI AND ALMOND LOAF (G)

1½ tablespoons dry yeast

¼ cup apple juice

2 tablespoons buckwheat flour

2 egg yolks

¼ cup maple syrup (optional)

¼ cup safflower oil

2 tablespoons oil

1 cup chopped onion

2 cups grated zucchini

½ teaspoon sea salt

½ cup brown rice flour

¼ cup buckwheat flour minus 2 tablespoons

½ cup maize flour

¼ cup roasted unhulled sesame seeds

¼ cup roasted slivered almonds

2 egg whites

Combine first three ingredients. Cover and set aside to rise. In a separate bowl combine next two ingredients and beat on a high speed until smooth and creamy. Drip in oil constantly beating.

Heat skillet, add oil and sauté onion until clear and lightly browned. Add grated zucchini and lightly sauté. Sprinkle in sea salt and remove from skillet. Combine next five ingredients and mix lightly with sautéed vegetables. (You may have to add ¼ cup apple juice if mixture is too thick.) Beat egg whites with a pinch of salt until peaked. Mix ⅓ of whites into batter and then fold in the remaining two-thirds of the whites very gently. Place in two oiled and floured pans two-thirds full, cover and rise. Bake in a preheated 180°C oven 40–50 minutes or until skewer inserted in centre pulls out clean. Place on rack remove from pans, cover with towel and cool.

Serves: 6–8.
Time: 1½ hours.

SATURDAY DINNER

SPINACH LASAGNE ROLLS

PASTA

16 curly edge wholewheat lasagne noodles

2 tablespoons oil

SAUCE

1⅓ cup oil

½ cup wholewheat flour

2 teaspoons sea salt

1 cup chopped basil

½ cup chopped parsley

FILLING

1 bunch spinach, blanched and chopped (2½ cups cooked and chopped)

2 tablespoons oil

1 cup chopped shallots

1 teaspoon minced garlic

1 tablespoon rinsed and chopped salted black beans

1 x 250 g cake tofu broken into small pieces

Pasta

Cook noodles in boiling water adding 2 tablespoons oil to water, until al-dente. Drain and rinse. As soon as you can, separate noodles and place in a single layer on flat surface.

Sauce

Heat deep skillet. Add oil and flour. Stir until smooth. Slowly add 2 cups noodle water, salt and continue to cook until mixture comes to the boil and thickens. Simmer 5 minutes. Combine sauce, basil and parsley and blend until smooth. Set aside in saucepan.

Filling

Drop spinach into boiling salted water and cook 3 minutes. Drain and rinse under cold water. Squeeze out all excess liquid and chop. Meanwhile, heat skillet. Add oil and sauté shallots, garlic, black beans and tofu. Add spinach and lightly sauté. Add ½ cup sauce, remove from heat and set aside.

Assembling

Oil a 20 cm (8 inch) round baking dish. Preheat oven to 180°C. Place 1 cup sauce in dish, set aside. Spread one-third of spinach mixture on each noodle to within 2 cm (1 inch) at one end. Roll up from the filled end, jelly-roll fashion. Lightly press uncovered portion against noodles to stick together. Place rolls upright in prepared baking dish. Cover and bake 45 minutes. Heat remaining sauce and serve.

Serves: 6–8.
Time: 90 minutes.

COUNTRY STYLE FISH WITH TERIYAKI SAUCE
500 g (½ lb) chopped bream or snapper
½ cup breadcrumbs and ½ cup ground walnuts
¾ cup water or soup stock
1 egg, beaten
1 cup minced onion
¼ cup sliced olives
1 teaspoon lemon rind
1 tablespoon grated ginger
½ cup chopped parsley
½ teaspoon basil
1 teaspoon prepared mustard
2 tablespoons oil
1 teaspoon sea salt or 2 tablespoons miso

TERIYAKI SAUCE (G)

1 cup miso
2 teaspoons grated ginger-root
2 cloves crushed garlic
1 teaspoon roasted sesame oil
1 tablespoon barley malt, rice syrup or maltose

Fish

Combine all the ingredients and blend until creamy. Preheat oven to 190°C. Oil 15 cm x 12 cm x 5 cm loaf pan, spoon into pan, cover and bake 15 minutes. Remove cover and bake until set and lightly browned. Remove from oven and cool before slicing.

Sauce

Blend first four ingredients together. Place in saucepan and simmer 10 minutes. Add sweetener and cook 5 minutes longer. Spoon over cut slices of loaf.

Serves: 4.
Time: 45 minutes.

DATE WONTONS
wonton skins*
250 g (2 cups) dried dates
90 g (¼ cup) chopped walnuts
1½ teaspoons grated orange rind
1 tablespoon orange juice
oil for deep frying

Chop dates finely or put through mincer. Add chopped walnuts, rind and juice. Fill by rolling a teaspoon of filling between the palm of your hands to form a cylinder. Place filling diagonally across wrapper. Moisten edges with water, fold point over and roll to form a tube. Stick a finger in each end of the tube and twist to seal. Deep fry 2–3 minutes. Drain and cool.

*Can be found in most Chinese food stores.

SUNDAY BRUNCH

NUT BURGERS
4 tablespoons grated cheese
4 tablespoons ground walnuts or almonds
1 cup grated carrot
2 tablespoons chopped onion
2 tablespoons chopped celery
1–2 teaspoons curry powder
4 slices wholewheat bread (crusts removed)
2 small eggs
breadcrumbs or cornmeal for coating
oil for deep frying

Grate cheese. Blend or process walnuts. Grate carrot. Chop vegetables. Mix all together. Blend or process bread and eggs together until very pasty. Add the first mixture and blend until smooth. Shape into burgers and place on oiled plate. Chill 15–30 minutes. Heat oil, roll in breadcrumbs and deep fry until golden.

Makes: 12.
Time: 15 minutes.

SPRING ONION SALAD (G)

1 teaspoon sea salt

2 bunches spring onions

6 tablespoons lemon juice

4 tablespoons shoyu

1 tablespoon prepared mustard

2 tablespoons tahini or almond butter

Bring salted water to the boil. Drop in whole spring onions and return to the boil. Cook 2 minutes. Dip the vegetables into a bowl of cold salted water. Drain quickly. Squeeze out excess liquid, cut off roots (reserve for another vegetable dish or soup) and cut onions into 5 cm (2 inch) pieces. Set aside.

Combine the rest of the ingredients and blend till creamy and smooth. Spoon over salad and serve with burgers.

Serves: 4–6.
Time: 10 minutes.

SWEET AND SOUR TURNIPS (G)

500 g (1 lb) turnips

2 tablespoons miso

1 tablespoon maple syrup, maltose or barley malt

$\frac{1}{4}$ teaspoon grated ginger

$\frac{1}{4}$ cup water

2 teaspoons lemon juice

chives

Cut turnips into 2 cm (1 inch) cubes. Deep fry until browned. Drain well and set aside. Combine next four ingredients in saucepan. Cover and cook until heated. Stir in lemon juice and turnips. Bring to the boil and serve with minced chives.

FORGET ME KNOTS

1 Mustard in all of the recipes refers to the whole mustard seed variety unless otherwise indicated. They should be visible.

2 Many salad ingredients are living things. Do not pack fresh fruits and vegetables together too tightly since they need oxygen to breathe. Refrigeration slows the rate of breathing and delays spoilage.

3 Before serving salad greens and some vegetables, they should be immersed into cold water and refrigerated with some moisture still clinging to them. This will keep them crisp.

4 Salad dressings should be made ahead of time and kept in glass containers until needed.

5 The main reason for cooking vegetables is to break down their cellular structures so that the vegetables are more digestible. The compound that makes vegetable tough, cellulose, can be softened by cooking.

6 Most vegetables are slightly acidic and these are soluble in water and volatile in cooking. They are leached out into the cooking water and escape easily in steam. Therefore, cook green vegetables with the lid *off* to allow the escape of volatile acids.

7 When cooking with fish remember the following points:

- Don't overcook your fish or it will toughen and lose its subtle flavour.
- Keep fish moist until ready to use.
- Fish to be cooked in oil or broiled should be thoroughly dried. If not, it will spatter and only be cooked on the outside.
- When freezing oily fish, dip briefly in lemon juice before freezing.
- Rubbing hands with salt removes the fishy smell.
- To de-smell pots and pans boil in vinegar and water.
- Fatty fish are best cooked by dry heat—either baked, broiled or grilled.
- When buying your fish, look for the one with bright clear protruding eyes. This is a sign of freshness.

——AUTUMN——

A time of gathering, autumn signifies the beginning of more inward, home-oriented projects. It is the season of the harvest—reaping the growth of spring and summer and preparing for winter.

Late corn, wheat, new season rice, pumpkin, young ginger-root, beans and nuts are all a part of the bounty. It's a good time to put some vegetables and fruits into preserving jars so that when winter comes and the fresh fruit and vegetable selection begins to dwindle, you can look into your pantry and have a wider selection to choose from.

Goals

Some of us would do well to cleanse our bodily systems, whether it be for one day or one week. A cleansing diet can be helpful at this time of the year or even a semi-fast to break those old habits and formulate new patterns. When over-indulging and too many late nights have begun to show signs of fatigue and over-weight, it's time to increase activity and decrease consumption. After the fast, you will be amazed at how much lighter and brighter you will feel. A simple routine of brown rice, vegetable juices or vegetable broths for 24 or 48 hours can make a lot of difference in the coming months ahead.

Then you can begin to look again at more protein, fats, wholegrains, pumpkins, land and sea vegetables (such as spinach and watercress), stews, pies and generally warming foods. Stuffed baked pumpkin is one of my all-time favourites, especially for this titillating time of the year.

	DINNER	BREAKFAST	LUNCH
MONDAY	Scalloped yams Noodles with caraway onion sauce Radish with miso sauce Sweet cucumber salad Fruit and nut bars **After dinner thought:** Soak chickpeas and barley		
TUESDAY	Carrot and apple tzimme Buckwheat stew Coleslaw Chickpea roll **After dinner thought:** Soak ½ cup dried chestnuts	Sweet buckwheat creme **After breakfast thought:** Tropical chutney	Tofu burgers Grilled pears/carob sauce Vegetable chips **Lunch after thought:** Chickpea roll for dinner
WEDNESDAY	Egg and lemon soup Stuffed envelopes Okra and tomatoes Mixed pickles **After dinner thought:** Soak 3 cups kidney or pinto beans in water	Creme of wheat, rye and rice	Chickpea patties with onion and garlic sauce Stir-fried chestnuts and Chinese cabbage
THURSDAY	Chestnut rice Poached snapper in sweet and sour sauce Bean sprout salad **After dinner thoughts:** Bake yams Prepare crepe batter	Oatmeal porridge **After breakfast thought:** Soak ½ cup dried chestnuts	Autumn bean salad Watercress dressing Broccoli noodle casserole
FRIDAY	Vegetable croquettes Miso relish sauce Spinach and pumpkin salad with plum dressing Clear soup with shredded herbed crepes Babka (from lunch)	Yam crepés	Vegetable creme soup Cabbage and water-cress salad **After lunch thought:** Babka
SATURDAY	Chokoes with lemon fish Sauce Bechamel Shish kebabs Baked rice and peas	Potato cake Miso topping **After breakfast thought:** Pickled red cabbage	Chestnut balls with creme of cauliflower sauce **After lunch thought:** Pumpkin creme pie
SUNDAY		BRUNCH Apple marmalade pancakes **After Brunch thoughts:** Olive bread Peanut pumpkin spead Apple apricot spread Almond-mushroom paté **Special Sundays** *Pickles* Miso Shoyu Lemon	

MONDAY DINNER

SCALLOPED YAMS (G)

1 kg (2 lb) yams or sweet potatoes

3 cups soy or nut milk (see page 150)

$\frac{1}{2}$–1 teaspoon sea salt

$\frac{1}{2}$ cup maltose, rice syrup or barley malt

Peel the yams and cut crosswise into 1.5 mm ($\frac{1}{16}$ inch) slices. Combine the yams and milk in a saucepan. Bring to the boil. Add the salt and other seasonings if desired. Preheat oven to 200°C. Oil a baking casserole (shallow sided), transfer the mixture to the dish, cover and bake 20 minutes. Reduce the heat to 180°C, uncover and bake until dry. Heat the sweetener, spoon over casserole and bake uncovered 10 minutes longer.

Serves: 6–8.
Time: 45–50 minutes.

NOODLES WITH CARAWAY ONION SAUCE (G)

250 g (8 oz) buckwheat or wholewheat noodles

2 tablespoons oil

5 cups sliced onion wedges

2 teaspoons grated ginger juice to taste

$\frac{1}{2}$ teaspoon tumeric

2 teaspoons cinnamon

1 teaspoon sea salt

2 cups soup stock (see page 147)

1 tablespoon caraway seeds

1 tablespoon kuzu or arrowroot

watercress for garnish

Heat pot of water. Add noodles. Bring to the boil. Add cold 'shock' water. Repeat three times. Simmer until 'al-dente'. Remove from heat, strain off liquid and reserve. Rinse *immediately* under cold water until noodles are cold. Set aside.

Heat wok or skillet. Add oil and sauté onions. Prepare soup stock and add it and the rest of the ingredients except kuzu. Cover and simmer 15 minutes. Dilute kuzu in cold stock or water, and stir into sauce. Bring to the boil. Taste and adjust seasoning. Heat noodles in strainer. Serve sauce over noodles; garnished with cress.

Serves: 6.
Time: 45 minutes.

RADISH WITH MISO SAUCE (G)

1 large white radish (daikon)

4 cups dashi stock (see page 147)

SAUCE

$\frac{2}{3}$ cup miso

1 egg yolk

$\frac{1}{2}$ cup soup stock (if necessary)

3 teaspoons grated lemon rind

Peel the radish and cut into bevel-edged cylinders. Make a dashi stock. Add the radish pieces, cover with drop lid (a drop lid is any lid that is smaller than the pot so it sits on top of the cooking vegetables) and gently boil 30 minutes or until radish becomes slightly translucent. Meanwhile prepare sauce. In the top of a double boiler soften miso, add egg yolk and a little water if too thick. Cook over boiling water until thick and creamy (about 2 minutes). Remove from heat. Put grated lemon rind in strainer and rinse briefly. Add to miso. To serve, top each individual serving with miso topping and garnish with shallots.

Serves: 6.
Time: 40 minutes.

SWEET CUCUMBER SALAD (G)

2 large apple cucumbers, sliced and salted

DRESSING

1 cup maltose, rice syrup or barley malt

$\frac{1}{2}$ cup shoyu

1 teaspoon ginger juice

$\frac{1}{2}$ teaspoon ground coriander

$\frac{1}{4}$ cup apple cider or brown rice vinegar

pinch of assorted chilli pepper

Cut the ends off the cucumbers. Dip the cut ends in salt and rub them into the exposed ends of the cucumbers. Discard the cut ends. Cut cucumbers lengthwise, remove seeds and slice. Toss with salt and set aside for a few minutes. Meanwhile, place the rest of the ingredients into a saucepan. Bring to the boil. Spoon over cucumbers after rinsing them and squeezing out excess liquid. Reserve extra dressing for another day.

Serves: 6.
Time: 15 minutes.

FRUIT AND NUT BARS

2 cups diced apples

1 cup chopped walnuts

½ cup chopped cashews

1 cup currants

2 cups rolled oats

½ cup wholewheat flour

1 cup diced dried mixed fruit (apricots, dates, prunes, peaches)

4 cups apple juice

2 teaspoons sea salt

Combine all ingredients together. Add more juice to form a thick batter. (Should not drop from the end of an inverted spoon.) Spread into a 22 cm x 33 cm x 2 cm (8½ in x 13 in x 1 in) oiled baking sheet, and bake at 180°C for 45–50 minutes. Cool and cut.
Serves: 16.
Time: 1 hour.

 **After dinner thoughts:**

1 Wash and bring to the boil, 2 cups chick peas in double the volume of water. Simmer 30 minutes without a lid removing residue from the top of the beans. Set aside for next day. Add more liquid if necessary.
2 Soak 2 tablespoons Chinese barley for Tuesday's dinner.

Why Fermented Foods?

Fermentation, the mysterious process that actually changes the nature of food, is performed through the action of yeast, bacteria and enzymes. It makes minerals more readily available and protein more easily absorbable by the body. Fermentation also aids directly in the digestion of other foods. The range of fermented foods includes: miso, shoyu, tempeh, umeboshi, yoghurt, cheese, sauerkraut, sourdough bread, buttermilk, pickles, wine, beer and vinegar (if they are made from naturally fermented fruit or grain). There are tribes in Africa who drink fermented camel's milk because as the desert heat increases, the camel's milk rapidly changes from fresh to sour, and from sour to curdled. They turn this into whey and curds. The Eskimos ferment seal oil and fish heads; the Japanese ferment soy beans.

If treated carefully after fermentation and not allowed to boil or to simmer for a long time, these foods maintain their rich enzymes, supply the lactic acid necessary for cell respiration, help to maintain a proper balance of acid in the colon and destroy harmful bacteria in the intestines.

Try making these foods called for in some of the recipes, not only for flavour, but also for health. Remember, most fermented foods need no

refrigeration, just keep them away from light and make sure they are well sealed. What better time to start your own pickles than in autumn, so as to prepare for the cold months ahead.

TUESDAY BREAKFAST

SWEET BUCKWHEAT CREME (G)

½ cup roasted buckwheat groats

2½ cups boiling apple juice

½ cup currants

1 teaspoon cinnamon

½ teaspoon sea salt

½ cup sunflower meal

If buckwheat is *not* a nutty brown colour then spread on baking sheet and roast in oven 5–10 minutes at 180°C or until lightly browned. Bring apple juice to the boil. Add the rest of the ingredients. Bring to the boil. Cover and simmer 20 minutes. Serve hot or cold.
Serves: 4.
Time: 20 minutes.

 **After breakfast thoughts:**

TROPICAL CHUTNEY (G)

1½ cups peeled, seeded and chopped apples

2 cups peeled, seeded and chopped mango

½ cup barley malt, rice syrup or maltose

½ cup sultanas

¼ cup chopped red pepper

¼ cup chopped onion

¼ cup apple cider vinegar

1 tablespoon lemon juice

2 cm (1 inch) pieces smashed ginger-root

1 teaspoon chilli, finely chopped (optional)

1 clove garlic, crushed

½ teaspoon sea salt

¼ cup slivered almonds

Combine all the ingredients except almonds in a saucepan. Cover and simmer 30 minutes, stirring occasionally. Add the almonds; cook uncovered 15 minutes more, stirring frequently to prevent sticking. Cool to room temperature and store in refrigerator until using. Good with fish or chicken dishes.
Makes: 2½ cups.
Time: 1½ hours.

TUESDAY LUNCH

TOFU BURGERS

2 cups water
2 cups bulghur wheat or 2 cups leftover grain
1 teaspoon sea salt
500 g pressed tofu (see page 85)
2 eggs, beaten (optional)
1 cup minced onion
1 teaspoon oregano
2 teaspoons basil
$\frac{1}{2}$ cup arrowroot flour

Bring water to the boil. Add bulghur, salt, cover and simmer 5 minutes. Remove from heat and let sit 5 minutes. Meanwhile mash tofu, add eggs and remaining ingredients except bulghur and flour. Mix cooked bulghur with tofu, and add just enough flour to bind mixture together. Shape into burgers, fry half of them in hot oil 3–4 minutes. (Reserve other half for another day.) Drain on paper towels and serve with sprouts, lettuce, tomatoes, picked red cabbage (see page 117) and vegetable chips.

Makes: 10 burgers.
Time: 45 minutes.

GRILLED PEARS (G)

3 ripe pears, halved and pitted
4 tablespoons mirin or sherry
$\frac{1}{2}$ cup chopped macadamia nuts
2–3 tablespoons chopped sultanas or currants
2–3 tablespoons tahini
1 teaspoon dry anise
1 teaspoon miso (optional) or a sprinkle of sea salt

CAROB SAUCE

1 tablespoon oil
1 tablespoon wholewheat flour
1 tablespoon carob powder
1 cup nut or soy milk (see page 150)
$\frac{1}{4}$ cup maple syrup
1 teaspoon vanilla

Preheat oven to 180°C.

Peel, halve lengthwise and core pears. Arrange them cored side up in a baking dish. Scoop out some of the centre. Blend the ingredients until well combined, spoon filling into fruit. Bake the pears covered 20 minutes.

Sauce

Warm oil in a saucepan. Mix the flour and carob and stir into the oil. Slowly add the milk, stirring constantly until thick, add maple syrup and simmer 2–3 minutes. Take off the heat, stir in vanilla and spoon over pears. (Thin with juice if necessary.)

Serves: 6.
Time: 30 minutes.

VEGETABLE CHIPS (G)

1 cup carrot sticks
$\frac{1}{2}$ cup beetroot sticks
sea salt
oil for deep frying

Cut vegetables into matchsticks. Heat oil and deep fry until lightly golden. Drain and serve with 'burger'.

 After lunch thought:

CHICK PEA ROLL (G)

2 cups dry chick peas (should have doubled in size) soaked the night before
2 tablespoons crushed garlic marinated in 2 tablespoons olive oil
1 cup diced onion
2–3 tablespoons lemon juice
$\frac{1}{2}$ cup tahini
$\frac{1}{2}$ cup chopped parsley
roasted unhulled sesame seeds

Marinate garlic in olive oil. Cook chick peas in pressure cooker 2 hours or until tender. Strain off excess liquid, save this for soup and mash chick peas. Heat skillet, add oil and sauté the garlic mixture on a low heat. Add onions and simmer until transparent. Blend together $\frac{1}{2}$ cup beans with the onion and garlic mixture, then add this to the rest of the ingredients except sesame seeds. (Reserve $1\frac{1}{2}$–2 cups of cooked chick peas for another day.)

When cool, shape into logs, and roll in roasted sesame seeds. Set aside for dinner.

Serves: 6–8.
Time: 2 hours.

Variation:
Mix in tofu sour creme (see page 54) and serve as a dip with crackers and raw vegetables.

TUESDAY DINNER

CARROT AND APPLE TZIMMES

4 cups grated carrot

1 cup grated apple

2 tablespoons Chinese barley (if available) soaked overnight in apple juice

3 tablespoons oil

2 cups apple juice

½ teaspoon sea salt

½ teaspoon cinnamon

½ teaspoon ginger powder

Combine all ingredients in a large pot. Cover and simmer after bringing it to the boil, for 1 hour or until barley is tender.

BUCKWHEAT STEW (G)

1 teaspoon chopped garlic

2 cups chopped onion

½ cup minced spring onion

8 cups boiling water

1 bouquet garni

2 tablespoons oil

2 cups buckwheat (roasted)

1 cup chopped coriander

Peel and chop garlic and the onion. Mince the spring onion. Bring water to the boil with the bouquet garni. Cover and simmer 10 minutes. Meanwhile, heat the wok. Add oil and sauté the garlic and onion until transparent. Add the buckwheat and lightly sauté. When the stock has cooked for 10 minutes, add stock to the onion bulghur mixture, sprinkle in a little bit of sea salt, cover and simmer 15 minutes. Taste and adjust seasoning with shoyu and sprinkle in coriander just before serving.

Serves: 4–6.
Time: 1 hour.

COLESLAW

4 cups grated cabbage

1 cup grated carrots

1 cup chopped parsley

sea salt to press cabbage

½ cup washed raisins or sultanas

ISLAND DRESSING (G)

2 tablespoons miso

4 tablespoons tahini or peanut butter

6 tablespoons oil

6 tablespoons minced onion

½ cup minced parsley

4 tablespoons minced celery

2 tablespoons minced pickles (optional)

watercress for garnish

Grate vegetables. Chop parsley. Toss cabbage with sea salt, and press until water comes out of the cabbage. Squeeze out and rinse with cold water. Drain.

Dressing
Cream together the first five ingredients until smooth. Stir in the celery and the minced pickles. Spoon over coleslaw and mix in raisins. Garnish with watercress.

Serves: 4–6.
Time: 30 minutes.

Chick Pea Roll
Prepared during lunch on Tuesday.

After dinner thoughts:
Soak ½ cup dried chestnuts in boiling water for Wednesday. They can be found in most oriental groceries.

Honey *played its role in Aboriginal myth through the story of Bolig-Bolig the honey man. One early writer recorded it like this:*
'At certain times of the year certain trees have a powdery substance on the leaves and this is sweetish to the taste. When the sun comes up the powder is gone. Aboriginals like the sweet taste and to be able to indulge their craving for it they had to get up at dawn to collect it, then it was put in paperbark containers and eaten. If there was no powder or honey or sweet powder on the leaves the people said that Bolig-Bolig, the honey man had been there first with his many bags.'
(From: Allen, Joyce and McKenzie, Valerie, A Taste of the Past, Early Australian Cooking)

WEDNESDAY BREAKFAST

CREME OF WHEAT, RYE AND RICE

2 cups mixed wheat, rye and rice

6 cups water

1 teaspoon sea salt

Toast grains separately until lightly golden. Then crack in blender or food processor. Bring water and salt to the boil. Stir in cracked grains, add salt and return to the boil. Cover and simmer, stirring occasionally.

Variations
- Serve with maple syrup mixed with tahini.
- Top with cooked fruit or fresh fruit.
- Mix in some dried fruit while cooking.
- For a savoury taste, mix in some miso or shoyu at the end of cooking.

Serves: 4.
Time: 1 hour.

WEDNESDAY LUNCH

CHICK PEA PATTIES (G)

2 cups cooked chick peas (from day before)

2 tablespoons pressed garlic

$\frac{1}{4}$ cup minced spring onions

$\frac{1}{4}$ cup grated carrots

$\frac{1}{2}$ cup minced parsley

2–3 tablespoons arrowroot flour or kuzu

1 teaspoon dill seed

1 teaspoon cumin

1 teaspoon coriander

oil for deep frying

Drain cooked chick peas several minutes before mashing.

Mash chick peas. Prepare vegetables. Combine the vegetables with the chick peas and add the remaining ingredients. (If you blend or use a processor you may find the mixture is too creamy and may not bind very well.)

Oil a tray or plate. Shape patties into small balls or flat patties. Heat oil. Prepare a draining rack. Deep fry till golden brown. Serve with onion and garlic sauce.

Makes: 12–15.
Time: 15 minutes.

ONION AND GARLIC SAUCE (G)

2 tablespoons brown rice flour

$\frac{1}{2}$ cup diced onion

1 tablespoon pressed garlic

2 teaspoons ginger juice

$1\frac{1}{2}$ tablespoons miso

1 tablespoon warm maltose, rice syrup or barley malt

1 teaspoon dry mustard powder

$\frac{1}{2}$ cup chopped celery

$\frac{1}{4}$ cup chopped parsley

$\frac{1}{4}$–$\frac{1}{3}$ cup water or stock

2 tablespoons brown rice or apple cider vinegar

chives for garnish

Heat skillet. Dry roast flour until it begins to smell nutty and changes colour slightly. Remove from heat. Cream together the next six ingredients. Stir in cooled flour. Place in a saucepan, add celery and $\frac{1}{2}$ cup water or stock. Stir ingredients while bringing to the boil. When the sauce thickens adjust liquid content, if necessary, with the rest of the water or stock. Remove from the heat, stir in vinegar just before using.

Serves: 4–6.
Time: 10 minutes.

STIR-FRIED CHESTNUTS AND CHINESE CABBAGE (G)

$\frac{1}{2}$ Chinese cabbage

$\frac{1}{2}$ cup sliced red pepper

1 cup soaked chestnuts ($\frac{1}{2}$ cup dried) from Tuesday

1 teaspoon minced garlic

1 teaspoon minced ginger-root

2 tablespoons sesame oil

1 tablespoon maltose, rice syrup or barley malt (optional)

1 tablespoon shoyu

1 teaspoon roasted sesame oil (to taste)

Slice cabbage very thinly on the diagonal. Bring chestnuts to the boil. Cover and simmer until tender or pressure cook 20 minutes. Drain and save liquid for desserts. Mince the garlic and ginger-root. Heat wok, add oil and sauté garlic and ginger until sharp smell disappears. Add the cabbage, pepper and stir-fry 2 minutes. Add the chestnuts and maltose and toss gently. Stir in shoyu and roasted sesame oil.

Serves: 4–6.
Time: 45 minutes.

WEDNESDAY DINNER

EGG AND LEMON SOUP (G)

4 cups soup stock (chicken or fish see page 147)
$\frac{1}{3}$ cup uncooked brown rice
sea salt to taste
2 eggs, separated
juice of $\frac{1}{2}$ lemon
fresh mint for garnish

Bring stock to boil. Add rice and salt. Return to the boil, cover and simmer 45 minutes. Beat egg whites until stiff, add yolks and beat until light. Gradually beat in lemon juice. (Adding a pinch of salt helps whites to peak.) Ladle about 1–2 cups of boiling soup into eggs, whisking continuously. Remove soup from heat, add egg mixture and stir vigorously. Keep stirring, taste and adjust seasoning. Garnish with mint.

Serves: 6.
Time: 1 hour.

STUFFED ENVELOPES (G)

vine leaves (1 pack)
2 tablespoons olive oil
2 cups chopped onions
2 tablespoons chopped currants
4 tablespoons minced parsley
2 teaspoons chopped dill
1 cup long grain brown rice
4 tablespoons roasted pine nuts
1 teaspoon chopped mint
sea salt to taste
2–3 cups water
juice of 1 lemon
$\frac{1}{2}$–$\frac{3}{4}$ cup olive oil

Rinse vine leaves and blanch in boiling water 3 minutes. Drain and rinse in cold water. Cut off stems. Set aside.

Heat skillet. Add oil and sauté onion until transparent. Add the next three ingredients, and sauté lightly. Cover with washed brown rice. Add the next two ingredients. Sprinkle salt on top, add water and bring to the boil. Cover and simmer 40 minutes.

Shaping leaves
Take leaf, smooth side down and place a teaspoon or so of stuffing in the centre. Fold *stem* end and then sides over stuffing and roll up tightly. Line a heavy skillet with a few vine leaves and pack rolls in tightly, seam side down. Sprinkle each layer with remaining oil and the lemon juice mixture. Add water to almost cover and place unfilled leaves on top of rolled leaves. Invert a plate on top to keep rolls in shape during cooking. Cover and bring to the boil. Simmer 45 minutes. Remove from heat, and leave aside for a few minutes. Garnish with lemon slices before serving.

Serves: 6.
Time: 2 hours.

OKRA AND TOMATOES (G)

750 g (1$\frac{1}{2}$ lbs) okra
sea salt
$\frac{1}{2}$ cup vinegar
1 cup olive or corn oil
2 cups chopped onions
1 cup skinned, seeded tomatoes
2 tablespoons chopped parsley
2 teaspoons maltose, rice syrup or barley malt
sea salt to taste

Remove stems from okra. Wash, drain and place in dish. Sprinkle with salt and vinegar and set aside for a few minutes. (This prevents okra from splitting during cooking.) Heat skillet. Add oil and sauté onions until lightly browned. Add the tomatoes, parsley, maltose, and sea salt. Simmer covered 15 minutes. Add okra to tomato mixture, placing them side by side. Cover with plate, press down, and add a little more water, if there is none left. Cover and simmer 20–30 minutes or until tender.

Serves: 6.
Time: 40 minutes.

As far back as the Stone Age, people were making a type of bread from grain. However, instead of grinding the wheat, they crushed it slightly and mixed it with water. This was then placed on hot stones and covered with hot ashes. The resulting loaf was gritty, and covered with ash, obviously unleavened . . .

MIXED PICKLES (G)

3 tablespoons sea salt
5 cups water
4 cups sliced zucchini
1 red capsicum, seeded
3 celery stalks, sliced
2 carrots, sliced
garlic cloves
hot chilli peppers, fresh or dried
few sprigs of fresh dill
5 cups vinegar
4 cloves
$\frac{1}{2}$ teaspoon peppercorns
2 bay leaves

Stir salt into water and bring to the boil. Set aside to cool. Prepare vegetables. Parboil carrots in salted water 5 minutes. Place all vegetables in bowl and cover with cool brine. Leave 24 hours, rinse in cold water and drain. Pack into sterilised jars, adding garlic, hot chilli pepper and dill. Bring vinegar, rest of ingredients to a boil and pour over vegetables. Seal and store at least one week.

After dinner thought:
Soak 3 cups kidney or pinto beans in boiling water.

THURSDAY BREAKFAST

OATMEAL PORRIDGE

2 cups rolled oats
5 cups boiling water
$\frac{1}{2}$ teaspoon sea salt
1 cup dried currants, raisins or dates

Dry roast oats until lightly toasted. Bring water to the boil. Remove from heat, stir in oats and continue to stir adding sea salt and dried fruit. Return to the boil, lower heat, cover and simmer with the lid slightly ajar for 15–20 minutes. (Adjust liquid content which will vary according to the dried fruit that you use.) Serve with maple syrup.
Serves: 4–6.
Time: 30 minutes.

After breakfast thought:
Soak $\frac{1}{2}$ cup dried chestnuts in water. Bring to the boil and let them soak for dinner.

THURSDAY LUNCH

AUTUMN BEAN SALAD (G)

3 cups beans soaked from the night before
1 bunch parsley
2 cups shredded cabbage
1 cup shredded carrot

WATERCRESS DRESSING (G)

3 tablespoons lemon juice
4 tablespoons minced umeboshi salted plums or pitted minced capers
$\frac{1}{2}$ cup oil
1 cup finely diced watercress
2–3 tablespoons shoyu (to taste)
few tablespoons warm water or stock to creme

Bring water and beans to the boil. Simmer covered until tender or pressure cook 30 minutes. Drain off excess liquid and save for soup or sauce. Chop vegetables, shred cabbage and carrot. Toss with half of the beans. Combine all the dressing ingredients and blend till creamy. (Adjust liquid content to make a thick but creamy dressing.) Blend into salad while beans are still warm. Set aside to cool or eat at room temperature. Keep other half of beans for another day.

Serves: 4–6.
Time: 1 hour.

BROCCOLI NOODLE CASSEROLE

4 cups chopped broccoli stems and flowerettes
1 tablespoon minced garlic
$\frac{1}{2}$ cup chopped onion
$\frac{1}{2}$ cup chopped spring onion
2 cups sliced mushrooms
$\frac{1}{2}$ cup chopped olives
2 tablespoons oil
1 teaspoon dried basil
$1\frac{1}{2}$ tablespoons chopped parsley
1 teaspoon oregano
$\frac{1}{2}$ cup toasted unhulled sesame seeds
1 package wholewheat spaghetti or macaroni

Top: Treasure Triangles with Mayonnaise Curry.
See page 100
Bottom: Corn Relish.   See page 91

Slice flowerettes off into small pieces. Chop broccoli stems into small pieces after peeling. Cut the rest of the vegetables. Heat skillet or wok. Add oil and sauté garlic until harsh smell disappears. Add the onions and fry till transparent. Add the mushrooms, olives, herbs and salt. Then add a few spoons of water, cover and simmer 10 minutes. Meanwhile bring a pot of water to the boil. Drop in noodles, and bring to the boil. Add cold water to stop the boiling, and repeat three times. Then taste and either remove from heat or continue cooking until desired consistency is reached. (The noodles should be firm but cooked.) Drain and mix into broccoli dish. Toast sesame seeds until they pop and sprinkle on top.

Serves: 4–6.
Time: 30 minutes.

THURSDAY DINNER

CHESTNUT RICE (G)

2 cups brown rice
$\frac{1}{2}$ cup soaked chestnuts (from breakfast)
$3\frac{1}{2}$ cups water or stock
$\frac{1}{2}$ teaspoon sea salt

Wash rice. Combine soaked chestnuts, rice, soaking water from chestnuts, more water if necessary and salt in a saucepan or pressure cooker. Bring to the boil, cover and simmer 50 minutes or alternatively pressure cook 40 minutes after pressure. Stir gently before serving. (Use less water if pressure cooking.)

Serves: 4–6.
Time: 1 hour.

POACHED SNAPPER IN SWEET AND SOUR SAUCE (G)

1 kg (2 lb) whole snapper
2 stalks shallots or spring onions
2 slices ginger-root
1 tablespoon mirin
1 tablespoon sea salt
2 tablespoons shredded ginger-root
2 tablespoons shredded spring onion
1 tablespoon shredded red hot pepper
2 tablespoons shredded green pepper
1 tablespoon oil
1 tablespoon mirin
10–15 cups water
4 tablespoons roasted sesame oil
4 tablespoons oil
6 tablespoons brown rice vinegar
6 tablespoons maltose, rice syrup or barley malt
1 tablespoon prepared mustard
$\frac{1}{2}$ teaspoon kuzu or arrowroot flour
1–2 tablespoons water or stock
2–3 sprigs coriander

Rinse fish. Rub with the first four ingredients inside and out. Let stand 20 minutes. Meanwhile, shred all the vegetables. Drain off fish, combine in pot, oil, mirin and water. When the water reaches boiling point, place whole fish in. (Water should cover fish.) Cover and when the water boils again, turn off heat. Let sit covered 15 minutes.

Remove fish to a serving platter. Heat the roasted sesame oil and spoon over the fish. Heat the wok, add the other oil and stir fry the vegetables. Add the next three ingredients and cook until the mixture boils and the sweetener dissolves. Dissolve the kuzu in the water, stir into wok and mix till thick and clear. Pour sauce over fish and garnish with coriander.

Serves: 4–6.
Time: 50 minutes.

BEAN SPROUT SALAD (G)

3 cups bean sprouts
2 tablespoons shoyu
2 tablespoons tahini
2 tablespoons brown rice vinegar or lemon juice
2–3 tablespoons roasted poppy seeds
2 cups chopped spring onions

Place sprouts in a colander and pour boiling water over them. Refresh quickly under cold running water. Drain and place in a bowl. Combine the remaining ingredients and mix well. Pour dressing over salad and allow to sit several minutes before serving.

Serves: 4–6.
Time: 5 minutes.

After dinner thoughts:
Bake 6 yams at 200°C for one hour or until soft for Friday's breakfast. Prepare crepe batter for breakfast, and dinner.

Behind: Pickled Red Cabbage.   See page 117
Left: Sesame Carrot.   See page 83
Right: Tofu Burger.

FRIDAY BREAKFAST

YAM CREPES

½ cup wholewheat flour

½ teaspoon sea salt

1 egg

1 teaspoon oil

2 cups soy milk (see page 150) or water

YAM TOPPING (G)

8 cups chopped yams (4 cups cooked)

1 cup apple juice

1 teaspoon cinnamon

4 cloves

1 teaspoon vanilla

3 tablespoons tahini

1 teaspoon miso (optional)

1 tablespoon grated lemon or orange rind

roasted and chopped almonds or walnuts

Bake yams at 200°C for 1 hour or until quite soft. Alternatively, use baked yams from last night. Heat the juice, cinnamon and cloves for 3 minutes. Strain off cloves and add vanilla. Peel the yams, blend until creamy and smooth, adding just enough juice to make a very thick purée. Blend in the tahini, miso and grated rind. Set aside.

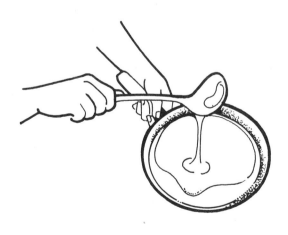

Crepes (Double recipe and reserve half for dinner) Sift flour and salt into a mixing bowl. Make a well in the centre and add the lightly beaten egg and oil. Add a small amount of soy milk or water and begin to stir until the batter is smooth and easy to pour. Cover and leave in a cool spot 15–20 minutes, or overnight.

Heat crepe pan, brush with oil. Ladle batter into pan. Immediately tilt and rotate pan to coat the bottom evenly with batter. Cook until the top of the crepe is no longer shiny and the bottom is golden. Turn crepe over, cook 30 seconds longer. Remove and stack on plate.

Place the crepes brown side down in a single layer, spread 2 tablespoons of yam topping over the centre and fold in half and then in quarters. Arrange rows of overlapping crepes in oiled baking dish. Cover. Bake until heated through. Sprinkle with cinnamon before serving, spooning heated maltose or maple syrup over cinnamon.

Serves: 6.
Time: 40 minutes.

FRIDAY LUNCH

VEGETABLE CREME SOUP (G)

2 tablespoons oil

3 tablespoons corn flour

4 onions, quartered

1 cup chopped celery

2 cups sliced cabbage

2 cups sliced carrots

1 cup cauliflower flowerettes

5–6 cups water or stock

1 tablespoon oil

1 cup brussels sprouts

1–2 teaspoons sea salt or 2–3 tablespoons miso

croûtons and spring onions for garnish

Heat skillet. Add 2 tablespoons oil and sauté the flour until the flour has changed colour slightly. Set aside.

Cut all the vegetables. Heat skillet or wok. Add oil and sauté the onions, celery, cabbage and carrots. Cover with water or stock, and simmer covered until tender.

Cook the cauliflower separately in a small amount of salted water. Repeat with sprouts. (Do not let sprouts turn dark green.) When the rest of the vegetables are tender, add the cauliflower and sprouts.

Cream together the roasted flour in a small amount of stock or water, making sure that they are both the same temperature to avoid lumps. Add this to the soup, season with salt and bring to the boil. Taste and adjust seasoning. Meanwhile fry or bake the croûtons and slice the spring onions. Serve on top of soup.

Serves: 4–6.
Time: 30 minutes.

CABBAGE AND WATERCRESS SALAD (G)

4 cups shredded cabbage

1 teaspoon sea salt

2 bunches watercress

1 tablespoon lemon rind

MISO DRESSING

$\frac{1}{4}$ cup oil or almond butter

1 tablespoon brown rice vinegar

1 tablespoon miso

Shred the cabbage and toss with sea salt. Press with a heavy weight.

When the water starts to rise to the top, strain off (reserve for soups) and rinse in cold water. Squeeze out excess liquid. Chop watercress, mix with cabbage and grated lemon rind.

Combine all the dressing ingredients and blend until creamy. Spoon over salad just before serving.

Serves: 4–6.
Time: 1 hour.

After lunch thought:

BABKA

$1\frac{1}{2}$ tablespoons dry yeast

$1\frac{1}{4}$–$\frac{1}{2}$ cups hot apple juice

3 cups wholewheat pastry flour or $1\frac{1}{2}$ cups pressed tofu (see page 85) and $1\frac{1}{2}$ cups wholewheat flour

$\frac{1}{2}$ teaspoon sea salt

1 tablespoon lemon or orange rind

4 tablespoons maltose, rice syrup or barley malt

2 teaspoons vanilla

3 tablespoons corn or safflower oil

FILLING

3–4 cups purée (see page 140)

1–2 cups crumb topping (see page 127)

2 cups roasted crushed walnuts

TOPPING

maple syrup

Yeasted Dough

Dissolve yeast in hot apple juice. Add enough flour to form a thin batter. Cover and set aside until bubbly. Combine the rest of the ingredients and beat with a wooden spoon until dough begins to leave the side of the mixing bowl.

Turn out onto floured board and knead 10 minutes or until dough is smooth and elastic. (Adjust liquid content.) Place in oiled bowl, brush surface with oil, cover and let rest while preparing filling.

Filling

Prepare apricot purée. Set aside to cool.

Prepare crumb topping. Set aside.

Roast nuts and crush while warm.

Putting it all together

Divide dough in half. Keep one half covered until using. Sprinkle arrowroot flour and roll out dough to 6 mm ($\frac{1}{4}$ in) thickness.

Spread purée over surface of dough. Sprinkle with crumb topping and crushed nuts. Roll up as for jelly roll.

Shaping

Twist dough in opposite directions, about 3–4 times. Place on oiled sheet or in round cake tin and join ends together. Cut 2.5 cm (1 in) slits with scissors. Cover with pan and allow to rise until almost doubled in size. Preheat oven to 190°C. Bake 30–45 minutes or until it sounds hollow when tapped.

Remove from oven and brush with warm maple syrup. Cool before serving.

Serves: 6.
Time: $1\frac{1}{2}$ hours.

---

*The **Cornish pasty** was devised for tin miners. It was a pasty wrapping filled with meat and vegetables, cooked slowly and taken to the pithead to send down to the miners still hot. The shape is like a half moon with the fastening curled into a crust along the curved side. This was because working with the tin ore left a certain amount of arsenic on the miners' hands. They could bite into the straight side and throw away the crust.*

FRIDAY DINNER

VEGETABLE CROQUETTES

3 cups wholewheat flour

1 cup kuzu or arrowroot flour

½ cup grated pumpkin or carrot

½ cup chopped shallots or spring onions

½ cup unhulled sesame seeds

½ cup chopped olives or other pickles

1 teaspoon sea salt

16 very small pickling onions

2 cloves crushed garlic

½–¾ cup oil

1 bunch chopped watercress or coriander

Sift flours into a mixing bowl. Grate and chop the vegetables. Peel the onions, crush the garlic, and set aside. Combine the flours, pumpkin, shallots, sesame seeds and sea salt with the flours. If the mixture seems too dry add water or soup stock until it begins to stick together. Form into 2 cm (1 inch) balls, then flatten slightly between the palms of your hands.

Heat skillet, preferably cast iron, add oil then sauté garlic and small onions. After the garlic has turned golden, remove from skillet. Add the balls, cover and simmer 15–20 minutes. Check and turn them over if necessary. Add more oil if necessary. When they are ready, add the watercress or coriander, and sauté lightly.

Serves: 6–8.
Time: 20 minutes.

MISO RELISH SAUCE (G)

5 tablespoons miso

3 tablespoons brown rice vinegar

2 teaspoons grated ginger-root

½ teaspoon dry mustard powder

2 tablespoons kuzu or arrowroot flour dissolved in a little cold water

2 cups water or leftover soup stock

Combine all the ingredients in a saucepan. Bring to the boil uncovered stirring until the mixture thickens and turns clearer. Garnish with spring onions, shallots or chives after spooning over croquettes.

Serves: 6–8.
Time: 5 minutes.

SPINACH AND PUMPKIN SALAD (G)

1 bunch of English spinach

1 cup chopped pumpkin or yams

½ cup minced onion

½ cup roasted unhulled sesame or sunflower seeds

oil for deep frying

PLUM DRESSING (G)

1 cup chopped onion

4 salted umeboshi plums

4 tablespoons shoyu

½ cup sesame oil

4 tablespoons chopped parsley

Wash spinach in a bowl of cold water to remove dirt that sometimes cling to the outer leaves. Bring a pot of water to the boil. Add salt, spinach and bring to the boil again. Remove spinach immediately, rinse in cold water, bathe and squeeze out excess water. Cut into 2 cm (1 inch) pieces. Meanwhile, heat oil and chop pumpkin into squares. Deep fry until golden brown. Drain on absorbent paper. Set aside. Lightly toast sesame seeds.

Serves: 6–8.
Time: 15 minutes.

Dressing
Chop onion. De-pit and mash plums. Blend all ingredients until creamy and smooth. Spoon over salad just before serving.

Serves: 6–8.
Time: 5 minutes.

CLEAR SOUP WITH SHREDDED HERBED CREPES

5 cups mixed stock (see page 147)

crepe recipe (see page 114)

½ cup minced parsley

1½ tablespoons minced chives or spring onions

1 tablespoon fresh chopped dill

Prepare mixed stock and set aside. Combine the crepe ingredients (if not already done) and add the parsley, chives and dill. Blend the batter until creamy. Transfer the batter to a bowl, cover with plastic wrap and let stand in a cool place for 30 minutes. (This is not necessary if prepared ahead of time.)

Crepes

Heat a 15–18 cm (6–7 inch) crepe pan (preferably steel) over moderately high heat until it is hot. Brush the pan lightly with oil, and remove from heat. Stir the batter, half fill a soup ladle with it, and pour the batter into the pan. Quickly tilt and rotate the pan so that the batter covers the bottom in a thin layer and return any excess batter back to the bowl very quickly before it starts to cook. Return the pan to the heat, loosen the edge of the crepe from the pan when you see it turning up (use a metal spatula) and cook until the underside is lightly browned. Turn the crepe and lightly brown the other side. Transfer the crepe to a plate or tea towel. Make crepes with remaining batter in the same way, brushing the pan with oil for each crepe if necessary.

Clear Soup

Strain the stock through a fine sieve into a bowl, pressing hard on the solids and let cool. Remove any fat. Heat and add seasoning to taste. Shred the crepes and sprinkle on top of the soup before serving.

Serves: 6–8.
Time: 45 minutes.

Serve Babka from lunch for dessert.

SATURDAY BREAKFAST

POTATO CAKE
1 kg boiling potatoes
sea salt to taste
5 tablespoons olive oil
3 crushed cloves of garlic

Put potatoes and enough cold water to cover in a large saucepan. Bring the water to the boil, and simmer the potatoes, covered partially 20 minutes.

Drain the potatoes, allow them to cool and chill them. (Must be *very* cold.) Peel, grate and sprinkle with sea salt.

Heat skillet, add 5 tablespoons olive oil, garlic and the potatoes, spreading them evenly and pressing them down with a spatula. Cook about 5–6 minutes or until the bottom is lightly browned and crisp. Invert the cake onto a plate and add the rest of the oil to the skillet. When the oil is hot again, slide the cake uncooked side down into the pan and cook it again another 5–6 minutes or until lightly browned. Slide the cake onto a platter and cut it into wedges. Decorate with watercress.

Serves: 4–6.
Time: 30 minutes.

MISO TOPPING (G)
1 bunch shallots
1 tablespoon oil
1 tablespoon miso
1 tablespoon tahini
1 teaspoon grated orange rind

Cut shallots into small pieces (use roots, white and greens). Heat skillet, add oil and sauté roots first. Then add greens and whites. Make a paste from the miso, tahini and orange rind. (Add water if necessary.) Add to shallots. Simmer on a low heat 5 minutes. Serve on potato pancakes. (Thin with liquid if necessary.)

 After breakfast thought:

PICKLED RED CABBAGE
2 cups brown rice vinegar
1 teaspoon cloves
1 teaspoon five spice powder
1 teaspoon ground ginger
1 teaspoon cinnamon
1 tablespoon sea salt
6 cups finely sliced red cabbage
2 cups onion rings

Combine first five ingredients together. Sprinkle cabbage with salt and press overnight. The following day, layer cabbage, onion and cover with 'spiced' vinegar. Cover with a plate or wooden cover that fits inside the bowl. Fill a plastic bag with water, fasten and put on top of the cover to act as a weight. Press 24 hours or longer. Keeps refrigerated up to 4–6 weeks.

*Around 300 B.C. in India, soldiers came across **honey** which had been made from 'a reed plant without the help of bees'. Up until that time they had been using honey from bees for sweetening and cooking. Interestingly enough, the Australian Aboriginal people obtained their sweetness by biting the head off the sugar ant and sucking the honey from its body. The honey is believed to be stored in the abdomen which swells up to the size of a grape.*

SATURDAY LUNCH

CHESTNUT BALLS WITH CREME OF CAULIFLOWER SAUCE (G)

leftover cooked chestnut rice from Thursday

1–2 tablespoons miso

grated orange rind

oil for deep frying

CAULIFLOWER SAUCE (G)

2 cups chopped cauliflower

1 cup chopped onion or spring onion

3 cups soup stock (see page 147)

1 tablespoon minced ginger-root or garlic

1 tablespoon oil

1 bouquet garni

2 teaspoons arrowroot flour or kuzu dissolved in ¼ cup cold water or stock

2–3 teaspoons sea salt to taste

grated carrot for garnish

Balls

The rice should be sticky for rice balls, and this is usually best obtained when the rice has been pressure cooked. If you don't have a pressure cooker, try soaking the rice overnight before cooking in the water in which you will cook the rice.

If the rice does not stick together several tablespoons of kuzu or arrowroot flour may be added to bind the mixture.

Mash the miso and orange rind into the cooked rice. Shape into balls or patties. When they are all shaped and ready for frying, heat the oil. Deep fry when the oil is hot until crispy and golden. Drain and serve while still hot with the sauce.

Sauce

Cut off the flowers from the stem of the cauliflower. Slice the stalks into thin strips on the diagonal and toss with salt. Press for pickle. Cut flowers into small pieces, and chop the onion as well. Prepare the soup stock of your choice. Heat the wok. Add oil and sauté the onions until they are transparent. Add the cauliflower and sauté a few minutes longer. Using just enough stock to cover the vegetables, pour over cauliflower and add the bouquet garni. Bring to the boil, cover and simmer 5 minutes or until vegetables are tender. Meanwhile, dissolve the kuzu in the cold water or stock. Blend the sauce discarding the bouquet garni, until creamy and smooth. Return the sauce back to the wok, bring to the boil and stir in the kuzu mixture.

Keep cooking until the mixture thickens and boils again.

Serve over the chestnut balls garnished with grated carrot.

Serves: 4–6.
Time: 35 minutes.

 After lunch thoughts:

PUMPKIN CREME PIE (G)

2 cups cooked mashed pumpkin (4–5 cups, raw and chopped)

100 g tofu

½ bar agar-agar

¾ cup apple juice

¼ cup maltose, rice syrup or barley malt

1 teaspoon cinnamon

½ teaspoon sea salt

1 teaspoon vanilla

4 tablespoons mirin (optional)

NUT CRUST

½ cup roasted unhulled sesame or sunflower seeds

1½ cups rolled oats

½ cup wholewheat flour

1 teaspoon sea salt

¼ cup oil (safflower or sesame is best)

⅓–⅓ cup apple juice to bind

egg white

1 teaspoon water

SECOND LAYER (G)

1 cup washed currants

¼ cup poppy seeds

pinch of sea salt

apple juice or cider

½ chopped orange

Chop pumpkin and steam *under pressure* 5 minutes or alternatively bake whole, covered until tender. Remove skin and mash or purée until creamy and smooth. Set aside. Meanwhile prepare pie crust. Roast the sesame seeds until they begin to pop. Blend with oats until the mixture is fairly fine. Add the flour and salt and mix well. Begin to add the oil and mix continuously stopping when the combination turns darker. Pick it up in your hands, squeeze it together and if it sticks to itself, the amount of oil is sufficient. Slowly add a few tablespoons of juice and stop when the dough begins to bind.

Lay down a sheet of greaseproof paper and roll out immediately. If the dough begins to crack, then add a touch more liquid. If the dough sticks to the paper then you have added too much liquid. Add a touch more *arrowroot* flour and try again. You must remember that the consistency will vary according to the weather, the temperature of the room, your hands and the ingredients. Preheat the oven to 200°C. Oil your pie shell 20 cm (8 inch) or 15 tart tins very well. Flip the greaseproof paper and dough into the shell and peel off paper.

Allow the dough to fall naturally into the shell before cutting off the excess. Trim edges, baste with egg white, and prebake 15–20 minutes. Roll out leftover pastry and cut into different biscuit shapes. Bake and reserve these for decorating the top of the pie.

Poppyseed Layer
Wash the currants. Place them in a saucepan with the poppyseeds, salt and apple juice or cider. Bring to the boil, cover and simmer 10 minutes. Remove lid, reduce excess liquid if there is any. Blend the mixture with the chopped orange until creamy. Set aside, or if the pie shell is ready, spoon into shell.

Pumpkin Filling
Bring a pot of water to the boil. Drop in tofu and bring it again to the boil. Rinse agar-agar under cold water and squeeze out excess water. Shred into a saucepan and cover with apple juice. Add the maltose, cinnamon and salt and bring to the boil. Cover and simmer 5 minutes. Combine the tofu, vanilla and mirin with the rest of the cooked ingredients and blend until smooth and creamy.

Putting it all together
Spread a thin layer of poppyseed filling over the bottom of the prebaked shell and cover with the pumpkin filling. Allow to set for a few minutes then decorate with biscuits, walnuts and more poppyseed filling. Brush biscuits with maple syrup.

Makes: 15 tarts.
Time: 1 hour.

SATURDAY DINNER

CHOKOE WITH LEMON FISH (G)

1 tablespoon mirin
1 tablespoon oil
1 tablespoon kuzu or arrowroot flour
1 tablespoon brown rice vinegar
1 teaspoon sea salt
500 g (1 lb) squid (allow 300 g for bones)
$\frac{1}{4}$ cup fish stock (see page 147)
oil for deep frying
3 chokoes
$\frac{1}{4}$ cup lemon juice
2 tablespoons mirin
1 tablespoon kuzu or arrowroot flour
1 tablespoon maltose, rice syrup or barley malt optional
$\frac{1}{2}$ cup minced spring onion
2 tablespoons minced ginger-root
2 teaspoons minced garlic
1 cup thinly sliced carrot sticks
reserved squash balls
1 cup boiled peas

Combine the first five ingredients in a glass or ceramic bowl. Wash and clean squid. Discard the head and contents of the sac. Slit the body sac lengthways and clean with kitchen paper.

Make diagonal slits on the inner surface scoring into a diamond pattern. *Be careful not to cut through the flesh.* Cut into bite size pieces.

Combine the squid with the first five ingredients. Mix and chill 15 minutes. Meanwhile, prepare the fish stock. (Ask the shopkeeper where you buy your fish for the leftover heads, tails and bones and cook a large pot of stock to use for other dishes as well.

Heat the oil. Drain squid and deep fry it just long enough for the squid to curl (about 30 seconds). Drain and reserve the oil after straining it. Steam chokoes under pressure about 15 minutes. Let them cool, halve them lengthwise and remove the seeds. Hollow out the shells with a melon baller, reserving the balls. Arrange the shells on a platter, cover with foil and newspaper to keep warm.

Combine the fish stock, lemon juice, mirin, kuzu and maltose in a bowl. Heat a wok, add 2 tablespoons of the oil used for the squid, then add the spring onion, ginger and garlic and stir-fry 1 minute. Add carrot sticks and the reserved squash balls. Stir-fry a few minutes longer. Meanwhile, drop the peas into boiling water and cook 5 minutes. Drain and stir into the vegetables along with the squid. Reserve fish broth mixture, spoon fish and vegetables into shells and serve with sauce, on the side.

Serves: 6.
Time: 1 hour.

SAUCE BECHAMEL

2 tablespoons brown rice or wholewheat flour

$\frac{1}{2}$ cup chopped onion

$\frac{1}{2}$ cup chopped spring onions

1 tablespoon tahini

$\frac{1}{4}$ cup chopped celery or watercress

1 teaspoon sea salt to taste

2 cups fish stock (see page 147)

2 teaspoons oil

Lightly roast the flour until it begins to smell nutty. Set aside. Chop all the vegetables. Heat skillet, add oil and sauté the onion and spring onions until they turn transparent. Then add the flour, tahini, salt and liquid. Cream with fish stock. Bring to the boil, cover and simmer with the lid ajar for 10 minutes. Taste and adjust seasonings. Serve alongside choko.

SHISH KEBABS

2 x 200 g pieces tofu

3 tablespoons prepared mustard

4 tablespoons sake or white wine

2 tablespoons brown rice vinegar

4 tablespoons oil

2 tablespoons maple syrup

1 teaspoon dry rosemary

1 teaspoon dry oregano

2 cloves minced garlic

2 teaspoons minced ginger-root

1–2 teaspoons sea salt or 3–4 tablespoons shoyu to taste

12 tomato wedges or eggplant

12 mushrooms, halved

12 sweet red pepper chunks

6 green pepper chunks

8–12 bamboo skewers or stainless steel (soak bamboo in water before using)

Press tofu to remove excess water for 20 minutes (see page 85). Drain and cut into 2 cm x 2 cm (1 x 1 inch) cubes. You can deep fry them at this stage if you like. Combine the marinade ingredients in a bowl, add the tofu cubes, sprinkle with salt and then add the rest of the vegetables. Toss lightly so that all the vegetables are

coated with the marinade. Put aside for at least 1 hour turning the tofu and vegetables occasionally. Prepare rice and peas.

Soak the bamboo skewers in cold water. Drain.

Skewer the tofu cubes on the skewers alternating with the vegetables to form a colourful arrangement. Cook under the grill until brown and fragrant, basting the vegetables with the marinade occasionally.

SAUCE

1 tablespoon kuzu or arrowroot flour

1 cup leftover marinade

Dissolve the kuzu in the cold water. Add the marinade and bring to the boil, stirring constantly. Taste and adjust seasoning. Remove from heat, sprinkle in some watercress or chives and spoon over kebabs, which is served on top of rice.

Serves: 4–6.
Time: 1 hour 15 minutes.

BAKED RICE AND PEAS

3 cups brown rice

15 cm (6 in) strip kombu sea vegetable

1 cup bonita flakes*

$4\frac{1}{2}$ cups water

1 cup fresh peas

Wash rice. Preheat oven to 190°C and roast rice on a 22 cm x 33 cm x 2.5 cm (11 inch x 16 inch x 1 inch) baking sheet with low sides. Meanwhile add kombu to water, and bring to the boil. Remove kombu, add fish flakes and bring to the boil. Let sit several minutes. When the flakes have settled to the bottom, strain off liquid. Bring liquid to the boil, add rice bring to the boil and cover. Bake in oven 45–60 minutes.

Meanwhile boil the peas in salted water 5 minutes uncovered. Rinse in cold water to stop from cooking. Mix rice with peas after rice is cooked. Press into bowl and mould onto plate.

*Found in Japanese and Chinese groceries.

SUNDAY BRUNCH

APPLE MARMALADE PANCAKES

2 cups brown rice flour

2 cups rolled oats

pinch of sea salt

1 teaspoon oil

2½–3 cups water or apple juice

1–2 tablespoons oil

MARMALADE (G)

8 cups grated peeled apples

1 orange

2 cups apple juice or cider

1 cup orange juice

orange peel from 1 orange

½ cup maltose, rice syrup or barley malt

1 teaspoon sea salt or to taste

1 tablespoon ginger juice to taste

Pancakes

Combine flour and oats. Add salt and mix oil and juice into batter until the consistency is pourable. Set aside 20 minutes.

Heat pan, add oil and ladle batter in. Cook till holes appear, then turn over and lightly brown. Serve with marmalade.

Marmalade

Grate apples. Chop orange. Measure juices into a large pot. Add apples, salt and bring to the boil. Cover and simmer. Meanwhile, cut orange rind into thin matchsticks. Combine with enough water to cover and bring to the boil. Throw away the water and repeat three times. Combine rind and maltose in a saucepan and bring to the boil. Lower heat and simmer until there is almost no sweetener left. Serve on top of marmalade. Blend half of the mixture and return to the pot with the other half. Squeeze in ginger juice and cook until the desired consistency is reached.

Serves: 4–6.
Time: 30 minutes.

After brunch thoughts

OLIVE BREAD (G)

3 cups wholewheat flour

1½ tablespoons dry yeast

1 cup hot apple juice

2 teaspoons maltose, rice syrup or barley malt

1 teaspoon sea salt

2 tablespoons oil

unhulled sesame seeds

STUFFING

1 cup olives

1 cup chopped onion

1 tablespoon olive oil

oil for glazing

Dough

Sift flour into a bowl. Dissolve yeast in ¼ cup hot juice, then add remaining juice and sweetener. Cover and set aside until bubbly. Combine salt with flour and mix. Make a well in the centre of the flour mixture, and pour in yeast mixture. Add oil gradually then beat with wooden spoon until dough begins to leave the side of the bowl. Knead 10 minutes. Shape into a ball. Oil bowl, put in dough, cover top of dough with oil. Cover bowl and set in a warm place to rise until doubled in size.

Stuffing

De-pit olives and chop. Chop onion. Heat skillet, add oil and sauté onions until they are translucent. Add olives and mix together with onions. Cool.

Shaping Dough

Punch down dough and turn out on lightly floured board. Press out into a rectangle. Roll out to 1 cm (½ inch) thickness. Spread onion and olive mixture over dough, leaving sides clear of filling.

Shaping and Decorating Breads:

1 For a nice finishing touch to any loaf, use a razor blade or scissors.
2 Cut or slash the top of the bread when it has almost completely risen in the pans or tins. Allow the bread to 'rest' for 10 minutes longer to allow the dough to open up.

Roll up dough from longer side and shape into a long loaf. Oil baking sheet and place bread seam side down. Make three slits diagonally across the top of the bread. Cover with a pan that does not touch the surface of the bread. Leave in a warm place until doubled in size.

Preheat oven to 190°C. Brush top with oil and sprinkle with sesame seeds. Bake 40–45 minutes or until bread sounds hollow when tapped.

PEANUT PUMPKIN SPREAD (G)

1 cup steamed or baked pumpkin
3 tablespoons peanut butter
1 tablespoon miso
2 tablespoons grated apple
1 tablespoon lemon rind

Cook pumpkin. Cream all ingredients together until a smooth paste is formed. Spread on bread with cucumber, sprouts and lettuce.

Time: 30 minutes.

APPLE APRICOT SPREAD (G)

4 apples
$\frac{1}{2}$ cup sultanas
2 cups dried unsulphured apricots
apple juice
$\frac{1}{2}$ teaspoon sea salt or 1 tablespoon miso
1 teaspoon cinnamon
$\frac{1}{2}$ teaspoon ginger
$\frac{1}{2}$ teaspoon coriander

Core and chop apples. (Peel if not organic.) Combine apples, sultanas, apricots and enough juice to cover fruit in saucepan. Bring to the boil, add the next four ingredients and simmer uncovered for 15 minutes or until it becomes very thick and spreadable. Cool and use as spread on bread.

Time: 25 minutes.

SPECIAL SUNDAYS

ALMOND-MUSHROOM PATÉ (G)

1 cup chopped onion
1 teaspoon chopped garlic
$2\frac{1}{2}$ cups (250 g, $\frac{1}{2}$ lb) halved mushrooms
2 tablespoons oil
$\frac{1}{2}$ teaspoon sea salt or 1 tablespoon miso
$\frac{1}{4}$ teaspoon tarragon
250 g ($\frac{1}{2}$ lb) blanched whole almonds, toasted
1 tablespoon mirin

Chop onions and garlic. Halve mushrooms and blend or chop very finely. Heat skillet, add oil, onions and garlic. Sauté until the onions are transparent.

Add the mushrooms, salt, tarragon and cook stirring occasionally until all of the liquid has evaporated.

Reserve $\frac{2}{3}$ cup almonds for garnish. Blend the remaining almonds to form a paste. Add cooked mushroom mixture and mirin. Mix until smooth. Cover and chill. Mound paté onto a serving plate. Garnish with reserved almonds.

Serves: 6.
Time: 15 minutes.

PICKLES

Foods to be pickled in miso (G)

1 Garlic
   Peel the outer skin for garlic cloves and parboil 3 minutes. Drain and dry 1 hour. Cut in half, tie together in cheesecloth and embed in miso 2–3 weeks.
2 **Celery**
   Cut stalks into 5 cm lengths. Embed in miso 48 hours. Serve as a snack.

When Australian troops were sent to the Boer War in the 1900s, each man was issued with a billy can and a packet of tea by the Inglis Tea Company. It was a flavoured tea, containing 10 per cent china green and it later became known as 'The Billy Tea', because it was brewed over a fire of gum leaves and twigs.

TOFU (G)

1 x 200 g cake tofu

1 cup miso*

1 teaspoon grated ginger

4 teaspoons sesame oil

2 tablespoons sake, dry sherry or mirin

Press tofu. Cut into 2 cm (1 inch) slices and drop in boiling water. Bring to the boil, drain and cool to room temperature. Combine all ingredients and make a bed of miso using half of the mixture. Place tofu slices on top and cover with remaining miso. Cover with cheesecloth and plastic to keep air out. Place in refrigerator for 12 hours. Remove tofu, wipe off miso and mix with grains, vegetables or grill on top side before serving.

*Use hacho, soba, kome or genmai miso for gluten-free diets.

SHOYU PICKLES (G)

seasonal vegetables

shoyu

ginger slices

brown rice vinegar

Mix equal parts water and shoyu in a glass jar or bowl. Slice seasonal vegetables (hard roots are best) and place in mixture. Add slices of ginger and several tablespoons vinegar. Press or marinate overnight. Can marinate for 2–3 weeks.

LEMON PICKLES (G)

4 small lemons

$\frac{1}{2}$ cup miso

2 tablespoons grated cheese or bonita flakes

2 tablespoons tahini or minced walnuts

$\frac{1}{2}$ tablespoon maple syrup

Japanese pepper to taste

Cut lemons crosswise into halves and scoop out fruit and pulp. Combine the rest of the ingredients and stuff the lemon halves. Join the halves together, and tie with four long strips of muslin. Place in steamer and cook 20 minutes. Hang up to dry in a cool, well ventilated place for at least 1–2 weeks (avoid sunlight). Cut crosswise into thin rounds and serve as a topping for casseroles, sprinkled into soups or salads or on top of crackers for hors d'oeuvre.

For a quicker version:

Add $\frac{1}{2}$ teaspoon grated lemon rind to ingredients. Omit steaming. Wrap miso-stuffed citrus and refrigerate at least 2 days. Serve the inside and use outside in soups or salads.

FORGET ME KNOTS

1 When baking, it is best to heat baking trays before oiling to allow oil to penetrate into trays and not the food.

2 When making stock, try to avoid the use of 'stock cubes' and canned soup stocks. Full of salt and monosodium glutamate (a chemically made substance which has been known to cause headaches, nausea and lockjaw), they are also filled with chemicals, artificial flavourings and sometimes even colouring.

3 Dry stale bread, at room temperature uncovered for several days or placed in an oven at 120°C until sufficiently dried, can be used as croûtons. Cut into 2 cm (1 inch) cubes, and toss with oil and garlic marinade (crush several pieces of garlic in salt and place in oil). Bake at 200°C until crisp.

4 Dry stale bread as stated above and after cutting into 2 cm (1 inch) cubes, heat skillet, add garlic oil and lightly fry. Drain before using.

5 For fibre and roughage which aid digestion, nibble on wholegrain sandwiches, seeds, dried fruits and nuts.

6 For a quick snack, popcorn can supply you with fibre, roughage and protein.

7 For in between meal pick-me-ups, try a bowl of soup, roasted nuts and seeds, or wholegrain sandwiches.

8 When purchasing dried fruit make sure that they have not been chemically treated. *Sulphur dioxide* is used as a preservative in dried fruit to prevent browning and oxidation of fruit, mould growth and loss of Vitamin C after drying. *Sorbic acid* is used as a preservative in dried tree fruit.

9 When creaming flour and liquid together they must both be the same temperature so that no lumps appear.

10 To prevent browning and to remove bitterness of yams and sweet potato, soak in 1 litre of water and 2 tablespoons vinegar for 30 minutes.

11 For a lighter pastry dough substitute half the amount of wholewheat flour with pressed tofu.

12 When marinating fish, chicken or vegetables use ceramic or glassware only.

WINTER

As winter approaches, the cold and wet weather usually brings the elements of rest, solitude, withdrawal and inward reflection. It's the season to spend more time at home with family and friends and a time also to be more physically active in order to keep warmth and energy flowing throughout the body.

The coldest and darkest of all the seasons, winter finds some of nature's creatures hibernating while 'mother' earth shows very little signs of activity. At best, it is a time of preparation for the rebirth and regeneration of the blossoms, the birds and the bees.

Goals

Two to three months before winter makes itself known, your diet should show signs of a change. More warming foods and winter cooking techniques; stewing, baking, deep-frying and more foods that lend themselves to longer cooking time, such as whole grains, which are not only good fuel but beneficial for the intestines as well. Combine beans and miso with grains to make a complete protein (contains all the essential amino-acids that your body cannot produce) and introduce more animal foods such as fish to keep your body warm. A greater abundance of root vegetables and those that grow close to the earth make good stews and hearty soups. The use of ginger and garlic are not only good for flavour but they also keep the blood circulating, producing warmth and vitality at the same time.

Many of the lunches are designed for home or portable lunch boxes. If you are working, then take soup along in a thermos. Use the sour dough bread for sandwiches, or if there is no time to bake some, buy some good wholemeal bread and combine the vegetables and beans for spreads.

	DINNER	BREAKFAST	LUNCH
MONDAY	Buckwheat nut loaf with lemon-garlic sauce Caraway salad with tahini creme dressing Yams a la wakame Apple almond mousse **After dinner thought:** Sourdough starter		
TUESDAY	Bean and vegetable cassoulet with dumplings Boiled watercress salad spring onion dressing	Fresh fruit jam Oat and barley porridge **After breakfast thought:** Soak 1 cup aduki beans	Four vegetable bake Broccoli miso soup Wrapped snacks
WEDNESDAY	Herbed rice Grilled fish with garlic sauce Creme of watercress soup Endive and fennel salad Winter dressing Sesame pretzels **After dinner thoughts:** Sourdough starter	Baked apples Eggs in the whole	Mushroom-barley soup Buckwheat rissoles **After lunch thought:** Brown rice
THURSDAY	Slimmer's cabbage pie Onion parsley sauce Peanut patties Onion and radish salad **After dinner thought:** Roast wholegrains for breakfast cereal	Whole grain porridge **After breakfast thoughts:** Sourdough rye bread Spiced fruit ring	Stuffed peppers Sweet and sour green beans
FRIDAY	Tempura (fritto misto) Sea salad Dipping sauce Pear custard	Sunflower-sultana porridge	Turnip slice Broccoli with black beans **After lunch thought:** Tofu whip creme for cake on Saturday
SATURDAY	Anise chicken Apple cake with tofu whip creme Leeks in piquant sauce Beetroot viniagrette	Granola **After breakfast thought:** Marinate chicken	Onion and carrot tarts Braised endive and mushroom **After lunch thought:** Filling for Danish pastries
SUNDAY		Sesame-oat waffles Apple sauce **After brunch thoughts:** Lemon meringue pie Danish pastries	

MONDAY DINNER

BUCKWHEAT NUT LOAF

$1\frac{1}{2}$ cups buckwheat (roasted)

$2\frac{1}{4}$ cups water

$\frac{1}{2}$ teaspoon sea salt

2 cups sliced mushrooms

1 tablespoon minced ginger-root

2 teaspoons minced garlic

1 cup diced onion

$\frac{1}{2}$ cup grated carrot

2 tablespoons oil

6 large cabbage leaves

1 cup roasted, ground almonds or walnuts

3 eggs, beaten

2 tablespoons miso

$\frac{1}{2}$ teaspoon each thyme, basil, oregano

$\frac{1}{2}$ cup chopped parsley

$\frac{3}{4}$ cup breadcrumbs

If buckwheat is not roasted, bake in 200°C preheated oven until lightly browned. Bring $2\frac{1}{4}$ cups water to the boil. Add buckwheat, salt, cover and lower heat, simmer 15 minutes. Meanwhile, cut the rest of the vegetables. Heat the 2 tablespoons of oil and sauté mushrooms 5 minutes. Remove from skillet or wok, set aside and add the 2 remaining tablespoons of oil to wok. Sauté the rest of the vegetables in order listed above. Cover and simmer 5 minutes.

Meanwhile, bring a pot of salted water to the boil. Add cabbage and blanch 1–2 minutes. Drain and rinse under cold water.

Oil bread tin. Preheat oven to 190°C. Line tin with cabbage leaves, covering the bottom and sides. Leave enough overhang to fold over and cover the top.

Combine half the buckwheat with the cooked vegetables and the roasted nuts. Beat eggs and miso, combine with buckwheat mixture and add the rest of the ingredients. Spoon into cabbage lined loaf tin ($9\frac{1}{2}$ cm x 23 cm) (4 in x 9 in), press down firmly and fold overhanging leaves over the mixture. Cover the pan with a double layer of oiled paper. Reserve other half of buckwheat for Wednesday.

Place the loaf pan in a baking dish and pour enough water into the baking dish so that it reaches halfway up the sides of the loaf pan. Bake 45–60 minutes or until firm to the touch. Cool before slicing.
Serves: 4–6.
Time: $1\frac{1}{2}$ hours.

LEMON AND GARLIC SAUCE (G)

2 cups (400 g) plain goat's milk yoghurt or tofu

3–4 tablespoons lemon juice to taste

1 tablespoon prepared mustard

$\frac{1}{2}$ teaspoon pressed garlic

2 tablespoons tahini

sea salt to taste

Combine all the ingredients and blend well. If using tofu, drop into boiling water before blending with other ingredients.

Makes: $2\frac{1}{2}$ cups.
Time: 5 minutes.

CARAWAY SALAD (G)

inside of cabbage (reserve outside leaves for buckwheat loaf)

1 cup grated carrot

1 tablespoon sea salt

1 tablespoon caraway seeds

DRESSING

2 tablespoons tahini

$\frac{1}{4}$ cup oil

1 clove of garlic pressed in sea salt*

$\frac{1}{4}$ cup minced parsley

Grate cabbage and carrots. Mix together with salt and press with a plate and heavy weight at least 30 minutes up until 24 hours. Wash cabbage, squeeze dry and toss with caraway seeds.

Blend all of the dressing ingredients together and mix into coleslaw at least 15 minutes before serving. Reserve extra for another day.

Serves: 4–6.
Time: 40 minutes.

*Press garlic on brown paper in sea salt to remove pungent oil.

YAMS A LA WAKAME (G)

1 kg (2 lb) yams

oil for deep frying

1 strip of wakame sea vegetable

Cut half of the yams into thin strips, like chips. Heat oil and deep fry until golden. Meanwhile preheat oven to 200°C. Drain chips, and set aside. Brush wakame with dry towel, and bake on the rack 5 minutes or until crisp. Bake the remaining yams for Wednesday's lunch.

Sprinkle wakame over chips *just* before serving.

Serves: 4–6.
Time: 15 minutes.

ALMOND APPLE MOUSSE (G)

1 cup apple juice

4 tablespoons almond butter

4 tablespoons barley malt, rice syrup or maltose

4 tablespoons kuzu or arrowroot flour

1½ cups apple juice

1 teaspoon cinnamon

1 tablespoon orange rind

2 teaspoons miso

1 teaspoon vanilla

Blend juice and almond butter until smooth. Place in saucepan with sweetener and heat. In another bowl or suribachi* combine the remaining ingredients. Add to first mixture and continue to cook over a medium heat, stirring constantly until the mixture thickens, boils and turns clearer. Remove from heat. Prepare topping. Serve warm on a cold night or cold on a warm night.

Serves: 4–6.
Time: 15 minutes.

*Japanese mortar and pestle (see page 37).

MOCHA CRUMB TOPPING

1 cup wholewheat flour

2 cups rolled oats

½ cup corn or maizemeal

2 teaspoons cinnamon

½ teaspoon sea salt

½ cup crushed walnuts or almonds

½ cup oil

4 tablespoons maple syrup

2 teaspoons vanilla

apple juice to bind (if necessary)

Roast flour until lightly browned. Roast rolled oats until fragrant. Combine all the dry ingredients. Beat oil, sweetener and vanilla together and combine with dry ingredients. Mix until it becomes sticky, adding a few drops of apple juice if not moist enough. *Do not saturate with too much juice* — texture should resemble a crumble. Bake on a cookie sheet in a 190°C oven 10–15 minutes and after cooling, sprinkle on top of mousse. For a delicious biscuit, add enough apple juice to bind. Spoon onto oiled cookie sheet and bake at 190°C for 20–25 minutes.

*For gluten-free substitute, substitute 1 cup millet flour for 1 cup wholewheat and 2 cups rolled rice flakes for oats.

Serves: 4–6.
Time: 15 minutes.

After dinner thoughts:

SOUR DOUGH STARTER

1 cup rye flour

slice of onion

1 tablespoon caraway seeds (optional)

warm water, cider or apple juice to form batter

Mix starter ingredients together. Leave covered in a warm spot to allow fermentation to occur 2–3 days. Stir daily. When it begins to smell slightly alcoholic and sour, bubbles should also appear on the surface. It is now ready for use. If you are not ready to use this starter immediately, place in glass jar and refrigerate after removing onion. Mix fresh flour and water every seven days into starter or use within seven days. This feeds the starter and keeps it fresh.

Time: 5 minutes.

TUESDAY BREAKFAST

FRESH FRUIT JAM (G)

8–10 cups fresh chopped fruit in season
4–5 cups dried fruit
apple juice to cover
½ teaspoon sea salt
1 tablespoon minced ginger-root
2 teaspoons cinnamon
1–2 tablespoons miso
3–4 tablespoons kuzu

Cut up any combination of fresh fruit in season (apples, pears) and 1 orange. Add half the amount in dried raisins, sultanas, currants or dates. Cover with apple juice. Add ½ teaspoon sea salt, 1 tablespoon grated ginger-root, 2 teaspoons cinnamon and bring to the boil. Cover and simmer 10 minutes or until fruit is tender. Remove cover, add miso to taste (1–2 tablespoons). Meanwhile, dissolve 1 tablespoon kuzu per 2 cups jam in cold water. Stir into jam until thick and creamy. Use over anything. Keep in *glass* jar in refrigerator.

Yield: 8 cups.
Time: 40 minutes.

OAT AND BARLEY PORRIDGE

1 cup rolled oats
1 cup rolled barley
½ cup ground sunflower seeds or cashews
½ cup roasted maize, corn or millet meal
1 teaspoon sea salt to taste

Lightly toast rolled oats and barley. Do the same with the meal. Bring water to the boil, stir in dry ingredients and return to the heat. Lower temperature, cover and leave lid slightly ajar. Simmer at least 40 minutes. You can do this overnight in a crock pot or thermos.

After breakfast thoughts:
Wash and pick through 1 cup aduki beans. Bring water and beans to the boil. If you have the time simmer without a lid 30 minutes. Remove from heat and set aside for the evening.

Serves: 4–6.
Time: 50 minutes.

TUESDAY LUNCH

FOUR VEGETABLE BAKE

2 cups chopped Chinese cabbage
2 cups chopped cauliflower flowerettes
½ cup small whole button mushrooms
½ cup mung or soy bean sprouts
3 tablespoons oil
4 tablespoons roasted sesame oil
½ cup wholewheat flour or brown rice flour
½ cup hot stock or water
3 cups hot stock or water
1–2 teaspoons sea salt to taste
bay leaf
roasted, ground sunflower seeds for garnish
parsley for garnish

Cut up vegetables and keep in separate containers. Rinse bean sprouts. Heat wok, add oil and stir-fry Chinese cabbage lightly. Meanwhile bring a pot of water to the boil. Drop in cauliflower pieces and simmer 2–3 minutes. Drain. Add cauliflower to cabbage and stir fry 2–3 minutes. Remove from wok.

Stir-fry mushrooms 2–3 minutes and remove. Stir-fry sprouts 1–2 minutes. (Add more oil if necessary.) Remove from wok. In a separate skillet add the 4 tablespoons of roasted sesame oil, and stir in flour. Toast, constantly stirring. Add the ½ cup *hot* stock or water and whisk quickly so that no lumps form. Stir in the remaining *hot* stock, add salt and bring to the boil. Preheat oven to 190°C. Oil baking dish, arrange vegetables in layers, pour sauce over the top and place bay leaf in the centre. Cover and bake 15 minutes. Remove cover and bay leaf. Serve garnished with seeds and parsley.

Serves: 4.
Time: 1 hour.

Top: Shish Kebabs.   See page 120
Bottom: Baked Rice and Peas.   See page 120

BROCCOLI-MISO SOUP (G)

2 cups broccoli

1 tablespoon oil

2 cups water

$\frac{1}{2}$ cup roasted unhulled sesame seeds

2–3 tablespoons miso

Separate broccoli flowers from the stems. Cut into flowerettes. Slice stem on the diagonal into 2 cm (1 inch) pieces after peeling.

Heat wok. Add oil and sauté broccoli stems. Add all but $\frac{1}{2}$ cup water and bring to the boil, cover and simmer 5–7 minutes or until stems are tender.

Roast sesame seeds in skillet until they begin to pop. Grind in a suribachi or blender. Drop broccoli flowerettes into soup, add the remaining $\frac{1}{2}$ cup of water and bring to the boil. Place miso in the suribachi with the ground seeds and $\frac{1}{4}$ cup hot broth. Purée. Add purée back to soup and remove from heat. Keep covered until serving. *Do not boil.* This will destroy the enzymes present.

Serves: 4.
Time: 20 minutes.

WRAPPED SNACKS (G)

Using leftover yams, root vegetables, rice ar any beans such as tofu as a base, combine the leftovers with miso (soy bean paste) and shoyu, along with any nut butter, lemon or orange rind, spices, herbs or salad dressing. Use any one of the suggested wrappers for a quick snack or easy lunch:

- blanched lettuce leaves (G)
- blanched spinach, silverbeet or cabbage leaves (G)
- Lebanese flat bread or pita bread
- leftover baked potato jackets (G)
- crepes (see page 114)
- pancakes (see page 121)
- stuffed onions, pumpkin or squash (G)
- nori sea vegetable (nori rolls and cones) (G)
- cucumbers (G)
- celery boats (G)
- brown rice wafers (G)

Top: Buckwheat Nut Loaf.   See page 126
Bottom: Lemon and Garlic Sauce.   See page 126

TUESDAY DINNER

BEAN AND VEGETABLE CASSOULET

Cassoulet is one of the most famous dishes in southern France. I have left out the usual sausage, preserved goose and ham bones. Have plenty of crusty wholemeal bread on hand to scoop up the broth with.

1 cup dry aduki beans

1 bay leaf

15 cm (6 inch) piece of kombu sea vegetable

2 cups onion wedges

1 cup chopped parsley

1 cup chopped parsnip chunks

1 cup chopped celery

4 cups pumpkin and carrot chunks

2 tablespoons minced garlic

4 large mushrooms

3 tablespoons oil

1 cup dry white wine or mirin

3 tablespoons miso

1 tablespoon prepared mustard.

1 tablespoon grated ginger-root

shell of gramma or Queensland blue pumpkin

DUMPLINGS

1 cup wholewheat breadcrumbs

2 tablespoons grated onion

2 tablespoons grated parsley

$\frac{1}{2}$ teaspoon thyme

$\frac{1}{2}$ teaspoon tarragon

1 teaspoon miso

1–2 tablespoons water (adjust accordingly)

1 egg yolk

maize or corn meal

oil for deep frying

Stew

Bring beans and soaking water to the boil. Simmer 30 minutes if not already done so. (Add more water if necessary so that beans are covered by at least 5 cm (2 inches) of water.) Skim off residue that collects on top. Add bay leaf, cover and pressure cook 30 minutes. If simmering, cook until tender (1 hour). Meanwhile cut the vegetables into large pieces. Cut the parsnips into irregular chunks by rotating the parsnip one-quarter to one-eighth turn with each cut. Mince the garlic. Heat skillet, add oil and sauté vegetables in order listed. Separately combine the next four ingredients and blend well. Set aside.

Dumplings
Meanwhile, mix the first five ingredients for the dumplings together. Dissolve the miso in water and yolk and add to the first mixture. Knead shape into small balls and roll in meal. Heat oil, deep fry until lightly browned. Drain.

Putting it all together
Drain the beans and reserve excess juice. Add beans to vegetables and a small amount of bean juice. Cover and simmer 20–30 minutes. Stir in wine mixture, taste and adjust seasoning. Place dumplings on top to warm. Serve garnished with spring onions or shallots in pumpkin.

Serves: 4–6.
Time: 1 hour.

BOILED WATERCRESS SALAD (G)

3 bunches of watercress

unhulled sesame seeds (toasted) for garnish

SPRING ONION DRESSING (G)

$\frac{1}{2}$ **cup tahini**

1 tablespoon minced spring onion

$\frac{1}{2}$ **teaspoon dry mustard powder**

2 tablespoons brown rice vinegar

2 tablespoons lemon juice

$\frac{1}{2}$ **teaspoon sea salt**

1 tablespoon shoyu

warm apple juice to cream if necessary

Salad
Bring a pot of salted water to the boil. Drop in watercress and blanch for 1 minute. Remove, drain and chop in 5 cm (2 inch) pieces.

Dressing
Combine all the ingredients and purée until smooth and creamy. Pour over warm vegetables and sprinkle sesame seeds on top before serving.

Serves: 4–6.
Time: 10 minutes.

WEDNESDAY BREAKFAST

BAKED APPLES

4 large apples

1$\frac{1}{3}$ cups granola (see page 138)

$\frac{1}{2}$ **teaspoon cinnamon**

$\frac{1}{2}$ **teaspoon coriander**

$\frac{1}{4}$ **cup tahini or peanut butter**

1 teaspoon orange or lemon rind

$\frac{1}{2}$ **cup warm barley malt, rice honey or maltose**

1 tablespoon oil

$\frac{1}{4}$ **cup apple juice**

Preheat oven to 180°C. Core apples and stand upright in a square or round baking dish. (Try out dish for size to assure that apples are tightly packed together.) To make filling combine the next five ingredients, and $\frac{1}{4}$ cup of sweetener together. Pack apples with filling. Combine the remaining sweetener, oil and apple juice. Blend. Pour over apples. Pierce apples with fork.

Cover and bake 15 minutes. Remove cover and bake, basting with juices until apples are tender. Serve warm or cool.

Serves: 4.
Time: 45 minutes.

EGGS IN THE WHOLE

4 teaspoons miso mixed with 4 tablespoons tahini

4 slices whole wheat bread or tofu

1 cup oil

4 eggs

shallots for garnish

Spread miso and tahini over bread slices. Cut a whole in the centre of each slice with a round biscuit cutter or small glass and remove the round piece of bread.

Heat skillet, add the cup of oil, put the bread in spread side up, and break an egg into each hole. Fry 2–3 minutes, or until bottom is nicely golden and egg is half done. Turn and repeat on other side or serve sunny-side up. Sprinkle with shallots.

Serves: 4.
Time: 10 minutes.

WEDNESDAY LUNCH

MUSHROOM BARLEY SOUP

3 dried Chinese or Japanese mushrooms

3 tablespoons barley

6 cups water

3 slices ginger-root

2 cups diced onion

2 tablespoons oil

2 tablespoons roasted brown rice flour

$\frac{1}{2}$ cup mushroom soaking liquid

3–4 tablespoons miso to taste

fresh watercress for garnish

Soak mushrooms in hot water to cover until soft (15–20 minutes). Slice finely, and reserve soaking water.

Combine mushrooms, barley, water and ginger-root in a saucepan. Bring to the boil, cover and simmer 40 minutes or until barley is tender (pressure cook 15 minutes). Remove ginger.

Dice onions. Heat wok, add oil and sauté onions. Add the flour and roast with onions. Heat the reserved mushroom liquid adding more if necessary to measure $\frac{1}{2}$ cup. Cream into flour mixture stirring so that there are no lumps. Add to the soup, and cook covered 10 minutes. Cream miso with $\frac{1}{4}$ cup soup. Stir into soup and bring to just under the boil. Remove from heat, garnish with watercress and serve with rissoles.

Serves: 4–6.
Time: 1 hour.

BUCKWHEAT RISSOLES

2 cups leftover buckwheat (Monday night)

2 cups onion slices

3 cups carrot sticks

$\frac{1}{2}$ cup sliced celery

$\frac{1}{2}$ cup chopped parsley

1 tablespoon thyme or curry

$1\frac{1}{2}$ teaspoons sea salt

3 cups wholewheat flour

2 tablespoons kuzu

water to bind

GINGER DIP (G)

1 teaspoon grated ginger-root

$\frac{1}{2}$ cup shoyu

2 tablespoons hot water

Combine all ingredients for rissoles. Add enough water or leftover soup so that the mixture *just* sticks together. (Not too wet.) Shape into rissoles.* Place on an oiled platter. Meanwhile heat oil. Prepare draining paper. Deep-fry several at a time. Cook on both sides until lightly browned. Drain and keep in a warmed oven till ready to serve.

*Squeeze mixture in your hand to bind. The shape should be irregular with carrot sticks and onions visible.

Dip
Boil water. Grate ginger-root and combine with shoyu. Add hot water just before serving.

Serves: 4–6.
Time: 20 minutes.

 After lunch thought:

BROWN RICE (G)

3 cups brown rice (short grain is best for winter)

$4\frac{1}{2}$ cups water

$\frac{1}{2}$ teaspoon sea salt

Wash rice until water is clear. Drain. Combine rice and water in saucepan. Add salt, bring to the boil. Cover and simmer 45–50 minutes. With a pressure cooker (use slightly less water) and pressure cook rice 45 minutes. Rice can also be roasted in the oven at 190°C until golden brown. Add to boiling water, cover and simmer on top of stove or bake 45 minutes. Stir, and reserve for dinner.

WEDNESDAY DINNER

HERBED RICE

2 teaspoons minced garlic

1 tablespoon chopped ginger-root

3 cups chopped onion

2 tablespoons oil

3 cups cooked brown rice (from lunch)

4 tablespoons chopped coriander

½ cup chopped parsley

1 teaspoon sea salt or 2–4 tablespoons shoyu to taste

Chop vegetables and place in separate bowls. Heat wok, add oil and vegetables in order listed above. Sauté until onion is transparent and smell is sweet. Add cooked rice, top with coriander and parsley. *Do not mix the rice.* Cover and warm. Season to taste and stir all ingredients together before serving.

Serves: 6.
Time: 15 minutes.

GRILLED FISH (G)

6 snapper or bream

sea salt

12 wooden or metal skewers

GARLIC SAUCE (G)

5 large heads of garlic

3 tablespoons olive oil

lemon juice to taste

parsley for colour

Fish
Scale and gut the fish if not already done. Sprinkle with liberal amounts of sea salt, rubbing inside as well as outside. Leave on a platter for 20 minutes. Rinse and wipe with paper towels. Sprinkle more salt over the fish, covering the tail and fin with extra salt to prevent burning. Soak bamboo skewers in cold water. To prevent the fish from curling up while cooking, insert skewer below the eye and bring it out just before the tail. Second skewer: insert directly below the first. Grill fish on both sides, turning when eye is white. Remove skewers and serve with sauce.

Sauce
Separate whole heads of garlic and peel each clove. Do not flatten the cloves to peel. Drop the cloves into

8 cups of lightly salted cold water and bring to the boil. Let the water boil vigorously 5 minutes. Drain. Repeat 3–4 times or until cloves are tender. Purée with oil adding lemon juice to taste and chopped parsley if you like a 'green' sauce. This sauce will be sweet in taste to offset the salty fish.

Serves: 6.
Time: 40 minutes.

CREME OF WATERCRESS SOUP (G)

1 cup chopped leeks

1 tablespoon oil

1 bunch of watercress

4 cups vegetable or chicken stock

1 bouquet garni

¼ cup brown rice, barley or wheat flour

sea salt to taste

Chop leeks. Heat deep skillet and add oil. Sauté leeks until sweet smell occurs. Add watercress and stock. Place bouquet garni in soup, bring to the boil, cover and simmer 5 minutes.

Meanwhile heat skillet and roast flour until lightly browned. Add 1 cup hot stock to flour and creme quickly so as no lumps appear.

Blend half of the remaining soup until cremy in blender or food processor. Return to pot, stir in creme mixture and bring to the boil. Lower heat and simmer 5 minutes. Season to taste. Garnish with sprouts or grated carrot.

Serves: 6.
Time: 20 minutes.

ENDIVE AND FENNEL SALAD (G)

4 cups chopped endive

2 cups chopped fennel

1 cup chopped celery

2 tablespoons minced chives or shallots

6 tablespoons pitted olives (preferably Italian), minced

WINTER DRESSING (G)

6 tablespoons olive oil

3 tablespoons apple cider vinegar

1 teaspoon dried oregano, crumbled

2 teaspoons prepared mustard

sea salt to taste

½ cup pine nuts

Chop all vegetables and combine in bowl. Toss lightly. Whisk oil, vinegar, oregano, mustard and salt in a small bowl. Just before serving whisk dressing again, pour over greens and toss well. Garnish with pine nuts.

Serves: 6.
Time: 5 minutes.

SESAME PRETZELS

6 tablespoons warm oil

⅓ cup warm maple syrup

2 teaspoons lemon or orange rind

2 cups sifted whole wheat flour (very finely milled)

½ teaspoon sea salt

6 tablespoons roasted ground sesame seeds

1 teaspoon vanilla or ½ teaspoon rose-water

TOPPING

4 tablespoons maple syrup

2 tablespoons cold water

Warm oil and sweetener together and beat until creamy. Add rind. Sift flour and salt. Add roasted seeds and vanilla. Combine the flour mixture with the oil mixture, adding cold water if necessary until dough is formed. Wrap in greaseproof paper and chill 15 minutes.

Roll into a log, cut into 16 pieces. Roll out each piece to thin log and shape into pretzels. Preheat oven to 160°C. Place pretzels on oiled sheet and bake 15–20 minutes or until lightly browned. Bring maple syrup and water to a boil. Brush each biscuit *immediately* after baking. Dry on rack with sheet underneath to catch drippings.

Makes: 16.
Time: 50 minutes.

 After dinner thought:
*Take sourdough starter (page 127) out of the refrigerator and mix:

1 cup rye flour

3 cups wholewheat flour

with the sourdough starter into a mixing bowl. Cover and set in a warm spot overnight. (Use for baking on Thursday.)

Roast grains in oven for breakfast cereal. Blend or process till cracked.

THURSDAY BREAKFAST

WHOLE GRAIN PORRIDGE

6 cups nut milk, soy milk (see page 150) or water

½ cup wholewheat berries (cracked)

½ cup whole oats (cracked)

½ cup barley (cracked)

¼ cup millet (cracked)

¼ cup roasted buckwheat groats (cracked)

½ teaspoon sea salt

Bring milk to the boil. Add cracked grains and sea salt to the pot. Return to the boil. Cover lower heat and simmer ½ hour.
Serves: 4–6.
Time: 45 minutes.
Variations
- Serve with maple syrup mixed with tahini
- Serve with cooked or raw fruit
- Mix in some dried fruit while cooking
- For savoury porridge add shoyu or miso at the end of cooking.

 After breakfast thoughts:

SOUR DOUGH RYE BREAD

Remove 1 cup starter from batter and place back in the refrigerator for next bread. *Remember:* if you do not use the starter at least once a week, add several tablespoons of wholewheat or rye flour and a little bit of water so that it doesn't go too sour. Stir and keep for the following week.

1 tablespoon dry yeast

½ cup warm apple juice or cider

1 cup rye flour

2 cups wholemeal flour

1 teaspoon sea salt

1–1½ cups water or apple juice

3 teaspoons arrowroot flour or kuzu

1 teaspoon water

corn or maizemeal

Dissolve the yeast in the ½ cup juice. Cover and set aside until frothy. Combine the sourdough starter, yeast mixture, rye flour, wholemeal flour and salt, adding just enough water or juice until a soft dough is formed.

Knead 15 minutes or until dough begins to feel sticky. Form into a ball. Oil bowl, place dough in bowl and turn to coat it. Cover and let the dough rise in a warm spot until almost doubled. (The warmer the room the faster the rise.) If you place the entire bowl in a plastic bag it will rise much faster. (If you don't want it to rise too quickly place in a very cold room.) At lunchtime or when the dough has sufficiently risen, punch down and shape into a round loaf.

Place on oiled cookie sheet which has been sprinkled with corn or maizemeal. Cover and allow to rise until almost double in bulk.

Preheat oven to 200°C. Place pan of water on bottom shelf in oven. Slash bread crosswise. Brush loaf with arrowroot mixture. Bake 15 minutes. Lower temperature to 180°C and bake another 25–30 minutes. Cool on wire rack.

Makes: 1 round loaf.
Time: 2 hours.

SPICED FRUIT RING (G)

3 cups apple juice
2 bars agar-agar
$\frac{1}{2}$ teaspoon sea salt
$\frac{1}{4}$ teaspoon ground cloves
3 cups chopped pears
1 tablespoon kuzu or arrowroot
$\frac{1}{2}$ cup apple juice
$\frac{1}{2}$ cup orange juice
mint leaves for garnish

Place apple juice in saucepan, rinse agar-agar under cold water and shred into juice. Add salt, $\frac{1}{4}$ teaspoon cloves and bring to the boil. Simmer until agar-agar dissolves. Meanwhile chop fruit, dissolve kuzu in apple juice and orange juice mixture. Stir into simmering agar-agar mixture along with chopped fruit. Blend. Pour into ring mould and chill until set.

Serves: 6.
Time: 30 minutes.
Setting time: 2–3 hours.

THURSDAY LUNCH

STUFFED PEPPERS (G)

4 sweet red capsicums
$\frac{1}{2}$ cup chopped spring onion
1 teaspoon chopped garlic
4 tablespoons chopped parsley
2 tablespoons chopped coriander
4 tablespoons grated feta cheese (optional)
2 tablespoons oil
1 teaspoon basil
1 cup cooked grains
sea salt to taste or shoyu
$\frac{1}{2}$ cup chopped almonds or macadamia nuts

Cut tops off capsicums and scoop out seeds. Chop all vegetables, grate cheese. Heat skillet, add oil and sauté spring onion and garlic. When onions are transparent, add the parsley, coriander and basil. Stir in grains (rice or buckwheat mixed together is delicious), cover and simmer 3 minutes. Add grated cheese and stuff into capsicums. Preheat oven to 190°C. Place peppers in oiled baking dish so that they stand upright and are pressing against each other. Cover and bake 15 minutes, remove cover and bake another 5 minutes. Sprinkle with crushed nuts before serving. (If using cheese omit salt.)

Serves: 4.
Time: 45 minutes.

SWEET AND SOUR GREEN BEANS (G)

500 g (1 lb) green beans
1 cup boiling water
1 teaspoon sea salt
1 bay leaf
3 cloves
4 tablespoons barley malt, rice syrup or maltose
3 tablespoons apple cider vinegar
3 tablespoons oil
roasted unhulled sesame seeds

Top and tail the green beans. Meanwhile boil water, add beans and the next three ingredients. Boil 2–3 minutes. Heat the sweetener, vinegar and oil together. Drain beans, add to maltose mixture. Cook 2 minutes.

(Reserve cooking water for onion parsley sauce for dinner.)

Roast sesame seeds in a dry skillet. Sprinkle over green beans before serving.

Serves: 4.
Time: 10 minutes.

THURSDAY DINNER

SLIMMER'S CABBAGE PIE (G)

12 large outside cabbage leaves
4 cups of any of the following vegetables:
diced onions
sliced leeks
chopped coriander or watercress
chopped cabbage
diced carrots
diced pumpkin
chopped grean beans
chopped brussel sprouts
chopped cauliflower
chopped broccoli stalks
leftover herbed rice from Wednesday
4 tablespoons oil
½ tablespoon Chinese five spice powder
3 eggs
½ cup soy or nut milk (see page 150)
sea salt to taste

Remove thick stems from cabbage leaves. Drop into boiling salted water and cook until almost tender. Drain and rinse in cold salted water. Oil a 20 cm (8 inch) pie dish and line it with the drained cabbage leaves, overlapping and hanging over the edge.

Preheat oven to 190°C. Cut vegetables. Heat wok, add oil and sauté vegetables starting from the ones that have the strongest odour (e.g. onions, leeks) and progressing onto the leafy greens and then the roots. Add 5 spice powder, cover and simmer 3–4 minutes. Remove from heat and place in a bowl to cool. Beat eggs and milk together. Add salt and other herbs if desired. Pour egg over vegetables. Mix again. Ladle into cabbage-lined dish and carefully fold over cabbage leaves so that the vegetables are completely enclosed. Bake 30–45 minutes. Prepare parsley sauce.

Serves: 4–6.
Time: 1 hour.

ONION PARSLEY SAUCE (G)

3 cups minced spring onions
1 cup minced parsley
1 tablespoon oil
½ cup roasted slivered almonds
1 tablespoon kuzu
1 cup soup stock (or greenbean water)
1–2 tablespoons shoyu

Heat oil and sauté spring onions until sweet. Add parsley and sauté a few minutes longer. Add almonds, and sauté. Dissolve kuzu in cold stock, add to vegetables and stir until clear. Season with shoyu. Serve over cabbage pie.

Serves: 4–6.
Time: 15 minutes.

PEANUT PATTIES (G)

½ cup brown rice flour
2 tablespoons ground brown rice or brown rice flour
1 teaspoon ground coriander
½ teaspoon cumin
¼ teaspoon turmeric
¼ teaspoon sea salt
1 cup water, nut milk or soy milk (see page 150)
1 teaspoon pressed garlic
1 cup minced onion
4–5 tablespoons roasted, ground peanuts
½–1 cup oil for frying

Combine all ingredients, except oil. Shape into patties. Place on oiled plate and chill 15 minutes. Heat oil and lightly fry until golden. Serve warm with prepared mustard.

Serves: 4.
Time: 25 minutes.

ONION AND RADISH SALAD (G)

2 cups sliced onion rings

2 bunches red radish cut into thin circles

1 cup chopped celery

PARSLEY DRESSING (G)

1 cup chopped parsley

1 x 200 g piece of tofu

1 tablespoon lemon juice

½ teaspoon crushed garlic

1 tablespoon tahini

2 tablespoons brown rice vinegar

¼ cup oil

sea salt to taste

alfalfa sprouts

Cut vegetables. Keep in separate bowls. Bring a pot of water to the boil. Add salt. Blanch onion rings, then drain and freshen in cold water. Bring water to the boil again, add onion rings and cook 3 minutes. Drain and refresh. Arrange the onions, radish and celery in layers. (Reserve radish tops if fresh for another day). Reserve some radishes for top of salad.

Chop parsley. Bring a pot of water to the boil. Add tofu and bring to a boil. Drain and combine with the rest of the ingredients, blending until creamy. Taste and season. (Adjust liquid content if necessary).

Pour dressing over vegetables and garnish with sliced radishes and sprouts.

Serves: 4.
Time: 15 minutes.

After dinner thoughts:

Roast ½ cup whole rye in 190°C oven, 10–15 minutes on baking tray. Repeat with ½ cup whole oats. Blend or process till cracked. Keep for breakfast or cook overnight in crockpot.

> **Mint**, *one of the more common herbs, is used in England with peas and new potatoes, while all over the Middle East, mint is one of the commonly used herbs; it goes into salads, soups, omlettes, tea and purées. In Spain where much of the cooking has been greatly influenced by the Arabs, it is also used in abundance. The Italians favour it in sauces and wild mint gives a characteristic flavour to vegetable soups. Chutney from pounded mint, mangoes, onion and chillies goes well with fish and curries. Mint is one of the most useful herbs for summer, adding that little bit extra to soups, salads, vegetables and purées.*

FRIDAY BREAKFAST

SUNFLOWER-SULTANA PORRIDGE

½ cup cracked rye berries (from previous night)

½ cup cracked whole oats (from previous night)

4–5 cups apple juice

½ teaspoon sea salt

1 teaspoon cinnamon or cinnamon stick

½ cup sultanas

½ cup roasted sunflower seeds

Bring the apple juice to the boil in a saucepan. Remove from heat, stir in roasted cracked grains, add sea salt, cinnamon and sultanas. Stir and bring to the boil. Cover and simmer at least 30 minutes, but the longer the better.

Roast sunflower seeds in a 190°C oven. When seeds are nicely golden in colour, sprinkle them quickly with shoyu and mix quickly. Place back in oven 2–3 minutes until dry. Add the roasted seeds just before serving. Cool and save extra (if there is any leftover) for other toppings, or as a snack for the family.
Serves: 4.
Time: 45 minutes.

FRIDAY LUNCH

TURNIP SLICE

2 cups diced onions

8 cups grated turnips

6 tablespoons oil

6 tablespoons roasted wholewheat flour

2 tablespoons miso

1 pre-baked pie shell (optional) (see page 142)

Cut onions. Grate turnips. Heat wok, add oil and sauté onions until browned. Add turnips and sauté lightly 1–2 minutes. Cover and simmer 3–4 minutes.

Meanwhile, heat skillet add oil and roast flour until lightly browned. Remove from heat and cool. Cream miso in 1 teaspoon water, add to turnip and onion mixture. Stir flour into vegetables. Preheat oven to 190°C. Oil a pie dish, spread vegetables on and bake 20–30 minutes or until firm. Cool and serve. If using pie shell pre-bake shell 15 minutes. Then spread with vegetable filling and bake again 15–20 minutes.

Serves: 4.
Time: 1 hour.

BROCCOLI WITH BLACK BEANS (G)

500 g (1 lb) broccoli flowerettes
2 tablespoons salted black beans
1 tablespoon oil
3 cloves garlic
2 slices ginger-root
¾ cup water or stock
1 tablespoon shoyu
1 teaspoon arrowroot flour or kuzu mixed with 2 teaspoons water

Cut the broccoli into 2 cm (1 inch) pieces. Rinse the black beans and crush them slightly. Peel garlic.

Heat a wok. Add the oil. Sauté the garlic and ginger until they are brown. Remove and discard.

Add the broccoli to the wok. Stir in the black beans. Add the stock and shoyu. Cover and simmer 7 minutes or until the broccoli is just tender. Stir in the thickening, and bring to the boil.

Serves: 4.
Time: 15 minutes.

After lunch thoughts:

TOFU WHIP CREME (G)
(For cake on Saturday)

boiling water
2 x 200 g pieces tofu
½ cup maple syrup
2 tablespoons tahini or almond butter
pinch of sea salt
1 cup apple juice
1 bar agar-agar
2 teaspoons vanilla or mirin

Bring water to the boil. Drop tofu in and bring to the boil. Drain. Combine with the syrup, tahini and sea salt. Blend until creamy. Set aside. Bring the apple juice to the boil. Meanwhile, rinse the agar-agar under cold running water. Squeeze out excess liquid and shred into boiling apple juice. Simmer until agar-agar dissolves (4–5 minutes). Stir occasionally.

Pour agar-agar into tofu mixture and blend. Stir in vanilla. Set aside to harden. When the mixture has set, beat again. Use immediately, or beat again before using. Refrigerate until cake is baked.

Time: 20 minutes.

FRIDAY DINNER

TEMPURA (FRITTO MISTO)

4–8 large prawns
2 onions
several sprigs of parsley
½ red pepper
½ green pepper
4 fresh mushrooms
1 carrot

BATTER

1 cup wholewheat low gluten flour
1 cup ice water or 1 egg yolk beaten and enough cold water to measure 1 cup liquid*
vegetable oil for deep frying

DIPPING SAUCE (G)

1 cup kombu stock (see page 147)
3 tablespoons shoyu
1 tablespoon mirin

*Will vary according to type of flour used.

CONDIMENTS

¼ cup grated daikon (radish)
2 teaspoons peeled and grated ginger-root
½ lemon or lime, cut into 4 wedges (optional)

Shell and devein the prawns, leaving the tail intact. Lightly score the under-belly to prevent curling. Cut onions in half lengthwise, stick toothpick in to secure pieces and then slice crosswise. Quarter green and red peppers. Remove seeds. Wash mushrooms and discard stems. Cut in half. Dry well. Slice carrot into matchsticks.

Prepare batter by placing flour in bowl. (Reserve 1 tablespoon.) Make a well in the centre of the flour and pour in the water or the egg and cold water mixture. Stir lightly, incorporating about half of the flour, leaving batter lumpy. (See pages 144–145.)

Combine the ingredients for dipping sauce in saucepan and heat. Heat oil and test with batter. It should sink and then rise *immediately*. Hold each prawn by the tail and dust in flour. Then dip into batter before frying. Repeat with onions, peppers and mushrooms.

Toss the carrot strips into the batter and let some stick together. Fry the bundles lightly.

Lay a sheet of tempura paper on bamboo. Arrange the vegetables and prawns. Serve hot with warm dipping sauce and add condiments to the sauce just before serving. Serve with **Samurai Soup** (see page 49).

Serves: 4.
Time: 25 minutes.

SEA SALAD (G)

60 g (2 oz) dried wakame

4 tablespoons brown rice vinegar

3 tablespoons shoyu

1 tablespoon maltose (optional)

2 cups orange segments

Soak the wakame in water 5 minutes. Remove any tough stems, and pat dry. Chop coarsely.

Combine the vinegar, shoyu and maltose in a saucepan. Heat. Chill. Peel orange. Slice thinly, and toss with the chopped wakame. Pour over dressing and serve at room temperature.

Serves: 4.
Time: 15 minutes.

PEAR CUSTARD

4 firm pears

juice of 1 lemon

2 cups water

$\frac{1}{2}$ cup maple syrup

5 cm (2 in) piece orange or lemon rind

$\frac{1}{4}$ cup tahini

$\frac{1}{4}$ cup maple syrup

2 eggs

1 tablespoon wholewheat flour

pinch of sea salt

1 bar agar-agar

Peel, halve and core pears. Drop them into a bowl of water and add the juice of 1 lemon. Set aside. Preheat oven to 180°C.

Combine water, sweetener and rind in a saucepan and bring to the boil. Drain pears, and poach 10 minutes or until they are just tender. Be careful not to over-cook them. Let pears cool in cooking liquid. Then transfer with a slotted spoon to drain on towels. Reserve liquid.

Cream the next five ingredients together and ladle into an oiled 20 cm (8 inch) pie dish. Arrange the pear halves cut side down onto the custard and bake 30 minutes or until golden and set.

Meanwhile, blend the poaching liquid and transfer to a saucepan. Bring to the boil. Rinse agar-agar under cold running water and squeeze out liquid. Shred into cooking liquid and simmer until agar-agar is dissolved.

Remove custard from oven, and cool on a rack. When it is *almost* cool, ladle over agar-agar mixture. Sprinkle crushed almonds on top. Cool to set.

Serves: 4–6.
Time: 1 hour.

SATURDAY BREAKFAST

GRANOLA

8 cups rolled oats or barley

2 cups wheat germ

1 cup coconut

$\frac{1}{2}$ cup buckwheat

2 cups chopped almonds

1 cup sunflower seeds

2 teaspoons vanilla

$\frac{1}{2}$ cup oil

$\frac{1}{2}$ cup maple syrup

$\frac{1}{3}$ cup apple juice

1 cup chopped dates

Preheat oven to 150°C. Combine first 6 ingredients in bowl. Toss. Combine next 4 ingredients and beat well. Pour into first mixture and place on baking sheet. Bake in a low oven one hour or until crunchy and golden. Stir every 10 minutes. Add chopped dates. Cool and store in air-tight containers.

Serve with soy milk or nut milk (p. 150) sour dough rye bread (p. 133) and fruit jam (p. 128).

Makes: 15 cups.
Time: 1$\frac{1}{2}$ hours.

⚙️ **After breakfast thoughts:**

For dinner:

1¼ kg (2½ lb) chicken or several small quails

MARINADE (G)

1½ tablespoons mirin
1½ tablespoons shoyu
1 tablespoon miso
2 teaspoons roasted sesame oil
1 tablespoon grated ginger-root
1½ teaspoons pressed garlic
2 tablespoons minced spring onion

Remove backbone and skin from the bird. Cut into bite size pieces through the bones. In a separate bowl combine the remaining ingredients. Add the chopped chicken or quail and marinate at least 4 hours. May be left up to 48 hours refrigerated.

SATURDAY LUNCH

ONION AND CARROT TARTS

BASIC PASTRY

2 cups wholewheat flour
⅔ cup water
¼ cup oil
¼ teaspoon sea salt
4 tablespoons ground unhulled sesame seeds (optional)

VEGETABLE FILLING

3 cups chopped onion
2 cups grated carrots
1 tablespoon chopped ginger-root
1 teaspoon ground coriander
1 tablespoon miso
3 tablespoons tahini

Pastry

Sift flour into mixing bowl. Bring water to the boil. Rapidly stir in oil and whisk until creamy. Add the salt and seeds to the flour and *immediately* pour in oil mixture all at once and stir with a wooden spoon. Knead several minutes. Cover and chill 15 minutes. Preheat oven to 190°C. Roll out pastry into a circle, 5 cm (2 inch) larger than the size of the tart shells. Oil shells, and line with pastry. Let the pastry stand 2–3

minutes to settle naturally into the shells. Press pastry into forms. Bake unfilled 10–12 minutes. Meanwhile prepare vegetable filling.

Vegetable filling

Combine first four ingredients in a saucepan. Add water to almost cover, and bring to the boil. Add a pinch of sea salt, cover and simmer 15 minutes. Remove cover, and reduce liquid if any remains. Cream miso and tahini together into a paste. Stir into vegetables until well combined.

Fill tarts with carrot mixture. Roll out a strip of dough 6 mm (¼ inch) thick. Cut strips 6 mm (¼ inch) wide. Lattice the pastry strips on top of the filling. Brush with egg yolk mixed with 1 teaspoon water.

Bake in 180°C oven for 15 minutes or until lightly browned. Cool on rack.

Serves: 4–6.
Time: 1 hour.

BRAISED ENDIVE AND MUSHROOMS (G)

8 dried Chinese or Japanese mushrooms, soaked
1 endive, separated, washed, drained and dried
1½ tablespoons oil
1 teaspoon sea salt
4 tablespoons shoyu
mushroom soaking water
2 tablespoons barley malt, maltose or rice honey
1 teaspoon roasted sesame oil
½ cup soup stock or water mixed with 2 teaspoons kuzu or arrowroot flour

Bring water to the boil. Add mushrooms and soak until soft. Squeeze out liquid, discard stems and slice into thin strips.

Wash, drain and dry endive. Heat wok, add oil and break up endive just before sautéeing. Mix rapidly in wok, coating with oil. Sprinkle salt over greens and remove from wok.

Combine shoyu, soaking water and sweetener in the saucepan. Add mushrooms and bring to the boil. Lower heat and reduce liquid until there is no more remaining.

Combine greens and mushrooms in saucepan or skillet. Add roasted sesame oil, and dissolve kuzu with ½ cup stock or water. Stir into vegetables, and continue to cook, stirring constantly until mixture thickens and turns clear.

Serves: 4.
Time: 20 minutes.

⊙→ **After lunch thoughts:**

FILLING FOR DANISH PASTRIES (G)

FOR SUNDAY

1 cup date and currant purée
2 tablespoons orange rind
2 teaspoons ground coriander
1 teaspoon cinnamon
$\frac{1}{2}$ tablespoon miso or $\frac{1}{4}$ teaspoon sea salt
$\frac{1}{2}$ teaspoon rose-water or 2 teaspoons vanilla

To make fruit purée, combine 2 cups of dates and currants in equal proportions. Cover with water or apple juice and bring to the boil. Add the rind, coriander and cinnamon and simmer uncovered until there is no more liquid left. Add the rest of the ingredients. Set aside to cool. Save filling for baking Danish pastries on Sunday.

Time: 15 minutes.

SATURDAY DINNER

ANISE CHICKEN

MARINADE (G)

$1\frac{1}{4}$ kg ($2\frac{1}{2}$–3 lb) chicken or quail
$1\frac{1}{2}$ tablespoons mirin
$1\frac{1}{2}$ tablespoons shoyu
$\frac{3}{4}$ tablespoon miso
2 teaspoons roasted sesame oil
1 tablespoon grated ginger
$1\frac{1}{2}$ teaspoons pressed garlic
2 tablespoons minced spring onion

COATING (G)

1 teaspoon Japanese lemon pepper
$\frac{1}{2}$ teaspoon anise
$1\frac{1}{2}$–2 cups brown rice flour

GARNISH

2–3 tablespoons minced chives

If not prepared after breakfast:
Remove backbone and skin from the bird. Cut into bite size pieces through the bones. In a separate bowl combine the next seven ingredients. Add the chopped chicken or quail, marinating it in the mixture. Make

sure that all the pieces are coated with the marinade. Set aside at least one hour. Maybe left up to 48 hours refrigerated. The longer marinated, the better the flavour.

Lightly dry roast the pepper until just warm. Then the anise, then the brown rice flour until it lightly browns. Combine all three together. Remove the chicken from the marinade and roll in flour mixture, shaking off excess and pressing the flour in.

Arrange the pieces on a lightly oiled heatproof platter or spinach leaves. Place in steamer. Cover and bring to the boil. Lower heat and simmer one hour or until tender. Stick with fork or skewer and when meat flakes it is tender enough. Serve warm or cool.

If there is left-over flour, shape into small balls adding *hot* water to bind. Drop into boiling water and cook until they rise to the top. Simmer several minutes and serve as dumplings in soup. (Use boiling dumpling water as soup or seasoning.)

Serves: 4–6.
Time: $1\frac{1}{2}$ hours.

APPLE CAKE

1 tablespoon barley malt, rice syrup or maltose
1 tablespoon dry yeast
$\frac{1}{2}$ cup warm apple cider
$\frac{1}{4}$ cup wholemeal flour
2 teaspoons oil
1 cup sliced apples
2 teaspoons cinnamon
$\frac{1}{4}$ cup crushed almonds or walnuts
$\frac{1}{3}$ cup hulled millet
1 egg, room temperature
$\frac{1}{2}$ cup maple syrup
1 teaspoon cinnamon
1 teaspoon coriander
2 tablespoons orange rind
2 tablespoons orange juice
$\frac{1}{2}$ teaspoon sea salt
$\frac{1}{4}$ cup warm oil
1 cup sifted wholewheat flour or
$\frac{3}{4}$ cup wholewheat flour and $\frac{1}{4}$ cup arrowroot flour

Combine the first four ingredients, cover and set in a warm spot until mixture bubbles. Meanwhile cook the next four ingredients together until apples soften. Set aside to cool. Roast millet in 190°C oven until lightly browned. Beat the egg and sweetener together 5 minutes. Add the yeast mixture and beat 1–2 minutes longer.

Add the cinnamon, coriander, rind, juice, salt and beat thoroughly. Slowly drip in the oil while beating. Sift flour and *fold* into batter, along with roasted millet.

Oil 20 cm (8 inch) spring form cake tin. Place cooked apple mixture in the bottom of the tin. Spoon over cake batter. Cover and set aside to rise in a *very* warm spot. Bake 30–40 minutes. For a layer cake double the recipe and bake in two separate cake tins (no higher than 5 cm (2 inch). Prepare Tofu Whip Creme (see page 137), if not already done.

Serves: 6.
Time: 2 hours.

SWEET GLAZE (G)

2 cups apple juice

1 tablespoon maple syrup

1 cup grated apple

2 teaspoons cinnamon

1½ tablespoons kuzu

1 tablespoon ginger juice

roasted crushed nuts for topping

whole roasted blanched almonds

Combine the first four ingredients in a saucepan. Cook until apple is tender (2–3 minutes). Dissolve kuzu in cold juice, add ginger juice and stir into saucepan. Bring to the boil. Mixture should thicken and turn clear.
Time: 10 minutes.

Assembling the cake:
Cover with creme. Prepare glaze and spoon over cake when slightly cool. Sprinkle on crushed nuts, and decorate with blanched almonds.

LEEKS IN PIQUANT SAUCE (G)

6 leeks

1½ cups chicken stock, vegetable stock or mirin (see page 147)

SAUCE (G)

1 cup tofu sour creme (see page 54)

2 tablespoons grated horseradish or 1 tablespoon wasabi horseradish powder

2 tablespoons brown rice vinegar

1 tablespoon pressed garlic

1 teaspoon prepared mustard

sea salt to taste

Combine leeks and soup stock in a large pot. Bring to the boil, cover and simmer 10–15 minutes or until tender. Preheat oven to 190°C. Meanwhile prepare sour creme. Blend all the sauce ingredients. Remove leeks from pot, drain and place in an oiled baking dish. Cover leeks with sauce and bake 10 minutes. Reserve cooking liquid for soup or sauce.

Serves: 4–6.
Time: 30 minutes.

BEETROOT VINAIGRETTE (G)

1 beetroot per person

watercress for garnish or lettuce cups

VINAIGRETTE DRESSING (G)

1 large garlic clove

1 teaspoon sea salt

½ teaspoon Japanese lemon pepper

1 teaspoon prepared mustard

1 egg yolk (optional)

2 tablespoons olive oil

2 tablespoons apple cider vinegar (optional)

2 tablespoons maple syrup (optional)

1 teaspoon lemon juice

2 tablespoons oil

Cut off greens from beetroots leaving 2 cm (1 inch). Place in steamer and steam under pressure 30 minutes.

Alternatively Bake covered until tender or boil in salted water 1 hour. Drain and cool. Peel off skin and slice into quarters. Place on watercress or lettuce cups.

While beetroots are cooking prepare dressing. Cover cutting surface with a brown paper bag. Place garlic and salt on paper and mince together until they almost form a paste. (Brown paper absorbs some of the pungent oil softening the strong garlic flavour). Transfer the garlic to mixing bowl along with the salt. Add the next four ingredients and whisk. Slowly add vinegar and lemon juice. Continue to stir while you drip in the remaining 2 tablespoons of oil.

Serves: 4–6.

Time: 1 hour.

SUNDAY BRUNCH

SESAME-OAT WAFFLES

$4\frac{1}{2}$ cups apple juice
3 cups rolled oats
1 cup unhulled sesame seeds
$\frac{1}{2}$ cup wholewheat flour
2 tablespoons oil
1 teaspoon sea salt

APPLE SAUCE (G)
8 apples
2 cups water
1 teaspoon cinnamon
$\frac{1}{2}$ teaspoon sea salt
$\frac{1}{2}$ tablespoon grated ginger juice (optional)
1 cup sultanas

Combine all ingredients for waffles and mix or blend until smooth. Set aside. Heat waffle iron, and cook 8–10 minutes.

Serves: 6.
Time: 15 minutes.

Apple Sauce

While batter is resting, core and quarter apples. Place all ingredients into a pressure cooker and pressure 10 minutes. Blend half of the sauce and stir with remaining sauce. Use as a topping on waffles, toast, pancakes or as a dessert by itself.

Makes: 4 cups.
Time: 15 minutes.

After brunch thoughts:

LEMON MERINGUE PIE

CRUST (PRESSED PASTRY)
1 cup rolled oats
$\frac{1}{2}$ cup wholewheat pastry flour
$\frac{1}{4}$ teaspoon sea salt
$\frac{1}{2}$ cup roasted unhulled sesame seeds
$\frac{1}{4}$ cup oil
apple juice to bind crust

FILLING (G)
1 bar agar-agar
3 cups apple juice
pinch of sea salt
2 tablespoons maple syrup
5 tablespoons arrowroot flour or kuzu
3–4 tablespoons lemon juice
1 tablespoon lemon rind
1 teaspoon vanilla

MERINGUE (G)
2–3 tablespoons maple syrup
2 egg whites
pinch of sea salt
1 teaspoon vanilla

Crust

Preheat oven to 190°C. Oil 20 cm (8 inch) pie pan. Combine oats, flour, salt and seeds and blend. Rub in oil until it resembles *moist* breadcrumbs.

Moisten with juice until it binds together. Press into oiled pie pan.* Bake 15–20 minutes. Set aside on cake rack to cool.

*Before baking brush egg white over crust to seal.

Filling

Wash agar-agar under cold water. Squeeze out excess liquid and shred into $2\frac{1}{2}$ cups apple juice. Place in saucepan and cook on a medium heat until mixture boils, reduce heat and simmer until agar-agar dissolves.

Dilute arrowroot in $\frac{1}{2}$ cup reserved apple juice and sweetener. Stir arrowroot mixture into agar-agar, and bring to the boil. Remove from heat after boiling, stir in lemon juice, rind and vanilla, cool slightly.

Pour into shell and set.

Meringue

Cook sweetener in a saucepan with candy thermometer until it reaches a temperature of 120°C.

Beat egg whites and salt together. Slowly drip in sweetener as soon as it reaches 120°C and continue beating until stiff peaks form. Add vanilla and beat some more.

Spoon on top of dessert. Bake at 200°C for 5 minutes. Turn off oven, open door and leave inside at least 15 minutes longer, to cool.

Serves: 6–8.
Time: 1½ hours.

DANISH PASTRIES

DATE FILLING (G)

1 cup date and currant purée
2 tablespoons orange rind
½ tablespoon miso or ¼ teaspoon sea salt
½ teaspoon rose-water
egg yolk for glaze

ALMOND FILLING (G)

½ cup chopped roasted almonds
¼ cup tahini or almond butter
2 tablespoons date or apricot purée
½ teaspoon cinnamon
½ teaspoon orange or lemon rind

PASTRY

1 cup sifted wholewheat flour
pinch of sea salt
1 tablespoon ground cardomon
2 teaspoons coriander
1 tablespoon dry yeast
1 cup apple juice or cider
2 tablespoons warm oil
1 egg (room temperature)

Filling (If not already prepared on Saturday)
To make fruit purée combine 2 cups dates and currants in equal parts. Cover with water and bring to a boil. Simmer uncovered until there is no more liquid left. Combine with the rest of the ingredients. Set aside to cool.

Almond Filling
Combine all ingredients.

Pastry
Sift flour, salt and spices into a mixing bowl. Warm

the juice and combine with the yeast. Set aside covered and when the mixture bubbles beat in the oil and egg. Beat several minutes until frothy, combine with flour mixture and knead into a dough. Chill covered 10 minutes or you may leave it in the refrigerator until you want to use it.

Time: 2 hours.

Shaping Dough

Envelopes   Roll dough into rectangle. Cut pastry into small squares. Fill in centre of square, fold in the corners. Top with blanched almond.

Windmills   Roll dough into rectangle. Cut squares. Slash into each square to the centre without cutting through centre. Place a dab of filling in the centre, and fold in one corner to centre of each piece.

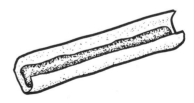

Birthday pretzel   Roll out double quantity of pastry 5–7 cm (2–3 inch) wide and very long. Spread the centre with filling. Turn the outer edge in but do not join them. Shape into pretzel.

After shaping, cover and let rise until almost doubled. Preheat oven to 200°C. Bake 15–20 minutes.

TEMPURA

The difference between 'tempura' and 'deep-frying' is that tempura uses a batter. Contrary to popular belief, the word 'tempura' is a corruption of the ancient Latin term *Quator Tempura*, meaning 'four times'. It was most likely brought to Japan by Portuguese sailors, who being good Catholics, did not eat meat on Ember days (which occurred four times each year).

About fat:
1 Butter has a low burning temperature which makes it unsuitable for deep frying.
2 The best oils to use for tempura are sesame, safflower and corn, as they have a high smoking point, and do not burn as easily as the others.
3 The smoking point of any oil will be lowered if water or food particles are allowed to enter and sit in the oil. *Keep oil clean!*

Tempura
1 Light batters or coatings protect fried foods by crisping the exterior while keeping the interior tender and moist. (Preserves vitamin C.)
2 Flour or meal can be applied to thin fish fillets, or tofu.
3 Heavier batters consisting of flour, beaten eggs, liquid, arrowroot or kuzu, ground nuts, seeds, grated cheese and spices are sometimes used.
4 Lighter batters consist of flour, sometimes eggs, and arrowroot or kuzu, combined with liquid such as water or beer. They have a sauce-like consistency and are usually reserved for deep-fried fish.

Oil preparation
1 Heat oil to temperature between 180°–190°C. Use a higher temperature for precooked foods, small fish and batter or crumb coated items that disintegrate if they do not crust immediately.
2 Test the temperature of the oil with a bread cube. The oil should bubble around at 190°C and will brown almost instantaneously at 200°C. Another way to test is by dropping some batter in the oil. If the batter does not rise immediately then the oil is not hot enough. If the batter does not drop down to the bottom of the pot, then the oil is too hot. If the oil is *smoking*, turn off heat, let oil cool down and *discard the oil*. It is not fit to use.

There are many ways to prepare a batter. Here are a few suggestions: (Use very finely milled flour only).

A–
$1\frac{1}{4}$–$1\frac{1}{2}$ cups wholewheat flour (low gluten)
$\frac{1}{2}$ teaspoon salt (optional)
1 cup cold water
1 egg

B–
$\frac{1}{2}$ cup wholewheat flour (low gluten)
$\frac{1}{4}$ cup brown rice flour
$\frac{1}{4}$ cup arrowroot flour
1–$1\frac{1}{2}$ cups cold water

C–
1–$1\frac{1}{2}$ cups cold water
$\frac{1}{2}$ cup wholewheat flour (low gluten)
$\frac{1}{4}$ cup maize (corn) flour
$\frac{1}{4}$ cup barley flour
1 tablespoon black sesame seeds

BEER BATTER
$\frac{1}{2}$ cup wholewheat flour (low gluten)
$\frac{1}{2}$ cup arrowroot
$\frac{1}{2}$ cup beer, room temperature
1 egg, separated
pinch of sea salt

A, B, and C
Mix dry ingredients together first. Then slowly add liquid folding with wire whisk, but not until smooth. Batter should be thick and lumpy enough to coat spoon but not cling to it. Refrigerate before using for a lighter, crisper texture.

Beer batter
Blend first three ingredients. Whisk egg white and salt until stiff. Fold into batter. Good batter for fish and chicken.

Making Tempura
1 When the oil is hot add batter coated foods one at a time and avoid over-crowding the fryer.
2 When the food stops bubbling intensely, it is ready to be removed.
3 When you take out a piece of tempura, make sure that you replace it with another piece *immediately*. Otherwise the temperature of the oil will rise and may cause the oil to burn.
4 As you approach the last piece of tempura, lower the temperature of the oil, so that when you remove all the food the oil has cooled slightly. Turn off the heat *before* removing all the tempura.
5 Drain food on draining rack attached to tempura pot or on old egg cartons or white paper towels. *Do not stack them on top of each other.* This will cause them to become soggy.

Cassoulet. See page 129

6 If cooking several batches, keep cooked food warm in 100°C oven with door ajar.

Storing oil

1 Allow oil to cool. Strain off into *glass* jar and refrigerate. Oil may be used several times. When it begins to get cloudy and slow, then it is time to change it.

Cleaning the oil

1 After using oil for fish, fry up a couple of slices of potato or ginger-root to clear the oil and change the smell. Discard potato or ginger, cool and re-use.

2 Sometimes particles appear that are difficult to strain off. Place several umeboshi plum pits in oil and deep-fry. Crumbs are attracted to the pits and cling to the surface. Discard the pits.

General hints

1 Sometimes when using oils for the first time they have a tendency to bubble when heated to high temperatures. This is caused by liquid in the oil left over from the pressing. Just heat oil to 180°C. Allow to bubble for several minutes, turn off heat and cool completely before using.

2 Cucumber, eggplant, zucchini and potato should be sprinkled with sea salt, set in a colander and allowed to drain for 15 minutes, rinsed and well-dried before using for tempura or deep-frying.

✄ FORGET ME KNOTS

1 To remove garlic sheath from cloves easily, place blade of knife over clove. Gently hit the blade with your hand and the sheath should separate from the clove. Peel.

2 In breadmaking, cake making and pastry, liquid content will vary according to the temperature of the room, the moisture in the flour and the air, and the general weather conditions of the day. Adjust accordingly.

3 Try to start the day with a warm drink which helps to start the digestive juices flowing. Activating the enzymes in the stomach, allows food to be digested more efficiently.

4 Kombu sea vegetable (kelp) not only makes a delicious soup stock, but the minerals also help soften dried beans or peas more quickly. Simply add a 15 cm (6 inch) piece of kombu to the cooking pot after boiling the beans without a lid for 30 minutes. Cover and simmer until tender. The minerals in the sea vegetable help to break the protein down in the beans. The cooked kombu will disintegrate into the beans or peas when cooked.

5 Always pick through dried beans and peas before washing for stones and twigs.

6 To freshen dry or slightly stale bread or rolls, place in brown paper bag, dampen outside with water and heat in 220°C oven 5–10 minutes or steamed covered without paper bag.

7 For baking bread, use lukewarm liquid with *fresh* yeast (26°–32°C) and warm liquid with *dry* yeast (40°–46°C).

8 Roll lemon on hard surface, and press down firmly to soften it for more juice.

9 To season beans: add a bay leaf and bouquet garni, an onion stuck with several cloves, ginger-root slices or garlic cloves to the cooking pot.

10 To aid in the digestion of beans, the use of spices, salt and pickles are recommended. Season beans with sea salt, miso or shoyu after the beans become tender.

11 Always cook in enamel, stoneware, cast iron, glass or ceramic utensils. *Never* in aluminium. Aluminium flakes off and enters your body with the food you eat. This aluminium can cause bloated intestines and general feelings of discomfort.

1   *Wholemeal biscuits from leftover pie dough.*
                                    See page 142
2   *Almond-mushroom pate.*   *See page 122*
3   *Nori roll.*   *See page 129*
4   *Vegetable tart with carrot topping.*   *See page 129*
5   *Vegetable tart with bughur topping.*   *See page 129*
6   *Vegetable tart with Tofu sour creme topping.*
                                    See page 129
7   *Vegetable tart with carrot topping.*   *See page 129*
8   *Fruit tart with dried fruit topping.* *See page 129*
9   *Vegetable piroshi and pastie.*   *See page 83*
10 *Vegetable piroshi and pastie.*   *See page 83*
11 *Vegetable piroshi and pastie.*   *See page 83*
12 *Mexican tomato sauce.*   *See page 97*
13 *Vegetable pie.*   *See page 139*
14 *Pita bread sandwich.*   *See page 78*
15 *Fruit and Nut bars shaped into cookies.*
                                    See page 107
16 *Mexican beans and salad in taco shell.*
                                    See page 96–97

──SOUPS──

Have you convinced yourself that you cannot cook a good pot of soup? Nonsense! If you can cut up vegetables, then you can cook a good, nutritious and hearty soup in a little more time than it takes to open up a can and heat it up. Many of us have forgotten that we do know how to cook, as a result of being surrounded by an overwhelming amount of instant, dehydrated and frozen foods.

Originally, soup was the dish that brought the family together. The sharing of the meal was centred around a large kettle of soup and in some cultures today, it is still the main part of the meal. It was and still can be a whole meal in itself. Just by combining grains, beans, vegetables and your favourite stock together, soup can become the main course. The complementary touch can be homebaked bread providing a warming meal on a cold winter evening or served chilled, a refreshing break for a lunch or as a light supper on a hot, balmy day.

Be brave and create your own soups and stews by combining leftovers with a strong stock, fresh vegetables and the finishing touches with a creative garnish.

VEGETABLE STOCK

500 g (1 lb) sliced onions

500 g (1 lb) chopped carrot

½ head chopped celery

small piece turnip or swede

bouquet garni

10–12 cups water

2 teaspoons salt

1 x 15 cm (6 inch) piece kombu sea vegetable (optional)

Place all ingredients in a large pot. (Include any leftover, uncooked vegetables.) Bring to the boil, half cover the pot and simmer at least 30 minutes to one hour or until stock has been reduced by one third. Strain off before using. Leftover vegetables can be puréed and mixed with miso and herbs for a spread or reheated and used as a sauce.

FISH STOCK

1½–4 kg (3–4 lbs) fish trimmings

10 cups water

vegetable parings (celery leaves, stalks, carrots, onions, parsley)

1 bay leaf

5 cm (2 inch) strip orange peel sliced into 6 mm (¼ inch) strips

1–2 teaspoons sea salt

Wash fish well and place in a large pot. Bring to the boil and skim off any residue that rises. Add rest of the ingredients, cover and bring to the boil. Simmer half covered at least 30 minutes or until reduced by one-third then strain.

DASHI SOUP STOCK

4 x 15 cm (6 inch) pieces of kombu sea vegetable

4 cups water

½ cup bonita fish flakes*

Soak kombu until soft. Score and combine with water in a saucepan. Bring to the boil and just before it boils, remove kombu. Add bonita, return to the heat, add ½ cup cold water and bring to the boil. Remove from heat, and allow flakes to settle to the bottom of the pan. Strain off and use. Kombu and flakes may be used again for stock. Kombu can then be used for sautéed vegetables with onions, carrots or pumpkin.

MIXED SOUP STOCK

This basic stock can be used for sauces, soups or broths. Combine raw or cooked fish, or the bones, heads and frames, chicken bones, carcasses, giblets or any leftovers and kombu. Mushrooms, vegetable peelings and sliced vegetables may be added in proportion of about two-thirds to the total quantity of animal parts. Use several slices of paper thin ginger root, sea salt and bouquet garni.

Combine all the above ingredients in a large pot, add sufficient water to cover and then slowly bring to the boil. Skim off residue on top, half cover and simmer several hours reducing to half the original volume. Strain and cool. Remove fat that has settled on the top of the stock.

IMPROMPTU CHICKEN STOCK

backs, bones, wings and trimmings of chicken

2 slices ginger

1 spring onion

4 cups water

1 teaspoon sea salt, to taste

Place the chicken parts, ginger and spring onion in a heavy saucepan. Add the cold water and bring to a brisk boil. Turn heat down and with a large spoon wrapped in cheesecloth skim off the residue.

When the liquid is clear, bring to the boil again, then simmer 1 hour. Allow the broth to cool. Line a strainer with several layers of cheesecloth and place over large pot or bowl. Pour in the broth and let it strain. Discard the bones. Cool and just before using skim off the fat that has accumulated on the top.

This stock keeps well for 5–7 days refrigerated in a *glass* container or bowl.

Alternative stock
Use 1 roasting chicken, 1½ kg and four slices ginger with 10 cups water. Follow recipe for Impromptu Chicken Stock.

Use 1 packet of 'instant dashi' stock (vegetarian or fish) to every four cups liquid. Contains no additives, preservatives or sugar.

* Bonita fish flakes, are made from the dried bonita which is related to the tuna. A strong flavoured fish, it can enhance any soup, vegetable dish or salad if lightly sprinkled on top.

SOUP GARNISHES

Garnishes will complement any soup or clear broth. Try any of the following:

- Freshly chopped herbs.
- Root vegetables cut into thin strips and parboiled to soften.
- Red, yellow or green capsicums roasted, peeled and seeded and then cut into thin strips.
- Fresh herbs such as parsley, fennel, dill and watercress.
- Raw eggs threaded in or grated after hard boiling.
- Leftover bread turned into croûtons.
- Pasta makes a most decorative garnish for clear soups.
- Dumplings made with flour, pumpkin or potatoes can add a hearty touch to any soup.
- Herbed crepes (see page 116) rolled and thinly sliced into narrow strips will make an attractive garnish to clear broths.
- Thinly sliced shallots or green beans will colour any clear or thick soup.
- Lemon or orange peel cut into thin slivers.
- Alfalfa, sunflower seed or buckwheat sprouts.

FORGET ME KNOTS

1 All stocks should be simmered and not allowed to boil rapidly. Hard boiling results in a thick and muddy-looking liquid, instead of a semi-clear stock.
2 Do not over-season stocks.
3 To keep any soup or stock from souring it should be boiled up once a day.
4 Soup with miso should *never* be boiled or simmered a long time. This will destroy valuable enzymes and B vitamins.
5 Firm vegetables such as carrots, onions, mushrooms, pumpkin, squash, turnips and swedes have a high starch content. These can make a good purée for a soup base.
6 Take yesterday's soup and purée it into today's.
7 A bouquet garni can delicately flavour most soups or stock. To prepare, combine several sprigs of parsley, 1 teaspoon dried thyme, celery and 1 bay-leaf. Tie together in double thickness cheese-cloth or muslin. Make several at once and store away until needed.
8 To cream a soup without adding countless calories use $\frac{1}{2}$–1 piece of tofu depending upon the amount of soup. Blend with $\frac{1}{2}$ cup of hot stock until smooth. Add this to the rest of the soup, season and bring to just *under* the boil. Thickness should be adjusted according to your preference.
9 Always put cut vegetables in separate bowls when preparing them for cooking.
10 Leafy vegetables should be immersed and washed quickly in a bowl of cold water to thoroughly remove all excess dirt and sandy particles.
11 Use leftover pies and pastries for soup. Just add water and bring to the boil. Cover and simmer 10 minutes then season to taste.
12 For a stronger tasting soup or stew, leave the cover slightly off the pot so that the soup reduces in volume and gets stronger in flavour.

BEVERAGES

When we share an evening with friends, they are usually surprised when I accept the odd glass of wine or beer. I don't think it's strange but I do find it difficult having to explain my so-called 'dualistic' behaviour. To me it's quite simple—drinking socially relaxes me and affords me the chance to share this feeling with my friends. So there is definitely truth in the old saying: 'A time and a place for everything'!

I do, however, discriminate in what I drink and I like to choose my beverages quite carefully. I am mostly attracted to imported beers because of their bitter taste, stronger beer flavour, and avoidance of added sugars. Sake, a natural rice wine, is another favourite but when a good quality white or red is offered I never refuse!

There is a top quality wine produced by the Botobolar Vineyard, located on the western slopes of the Great Dividing Range near Mudgee, NSW. This vineyard grows 23 hectares of grapes without using pesticides, combined with herbs, fruits and some vegetables. Moisture is conserved by a mulch of straw. The herbs sage, pennyroyal and hyssop are planted under the vines as beneficial companions. Much care and love is given to these vineyards, as evidenced by their fine wines.

I'm certainly not saying that you should immediately start to indulge in daily or even weekly drinking habits, but if the occasion calls for it, think about quality as well as quantity and you will enjoy it more without having to indulge in quite as much.

ALMOND MILK AND CASHEW MILK (G)

$\frac{1}{2}$ cup blanched almonds or $\frac{1}{2}$ cup cashews

2 tablespoons date purée (see page 140)

$1\frac{1}{2}$ cups hot apple juice or water

Blanch almonds, remove skin and place in blender with dates. Add $\frac{1}{2}$ cup boiling liquid, and blend slowly adding the remaining liquid as the mixture becomes creamy. Follow same method for cashews, but do not blanch. Just heat in oven for a few minutes.

SOY MILK (G)*

1 cup soy beans

2 quarts water

4 cups water

Soak beans at room temperature in 2 quarts of water until they are 3 times the original size (6–8 hours in warm weather or 10–12 hours in cold weather). Drain the beans, and combine them with $2–2\frac{2}{3}$ cups of water in blender and purée until smooth. Heat $\frac{1}{2}$ cup water in large pot and when water is very hot add puréed beans.

Cook on medium heat stirring constantly or beans will stick to the bottom of the pot. When foam suddenly rises to the top, turn off immediately and pour through muslin cloth, twist closed and press sack of beans against colander or strainer to drain milk.

When there is no more milk left to drain, pour it into cooking pot and bring to the boil stirring constantly to prevent sticking. Reduce heat and simmer 7–10 minutes. Serve hot or cold. If you are using organic soy beans, you may experience the milk being slightly bitter. Add 10 per cent tahini as well as other flavourings to remove the bitterness.

The part that is left-over is called okara and is very rich in nutrients. Try using it in breads, cakes, burgers, casseroles, soups, and pâtés.

Fresh soy milk is now available in many natural food stores.

INSTANT SOY MILK (G)

3 cups water

1 cup soy flour

$\frac{1}{4}$ teaspoon sea salt

3 tablespoons maple syrup

1–2 teaspoons vanilla

Beat water and soy flour together with beater. Place in saucepan and bring to the boil, stirring occasionally. Add salt, and simmer uncovered for 20 minutes.

Strain through cheesecloth to remove pulp. (This can be used in soups, or for making bread or patties.)

Cool. Whisk in sweetener and vanilla. Bring to a boil and cool.

Can be kept up to one week refrigerated.

INSTANT NUT MILK (G)

1 cup hot apple juice

2 tablespoons nut butter
(tahini, almond, cashew)

pinch of sea salt or shoyu

Blend ingredients together. Use in place of 'soy milk' if time is short.

OAT MILK

4–5 cups apple juice

$\frac{1}{2}$ cup rolled oats

pinch sea salt

Bring apple juice to a boil. Add oats, cover and simmer over low heat 20 minutes. Blend all together and use in place of milk for smoothies and shakes.

SUNFLOWER MILK (G)

$\frac{1}{2}$ cup sunflower seeds

$2\frac{1}{2}$ cups hot apple juice or water

2 tablespoons date purée (see page 140)

Heat sunflower seeds in oven for a few minutes. Blend. Add hot liquid slowly along with date purée until mixture becomes creamy.

SOY, NUT OR SUNFLOWER MILK DRINKS

CAROB SHAKE (G)

$\frac{1}{2}$ cup soy milk

2 tablespoons carob powder dissolved in 2 tablespoons hot apple juice

$\frac{1}{2}$ cup apple juice

2 tablespoons tahini

1 teaspoon shoyu

1 tablespoon vanilla

Prepare milk. Blend all ingredients until smooth.

COFFEE SHAKE

1 glass milk (see page 150)

2 tablespoons tahini

**2 teaspoons instant grain coffee dissolved in
2 teaspoons hot apple juice**

warm maple syrup to taste

1 tablespoon carob powder

pinch of sea salt

1 teaspoon vanilla

Prepare milk. Blend all ingredients until smooth.

DATE SHAKE (G)

1 cup soy milk (see page 150)

½ cup chopped cooked dates

2 tablespoons tahini

¼ tablespoon shoyu

1 teaspoon vanilla

1–2 teaspoons grated orange rind

Prepare milk. Blend all ingredients until smooth.

ORANGE SHAKE (G)

1 glass nut milk (see page 150)

juice of 1 orange

1 tablespoon tahini

1 egg yolk (optional)

**warm maple syrup or fresh fruit
to taste**

Prepare milk. Blend all ingredients until smooth.

APPLE BLOSSOM DRINK (G)

½ apple

juice of ½ orange

carrot juice

Juice apple and orange first. Pour them into a glass and fill with carrot juice.

SODA (G)

To make a soda combine any fruit juice or maple syrup (to taste) together with sparkling mineral water.

FRUIT COMBINATIONS FOR SHAKES

There are many possibilities that you can experiment with. The following are just a few examples.

- strawberry–apple
- carrot juice–apple
- sultana–date–apple
- melon
- peach–strawberry–apple
- plum–raisin–date
- lemon–date–apple

SUMMER COOLER (G)

2 cups fresh carrot juice

2 cups nut milk (see page 150)

½ teaspoon fresh lemon juice

APRICOT APPLE COOLER (G)

1 cup apricot nectar

1 cup apple juice

2 cups soy milk or nut milk (see page 150)

1 teaspoon orange juice

mint sprig for garnish

MELON COOLER (G)

3 cups peeled chopped melon

2 cups cashew milk (see page 150)

1 teaspoon barley malt

1–2 teaspoons lemon juice

ORANGE JUICE COOLER (G)

3½ cups soy milk (see page 150)

¾ cup orange juice, freshly squeezed

SUMMER DELIGHT COOLER (G)

2 cups peach, apricot or nectarine slices

2 cups almond milk (see page 150)

**3 teaspoons barley malt, rice syrup or
maltose**

peach, apricot or nectarine slice for garnish

Combine ingredients and blend. Pour into chilled glass and garnish with mint, fresh fruit or peel. All the drinks make 4 cups.

APPLE AND DATE SMOOTHIE (G)

1 cup soy milk (see page 150)

$\frac{1}{4}$ cup tahini or almond butter

$\frac{1}{2}$ teaspoon shoyu

2 grated apples

4 tablespoons warm maple syrup

$\frac{1}{2}$ cup cooked chopped dates

1 teaspoon vanilla

APPLE SMOOTHIE (G)

$\frac{1}{2}$ cup cashew milk (see page 150)

$\frac{1}{2}$ cup apple juice

$\frac{1}{2}$ cup grated apples

1 teaspoon cinnamon

pinch of sea salt

Prepare milk. Blend all ingredients together until smooth.

FRUIT SMOOTHIE (G)

1 cup sliced peaches or apricots

1 cup nut milk (see page 150)

$\frac{1}{2}$ cup orange juice

$\frac{1}{2}$ teaspoon cinnamon

Prepare milk. Blend all ingredients together until smooth.

PEACH SMOOTHIE (G)

1 cup cracked ice

1 cup unflavoured goat's milk yoghurt*

2 cups sliced peaches

1 teaspoon vanilla extract

$\frac{1}{4}$ cup sultanas, currants or carob powder

STRAWBERRY-BANANA SMOOTHIE (G)

1 cup cracked ice

1 cup unflavoured goat's milk yoghurt*

2 cups sliced strawberries

1 banana, peeled and sliced

$\frac{1}{4}$ cup sultanas or $\frac{1}{4}$ cup carob powder

Blend all ingredients until smooth.

* You may substitute nut milk or soy milk (see page 150) for any goat's milk recipe. Just reduce the ice by $\frac{1}{2}$ cup.

VANILLA SMOOTHIE (G)

$\frac{1}{2}$ cup almond milk (see page 150)

$\frac{1}{2}$ cup apple juice

2 tablespoons date purée (see page 140)

1 teaspoon cinnamon

1 teaspoon vanilla

pinch of sea salt

Prepare milk. Blend all ingredients together until smooth.

YOGHURT SMOOTHIE (G)

$1\frac{1}{2}$ cups milk, soy or nut (see page 150)

1 teaspoon carob powder

$\frac{1}{3}$ cup warm maple syrup

$\frac{1}{4}$ cup yoghurt

Prepare milk. Blend all ingredients together until smooth.

HOT TODDY

4 cups apple juice or cider

4 teaspoons maple syrup

1 tablespoon mirin

1 tablespoon lemon juice or to taste

cinnamon stick for stirring

Mix all ingredients together. Heat and serve with a cinnamon stick.

SPICED BREW (G)

1 cup tea

6 cloves

1 cinnamon stick

1 tablespoon lemon juice

1 cup apple cider

pinch of sea salt

8 cooked dates or prunes

1 cup water

1½ tablespoons maple syrup

Combine all ingredients together, cover pan and simmer 5 minutes. Remove cinnamon stick if desired before serving.

GINGER-APPLE BEVERAGE (G)

1 litre water

2 tablespoons kukicha tea

2 cups apple juice

1 teaspoon ginger juice

Boil water. Add kukicha tea, lower heat and simmer 5 minutes. Add apple juice and ginger juice.

MU/APPLE BEVERAGE (G)

1 litre water

1 teabag Mu tea

apple juice

Boil water and tea bag together. Simmer 10 minutes, or reduce to half volume for extra strength. Combine with equal parts juice and drink warm. Can be served plain or as a base for a punch. Just add apples, lemons and oranges. Cook with cinnamon stick for extra flavour.

CAROB SHAKE

1 tablespoon instant grain coffee

4 tablespoons carob powder

½ cup hot soy milk (see page 150)

2 cups hot apple juice

Blend all ingredients until smooth and frothy. Serve warm in cool weather.

APPLE-MINT TEA

½ cup chopped fresh mint

2 cups water

1½ litres apple juice or cider

¼ cup lemon or orange juice

¼ cup maple syrup

Place mint in an enamel or glass teapot only. Bring water to the boil. Remove from heat and wait until it stops boiing. Pour it over the mint and cover. Steep for 5 minutes. Strain and mix with the juices and sweetener. Serve hot or cool. Add grated ginger root juice in the winter time instead of orange or lemon.

SUMMER DELIGHT (G)

3 cups bancha, kukicha, hojicha or genmaicha tea

3 cups apple juice

juice of 1 lemon

Bring water to the boil. Add kukicha and simmer 5–10 minutes or alternatively boil water, take off the boil and pour water over bancha, hojicha tea or genmaicha (these last three get bitter if brewed). Cool. Mix the tea and apple juice together in a jar or pitcher. Cut the lemon in half, squeeze out the juice and add the rest of the lemon. Chill.

An alternative to caffeine

One of the world's most popular addictions, caffeine is found in chocolate, cocoa, coffee, tea and soft drinks. Aside from caffeine being responsible for over-stimulating your nervous system, it fosters the production of more adrenaline and speeds up your heart beat. The big attraction to caffeine is the ability to 'think more clearly' and 'that get up and go feeling' anytime of the day or night. But at what price? It is also responsible for sleeplessness, irritability, anxiety, irregular heartbeat and nervousness. Recently it has even been linked to birth defects.

It would be far better to switch over to herbal teas, Japanese or Chinese teas or grain coffees, usually made from ground roasted beans, grains and bitter vegetables such as chicory and dandelion. Grain coffees come in both instant and regular varieties for you to choose from.

SELECTED RECIPES FROM LEADING WHOLEFOOD AND MACROBIOTIC RESTAURANTS

These recipes are daily favourites at the 'Good Earth Restaurant', 34 Hindley Street, Adelaide, run by Diane and Peter.

PUMPKIN LEEK BAKE

BASE

$\frac{1}{4}$ cup long grain organic rice

$\frac{1}{2}$ cup buckwheat

1 small egg

shoyu to taste (approx. $1\frac{1}{2}$ tablespoons)

TOPPING

$1\frac{1}{2}$ kg pumpkin

1 bunch leeks

2 cups grated mature cheese

safflower oil for sautéeing

Base
Boil rice gently in $\frac{3}{4}$ cup water until dry and tender. Boil buckwheat in $\frac{3}{4}$ cup of water for 10 minutes or until glutinous.

Combine the rice, buckwheat, egg and shoyu well in a bowl. Spread the base in a medium baking dish to a depth of 1.2 cm ($\frac{1}{2}$ inch). Bake at 200°C for 20 minutes or until set.

Topping
Peel the pumpkin and dice into 2.5 cm (1 inch) cubes. Place in boiling water which has had shoyu added. Cook for 5 minutes or until pumpkin is half cooked. Drain very well. Peel the leeks. Chop diagonally into 1.2 cm ($\frac{1}{2}$ inch) strips. Wash very well. Sauté in oil until glassy but firm. Drain well. Combine pumpkin, leeks and one cupful of cheese. Place on the cooked base. Cover with the other cupful of cheese. (This amount could be reduced if desired.) Bake at 180°C for 30 minutes. Serve with natural yoghurt and/or extra shoyu.

Serves: 6.
Time: 1 hour and thirty minutes.

SPINACH ROLLS

FILLING

3 medium carrots

$\frac{3}{4}$ cup sesame seeds

$\frac{1}{2}$ cup bughur wheat

1 medium onion

3 cloves garlic

$1\frac{1}{2}$ sticks celery

75 g bean sprouts

oil for sautéeing

pepper and shoyu

LEAVES

18–24 medium-large spinach leaves.

SAUCE

$\frac{1}{2}$ cup tahini

$1\frac{1}{2}$ cups water

1 teaspoon maltose

juice of 1 medium lemon

Filling
Boil carrots until soft. Drain well then purée in kitchen whizz. Toast sesame seeds in medium oven until brown. Cover the bughur with water in a saucepan and boil hard until all moisture has been absorbed. Allow to drain well.

Sauté coarsely chopped onions and garlic. When translucent add finely chopped celery, bean sprouts and sauté for one minute. Combine with the carrot, sesame and burghur. Add pepper and shoyu to taste.

Leaves
Blanch each leaf for no more than one minute, until just tender. Remove and drain. Place about $1\frac{1}{2}$ tablespoons of mixture on each leaf (depending on size of leaf) in a sausage shape and roll as you would a parcel.

Cooking
Either steam spinach rolls for 10 minutes or bake in a moderate oven of 180°C for 20 minutes.

Note The baking dish must be covered and have 1.2 cm ($\frac{1}{2}$ inch) of water with shoyu added to the bottom.

Sauce
Combine tahini and water in a saucepan along with the maltose. Heat and stir until an even consistency. Cool. Add lemon juice and immediately beat until fluffy and 'set'. Do not reheat.

Serving
Give each person 3–4 rolls depending on size.

Place them on a small bed of rice.

Place about 2 teaspoons of sauce along each roll.

Do not reheat sauce, place it cold on the hot rolls.

Do not drown the rolls with sauce.

Serves: 6.
Time: 1 hour.

ENDIVE SALAD

2 endives

1 medium cucumber

2 sticks celery

6 radishes

DRESSING

1 teaspoon maltose

water, hot

3 teaspoons shoyu

1 teaspoon brown rice vinegar

Remove endive stalks. Chop coarsely and wash very well. Remove skin and seed of the cucumber and cut into strips 6 mm x 5 cm ($\frac{1}{4}$ inch x 2 inch). Chop celery diagonally into 6 mm ($\frac{1}{4}$ inch) pieces. Slice radishes finely. Combine all ingredients and toss as a salad.

Dissolve maltose in $\frac{1}{2}$ cup hot water. Add shoyu and vinegar and cool the dressing.

Serving
Pour over salad and refrigerate or let stand for 30 minutes to marinate before serving.

Serves: 6.
Time: 40 minutes.

The following recipes are some of the favourites at 'Billies Natural Food Restaurant', 38 St. Pauls Street, Randwick, NSW.

FAVOURITE PUMPKIN SOUP

1 butternut, seeded, skinned and chopped

1 cup chopped onion

8 cm (3 inch) piece of ginger, skinned and diced

1 teaspoon finely ground coriander

strip of wakame

1 teaspoon sea salt

$\frac{1}{2}$ squeezed orange/lemon

shoyu to taste

Sauté pumpkin, onion, and ginger for 4 minutes. Mix in coriander then add water or stock to cover. Add wakame and salt. Simmer for 35–40 minutes. Blend pumpkin, trying to keep the onion separate so as to provide an interesting texture. Check seasonings and add juice and shoyu. Simmer for 5 minutes.

Serves: 4–6.
Time: 1 hour.

SPINACH TOFU LASAGNE

1 cup onions, chopped

2 cloves garlic, minced

2 cups carrots

2 cups courgettes (zucchini)

$\frac{1}{2}$ kg mushrooms, sliced roughly

6 dried Japanese or Chinese mushrooms, soaked and sliced

pinch nutmeg

2 teaspoons basil

2 teaspoons oregano

1 teaspoon salt

1 kg red tomatoes, skinned and chopped

1 tin tomato paste (optional)

1 cup mirin, red wine or sherry

olive oil

one packet/12 pieces wholewheat lasagne

Sauté in a scant covering of olive oil the first six ingredients in the order they are given for 5 minutes. Add herbs, salt, tomatoes, wine and simmer 30–40 minutes.

Cook pasta in a large pot of salted, oiled (1 teaspoon oil) water for 10 minutes. Drain and rinse in cold water.

TOFU MIXTURE

1$\frac{1}{2}$ bunches spinach, cooked and chopped

1 teaspoon salt

2 x 200 g pieces of tofu

shoyu to taste

2 cups ground peanuts

1 cup breadcrumbs

Blend spinach, salt, tofu and shoyu to a cream. Combine peanuts and breadcrumbs.

To assemble
Sparingly coat the bottom of a 33 cm x 23 cm (13 inch x 9 inch) pan with the vegetable mix. Then add one-third of the tofu, followed by the pasta. Repeat tofu, vegetables and pasta twice more. Top with the nut crumb mix.

Cover and bake for 45–50 minutes at 160°C. Uncover for the final 15 minutes to brown. Let sit for 10 minutes to let the flavours and consistency 'marry and mature'.

Serves: 6.
Time: 1 hour 45 minutes.

WATERMELON SORBET

10 cups watermelon, cubed and depipped
3 cups orange juice
3 cups water
3 teaspoons sweetener (maltose, rice syrup or malt)
dash of vanilla
pinch of shredded coconut
pinch salt
2 bars of agar-agar, rinsed and squeezed

Combine all but the agar-agar and simmer till reduced by half. Put the shredded agar-agar in for the final 10 minutes.

Pour into individual dishes and serve as a jelly or add 1 tablespoon creamed tahini, pour into a large container and partially freeze. Before it totally freezes, blend into a smooth consistency and refreeze.

Garnish with a wedge of watermelon and a twist of orange.

Serves: 6.
Time: 45 minutes.

The Beggars Banquet was first opened by Pamela Murphy and Feiko Bouman in 1969 and was Australia's first restaurant to offer macrobiotic food.

Here is a meal which includes some of the favourite dishes from Sydney's 'Beggars Banquet' at 94 Evans Street, Balmain.

CREAM OF PARSNIP SOUP

1 tablespoon safflower oil
2 onions, chopped
4 cups chopped parsnip
6 cups kombu stock (see page 147)
½ cup rolled oats
1 bay leaf
sea salt
ground black pepper
2 tablespoons tahini
chives or onion greens to garnish

In a large heavy pan, warm the safflower oil and sauté gently chopped onion until translucent. Add chopped parsnip and continue to sauté for 5 minutes. Add the kombu stock, rolled oats and bay leaf, bring to the boil and then simmer for ¾ hour. Cover pan with lid while cooking. Stir soup from time to time to prevent mixture from sticking to the bottom.

When the soup is cooked, remove bay leaf and then it can be blended or pushed through a sieve. Return soup to pan, reheat. Season with sea salt and ground black pepper to taste and stir in tahini. Serve with sliced onion greens or chives sprinkled on top.

Serves: 6–8.
Time: 1 hour.

LOOBE-BE-SLIK

1 cup blackeyed beans
1 cup brown lentils
15 cm (6 inch) piece of kombu
1 bunch spinach (English or silverbeet)
1 large onion
2 cloves garlic
safflower oil
juice of 1 lemon
2 teaspoons dried mint
1 teaspoon sea salt

Soak the beans, lentils and 15 cm (6 inch) piece of kombu for 1 hour in 3 separate bowls. Drain the beans and lentils, discarding their soaking water. Finely slice the piece of kombu and return it to its bowl and retain its soaking water.

Wash the spinach and separate stalks and leaves. Cut both finely, but keep separated. Cut onion and garlic finely too. You will need a large heavy pan to cook this dish. Warm the pan and add enough safflower oil to thinly cover the bottom. Sauté the onion first until slightly brown. Then add spinach stalks and garlic and sauté a little longer until they begin to limp. Add the beans, mint, kombu and ½ teaspoon salt and enough water to just cover everything in the pot. (Use up the water from soaking kombu as part of this liquid.) Bring to the boil, cover and simmer briskly for 10 minutes. Add the lentils, remaining salt and once again just enough water to cover. Do not stir the beans and lentils during cooking. Simmer briskly with the lid slightly askew, so that the pot is not completely covered for a further 30 minutes. By now the beans and lentils should be soft and only a little liquid left. If too much liquid is remaining, remove lid and turn up heat until it is reduced. At the end of cooking, remove from heat, cover pan completely with lid and leave to stand for 10 minutes or so.

Cook spinach greens separately in a steamer. To serve, mix lemon juice to taste through the bean mixture and this will also mix together all the ingredients in the pot.

Do this mixing with a light hand and a pair of chopsticks so as not to mash the beans. Turnout onto a large serving platter, sprinkle the steamed greens on top and squeeze a little more lemon juice over everything.

Serves: 6–8
Time: 1 hour.

MUSHROOM FRITTERS

250 g fresh mushrooms

1 small onion

1 clove garlic

1½ tablespoons shoyu

1 egg (optional)

a little wholemeal flour

safflower oil

Finely dice the washed mushrooms, onion and garlic. In a bowl mix them all together with shoyu and leave to marinate for 1 hour or more. If possible, press the mixture by covering with a plate on which you then stand a heavy object, such as a jar of water, while the mushrooms are marinating.

Then remove the plate and break an egg or add ¼ cup water to the mushrooms and mix well with a fork. Mix in enough wholemeal flour to make a batter. Heat enough safflower oil in a frying pan to allow you to pan fry spoonfuls of the mixture. They need to be flipped over half way through cooking. You may need to cook the mixture in three batches. Allow the fritters to drain well on kitchen paper.

Makes: 12.
Serves: 3–4.

APRICOT AND PRUNE MOUSSE

1 cup sundried apricots

1 cup sundried prunes

4 cups water

1 orange

pinch sea salt

¾ cup cashew nuts

1 cup cooked oats

1 bar agar-agar

In a saucepan bring apricots, prunes and water to the boil, cover and simmer for 5 minutes. Leave covered overnight. In the morning the fruit will be soft and the stones easily removed. After doing this add the agar-agar, which should be squeezed briefly under running water and torn into pieces.

Bring this fruit mixture back to the boil and simmer gently till agar-agar has dissolved. Add juice of orange and pinch of salt. Place cashew nuts and cooked oats (porridge left over from breakfast) in blender and add enough of the hot fruit mixture to enable you to blend to a smooth cream.

Add the rest of the fruit mixture and blend again. You may need to blend the mixture in two batches, the first can be held in a large mixing bowl and then mix the second batch into it well. Pour mixture into cups or small moulds and leave to set. When cool refrigerate till needed. To serve, unmould and decorate, perhaps with slithers of almonds.

Serves: 6.
Time: 30 minutes.

APPLE HALWAH

2 tablespoons safflower oil

1 cup wholemeal flour or wholemeal semolina

2 apples (Jonathans if possible)

4 cups of water

½ teaspoon salt

¾ cup sultanas

1 or 2 teaspoons cinnamon

walnuts to garnish

In a heavy saucepan, warm the oil and in it roast the flour or semolina, stirring constantly until it has a nutty fragrance. Remove from heat and allow to cool. Cut the apples into small pieces, place in the pan with the roasted flour or semolina and add one cup of cold water. Mix until it is smooth and lumpless. Then add 3 cups boiling water and the salt. Bring to the boil stirring constantly, reduce heat to lowest possible, cover pan and cook for about 20 minutes, until apples are soft. You will need to give the mixture a good stir a couple of times during cooking. Add sultanas and cinnamon, remove from heat and allow to stand with lid on for 5 minutes. Stir well and pour into a large dish or individual moulds. Cool and refrigerate. Serve garnished with walnuts.

Serves: 6.
Time: 30 minutes.

These recipes are some of the favourite from Brisbane's 'Food from the Fields' at 76 Wickham Street, Fortitude Valley.

BAKED PUMPKIN GRATIN

1 kg (2 lb) raw cubed pumpkin, cut in 12 mm ($\frac{1}{2}$ inch) cubes

**mix in a large bowl with:
2 tablespoons finely chopped parsley**

1 teaspoon finely chopped and crushed garlic

1 teaspoon cinnamon

$\frac{1}{2}$ cup wholewheat flour

salt (optional)

Toss all ingredients well until coated lightly. Oil 4 small or 1 medium large ovenproof casserole(s) with olive oil or sesame oil. Place pumpkin mix in casserole and sprinkle lightly with a little more oil.

Bake at 160°C (325°F) for 2–2$\frac{1}{2}$ hours until a crust forms on top.

Serve hot with wholemeal toast.

Serves: 4.
Time: 2$\frac{1}{2}$ hours.

CHICK PEA/SOYA/OAT PATTIES

2 cups chick peas

1 cup soy beans

1$\frac{1}{2}$ cups water

$\frac{1}{2}$ cup brazil nuts

1 tablespoon oil

1 dessertspoon salt

1 medium size onion

3–4 cloves garlic

$\frac{1}{2}$–1 teaspoon sweet basil

1 cup rolled oats

SAUCE

2 onions, finely chopped

4–6 skinned tomatoes

1 dessertspoon fresh basil (chopped)

salt

Patties
Soak chick peas and soy beans in boiling water overnight. Place soaked peas and beans in blender and add the rest of the ingredients. Blend all till a fine

consistency. Mix in a bowl with 1 cup rolled oats. Leave standing 15–20 minutes. Drop by spoonful onto a lightly oiled frypan or onto oiled baking trays. Cook in frypan (medium heat) 10 minutes each side until browned, or in oven 190°C (375°F) turning once to brown both sides. (Unused mixture can be stored in an airtight container in refrigerator or freezer.)

Sauce
Lightly stir-fry onions, add chopped and skinned tomatoes, basil (or $\frac{1}{2}$ teaspoon dried) and a little salt. Simmer until tomatoes break up. (Alternately, purée all in blender and heat slowly. Simmer for 15–20 minutes).

Serve patties with lightly steamed vegetables or salad.
Serves: 4.
Time: 1 hour.

PEACH PARFAIT

6 large cling peaches or 8 smaller slipstone peaches

1 ripe banana

a little maple syrup (1 teaspoon)

1 dessertspoon lemon juice

Wash peach skins and steam for 45 minutes until very soft. Place in colander (without stones) and purée with banana, maple syrup and lemon juice.

Pour into champagne or parfait glasses and chill thoroughly. Sprinkle top with slivered almonds, chopped nuts or coconut.

Serves: 4.
Time: 1 hour.

POTATO AND FRESH HERB SOUP

4–6 chopped onions

4–6 crushed cloves garlic

1 bunch chopped shallots

some fresh chopped chives

some fresh chopped basil leaves

some fresh chopped fennel or dill

some fresh chopped sweet marjoram

some fresh chopped oregano

some fresh chopped comfrey leaves

1 teaspoon salt

1 bunch chopped parsley

finely chopped celery

6–10 potatoes

Add some water to just cover all herbs and simmer all while preparing potatoes. Scrub and/or peel 6–10 potatoes, dice into 12 mm ($\frac{1}{2}$ in) cubes. Place in large saucepan with herbs and add enough water to just cover. Bring to the boil and keep on rolling boil until potatoes are softened. Mash potatoes with a masher until soup is thickened. (Purée in blender if a more fine consistency is required.) Leave to simmer at least 45 minutes so that the herbs' flavour is sufficiently infused. Serve with rye bread and thin slices of avocado.

Serves: 4.
Time: 1 hour.

RATATOUILLE

4–6 brown onions

4–6 tomatoes

2 cloves garlic

$\frac{1}{2}$ teaspoon dried basil

4–6 zucchinis

2–3 eggplants

3–4 red capsicums

2 tablespoons olive oil

In large saucepan, blend onions, tomatoes, crushed garlic and $\frac{1}{2}$ teaspoon dried basil. Simmer for 10 minutes (add a little water to prevent sticking).

Add zucchinis, eggplants, capsicums and enough water or tomato juice to not quite cover vegetables. Bring to the boil and then cover and simmer for 30 minutes, stirring occasionally. Add salt to taste. Serve with cooked brown rice. (See page 52.)

Serves: 4.
Time: 1 hour.

GARBANZO/OAT WAFFLES

$2\frac{1}{4}$ cups water

$1\frac{1}{2}$ cups rolled oats

1 cup soaked garbanzos (chick peas) ($\frac{1}{2}$ cup dry)

1 tablespoon oil

1 tablespoon maple syrup

$\frac{1}{2}$ teaspoon salt

SOY/OAT WAFFLES

$2\frac{1}{4}$ cups water

$1\frac{1}{2}$ cups rolled oats

1 tablespoon oil

1 cup soaked soy beans ($\frac{1}{2}$ cup dry)

$\frac{1}{2}$ teaspoon salt

SOY/MILLET WAFFLES

$2\frac{1}{4}$ cups water

$1\frac{1}{4}$ cups millet flour

1 cup soaked soy beans

1 tablespoon oil

$\frac{1}{2}$ teaspoon salt

Blend all ingredients in blender until light and foamy (1 minute) and let stand while waffle iron is heating to thicken. Blend briefly then pour into a jug. Oil waffle iron and keep on medium heat. Cook each waffle for about 8 minutes. Do not open iron while cooking. Serve hot with following fruit toppings.

Date and Coconut Spread
Cook some dates in enough water to three-quarter cover them, until very soft. Mash with a fork and mix in enough dessicated coconut to make a moist spreadable consistency; also add 1 dessertspoon lemon juice.

Apple Spread
Wash, peel and core apples. Cook until soft on their own or with any other fruit (peaches, pears, sultanas) and purée in blender.

Serves: 4.
Time: 15 minutes.

Tempura.   See page 137

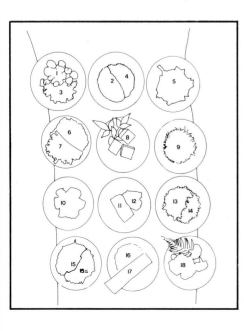

1 dried chestnuts
2 unhulled sesame seeds
3 kombu sea vegetable strips
4 natural black sesame seeds
5 soaked wakame sea vegetable
6 shaved bonita fish flakes
7 non sea vegetable strips
8 tofu (soy bean curd)
9 kukicha twig tea
10 umeboshi salted pickled plums
11 tempeli (fermented soy bean food)
12 mugi (barley) miso (soy bean paste)
13 kuzu (starch)
14 azuki beans
15 genmai-cha tea (roasted rice and green tea)
15a genmai-cha tea (roasted rice and kukicha tea)
16 agar-agar flakes
17 agar-agar bar
18 Japanese dried Shitake mushrooms

GLOSSARY

Agar-agar
A processed sea vegetable gelatin blended from eight different seaweeds. High in minerals, it can be used to replace gelatin for making jellied desserts or savory dishes. Refreshing on a hot summer day.

Arrowroot-flour
A flour containing a high percentage of starch processed from the root of a native American plant. Used as a thickening agent and similar to kuzu or cornstarch when cooked, it can be substituted for either one when making sauces, gravies, desserts or stews.

Bancha tea
This delightful beverage is made from three-year-old leaves and twigs of a Japanese tea bush. Said to be high in minerals, especially calcium, it has been roasted to eliminate tannic acid which is believed to be harmful to the system.

Barley
One of the seven grains that is high in natural sugars, easy to digest and used medicinally for many centuries in the form of barley water for digestive problems. Used in making Mugi Miso, it can be used in soups, stews, desserts or as a breakfast cereal.

Barley malt extract
Sweetener made from sprouting barley, which is cooked into a sweet syrup to which nothing is added.

Bean curd see **Tofu**.

Bifun
Thread-like noodles made entirely from rice. It cooks quickly and easily in boiling water and has a variety of uses in vegetable dishes, soups and salads. Low in calories, it is ideal for weight watchers as well as health conscious people.

Black beans (salted)
These beans have been fermented, salted and dried. Mainly used as a seasoning agent with fish or seafood, they should be rinsed before using.

Bonita fish flakes
Shaved (Katsuobushi) from fermented Bonita, are dried, and mainly used best in soup stocks, garnish for salad, bean curd dishes and noodles. It is said to be able to sustain one for forty days without other foods.

Buckwheat
A small triangular-shaped grass, it is high in protein and can be used to keep warm in cold weather. It is the staple grain of the Russian people, and is the principle food of the Russian army.

Carob powder
Used in place of chocolate and cocoa (3 tablespoons carob equals one square of chocolate). It is ground from the pods of the carob tree and is rich in minerals and natural sugars and low in fat.

Chilli pepper, assorted
Made from a combination of chilli, sea vegetables, berries and orange peel, it is much milder in effect and therefore more suitable for cooking. Use it in place of regular chilli powder. Found in oriental groceries.

Chinese mushrooms, see **Shitake**.

Cooking wine
Cooking wine refers to Mirin, which is rice wine or dry sherry, made from grapes. Either one will be suitable for the recipes which call for 'cooking wine'.

Coriander
Also known as Chinese Parsley, fresh coriander is much stronger and more distinctive in flavour than the ordinary varieties of parsley.

Daikon
This oriental white radish aids in the digestion of fatty foods and also helps eliminate excess fluid from the system. It is high in Vitamin C and can also be found in the form of dried pickles.

Deep fry
Cooking foods in heated oil of temperatures around 180°–190°C without a batter.

Dried mushrooms (shitake)
These very special mushrooms can not be substituted because of their unique flavour and special characteristics. They range in colour from black to mottled brown and in size from 2–5 cm. Sold packaged in oriental groceries or some natural food stores, they keep almost indefinitely in a covered container at room temperature. Before using, soak in hot water at least 15 minutes and trim off woody stems.

Ginger root
This common root is used mostly in Asian countries in the form of spices for various dishes. The younger plant has almost no visible skin and is best used for grating whereas the more popular, older variety is more stringy and coarse and more suitable for slicing, chopping or mincing. It is used as a seasoning agent as well as a subduer of undesirable tastes, such as fishiness and the raw taste of some vegetables. It is useful when serving tempura for digestion of oily foods. Two parts powdered ginger may be substituted for one part freshly grated. (Young ginger is available in the autumn.)

Japanese mushrooms, see **Shitake**.

Japanese pepper (Sansho)

Known as a lemon pepper, it is much milder than ordinary pepper and much more soothing to the system. Use it in place of pepper. (The lemon pepper available in regular groceries and supermarkets is not the same.) This is available in Japanese and oriental groceries, and does not contain any additives.

Kelp powder

Usually a naturally sun-dried form of kelp, it can be used in place of sea salt to flavour soups, salads, casserole dishes and grains. High in iodine, it is usually found in a powdered form.

Kombu

Sea vegetable that is used mainly in soup stocks to enhance flavour. It contains glutamic acid which is directly involved in mental activities carried on in the brain.

Kuzu

A high quality starch which grows in the mountains of Asia and throughout the US, it is somewhat like arrowroot or gelatin. Kuzu is a very nutritious food and serves a medicinal purpose especially for stomach or intestinal complaints.

Malt

A grain honey made from sprouted barley, or rice. Use two times the amount called for if substituting for maple syrup or honey.

Maltose

Somewhat similar to Barley Malt Extract, it is made by germinating wheat, then mixing it with cooked sweet rice, and allowing it to *ferment* at a warm temperature until the starch has been converted to sugar. At this point, the fermentation is stopped by cooking. It is very similar to the Japanese Rice Syrup, and can be found in Asian food shops.

Millet

Small yellow grain, sometimes referred to as 'poor man's rice', it is widely used in China, Africa and Japan. It contains no gluten, high protein, calcium and lecithin. It can be used in soups, stews, or as a separate grain and in cakes to lighten and give a nicer flavour.

Mirin (wine used in cooking)

This unique seasoning is made from rice, rice koji, and salt through a process of *natural* fermentation. It is a cooking wine and may be used in place of sherry.

Miso

A soy bean purée made from Soy beans, grain, sea salt, water and koji (enzyme), it is prized for its ability to aid in the digestion and assimilation of other foods. It consists of natural digestive enzymes, lactic acid bacteria (lactobacillus), salt resistant yeasts, and mould and other micro-organisms present in koji. Lactic acid bacteria are one of the basic factors which make miso and yogurt excellent aids to digestion. It contains B12, all essential amino-acids, 5 per cent natural oils, can prevent radiation sickness, and neutralises the effects of air pollution and smoking.

Mushrooms, see Shitake.

Mu tea

A blend of nine or 16 herbs, it can be used medicinally for weak persons or for women who suffer from menstral problems. Also a delicious tea.

Noodles

The best noodles to use today are made from wholewheat or a combination of wheat and buckwheat flour. Some oriental shops also carry bean threads, or vermicelli which are processed from the starch of mung or green bean, and sometimes sweet potato as well. The wholewheat and buckwheat varieties can be found in most natural foods shops which import several varieties from Japan and Italy.

Nori

A sea vegetable that comes in sheets usually darkish in colour, it is frequently used as a wrapper for rice in Japanese restaurants. It can also be used as a vegetable, or as a garnish sprinkled or cut into thin strips over grains, beans or noodles.

Oriental sesame oil

This dark brown oil, with its strong and nutty flavour, is available in Oriental groceries and in some natural food stores as well as speciality delicatessens. It is made from toasted sesame seeds.

Rice syrup

Made from barley malt and rice.

Rosewater

This flavouring liquid is similar to vanilla in that it greatly enhances any sweet recipe with a unique and vital flavour. If using in place of vanilla, use half the amount.

Saifun

Translucent noodles which are made from green bean or mung bean starch. They can be used in much the same way as Bifun.

Sake

Rice wine containing 15 per cent alcohol and widely used in cooking in place of Mirin.

Salt plums, see Umeboshi.

Sea salt

Sea salt which has not been stripped of essential minerals, bleached or refined in any way. It is more desirable than the processed refined table salt which is depleted of minerals and is loaded with additives.

Sea vegetables
Various endless varieties. Those used in this book can be found growing all around the coastal waters, near the rocks and can be easily picked not far from shore.

Sesame oil, roasted
Light brown in colour and highly aromatic, it is made from roasted sesame seeds. The thicker it is the better the flavour. Roasted sesame oil is best used as a seasoning, before or after cooking because it has a tendency to burn too quickly when heated. It imparts a delicious flavour to most dishes.

Sesame paste (butter)
An extremely rich and tasty food, it can be used primarily as a salad dressing, a spread for bread and as a base for smoothies and shakes. Stir well before using as the 'paste' settles to the bottom and the 'oil' rises to the top. If you don't have sesame paste, substitute any other nut butter.

Sherry, dry
Cooking wine made from grapes. Can be used in place of Mirin.

Shitake mushrooms
These wonderfully flavoured dried mushrooms, are imported from China and Japan, ranging in size, shape and colour. They can enhance any meal and should be soaked in warm water until tender. Use the soaking water for soups or sauces. They keep indefinitely at room temperatures and aid in the elimination of excessive animal fats from the system.

Shoyu
This is a natural soy sauce made from fermented soy beans, sea salt, wheat and a special bacteria (koji). It is one of the staple foods in Asian cooking. Sometimes confused with 'tamari', (which is a thicker form of Shoyu made without wheat; and good for gluten-free diets). It is also completely free of chemicals.

Sourdough
A mixture of fermented grain, flour and water used as a natural yeast for leavening.

Tahini
Paste made from sesame seeds, it is high in calcium, and protein and is extremely rich, tasty and aromatic. It can be used for spreads, salad dressings, sauces or soups. If not available use almond or peanut butter as a substitute.

Tempeh
A third world soy bean product, it is slowly making itself known in Western countries, especially America and Australia. It can be used in soups, salads, vegetable dishes as well as a filling in sandwiches. It s versatility is unlimited.

Tofu
Made from soy beans, water and a natural coagulating agent derived from sea salt called 'nigari', it can be boiled, marinated, steamed, simmered, stir-fried, shallow or deep fried with tasty results. High in protein, low in fats it is the ideal diet food.

Umeboshi plums
Pickled salted plums, they have the ability to relieve stomach upsets, digestive disturbances and can act as a seasoning agent as well. Sour and salty in taste and flavour, they will add zest to any salad dressing, soup or vegetable dish.

Wholefoods
These are foods that have not been processed or refined in any way as to remove part of the nutritious quality that usually aids in digestion, by supplying essential minerals, cellulose and fibre for better absorption and assimilation. The difference between sugar, white flour, wholegrains and wholewheat flour cannot be debated.

Vinegar, brown rice
This vinegar is made by a special process in Japan. It is organic, completely natural in ingredients and production an excellent pickling agent, and its preserving ability will add days to the life of cooked grains and vegetables. Through its large content of amino-acids, which work successfully at dissolving excess lactic acid, it can help to alleviate such conditions as arteriosclerosis and high blood pressure, and minor complaints like nervousness irritation, stiff muscles and fatigue.

BIBLIOGRAPHY

ABEHSERA, Michel, *Cooking With Care and Purpose*, Swan House Publishing Co. Brooklyn, New York, 1978.

AIHARA, C., *The Calendar Cookbook*, George Ohsawa Macrobiotic Foundation, Oroville, California, 1979.

ALLEN, J. and McKENZIE, V., *A Taste Of The Past*, A. H. & A. W. Reed Pty Ltd, 1977.

BENDER, A. E., The Fate of Vitamins In Food Processing Operations, in University of Nottingham, *Proceedings On Vitamins* pp. 71–72.

BUMGARNER, M. A., *The Book of Whole Grains*, Grass Roots Books, 1977.

COBLIN, A., *The Book of Wholemeals*, Autumn Press, Brookline, Massachusetts, 1979.

DOWNES, J., *Natural Tucker*, Hyland House Publishing Pty Ltd, Melbourne, 1978.

DUQUETTE, S., *Sunburst Farm Family Cookbook*, Woodbridge Press Publishing Co., 1976.

ESKO, W. & E., *Macrobiotic Cooking For Everyone*, Japan Publications, Japan, 1980.

FAO/WHO, *Ascorbic Acid, Vitamin B-12, Folate and Iron*, p. 41.

FORD, HILLYARD, and KOOCK, *The Deaf Smith County Cookbook*, Collier MacMillan, New York, 1973.

HARRIS, R. S. and VON LOESECKE, Harry, eds., *Nutritional Evaluation of Food Processing*, Wiley, New York, 1960 pp. 1–4.

HAYDOCK, Y. & B., *Japanese Garnishes—The Ancient Art of Mukimono*, Holt, Rinehart, and Winston, New York, 1980.

JONES, Anita W., *Door to Chinese Festivals, Feasts and Fortunes*, Mei Ya Publications, 1971.

KUSHI, A. T., *How To Cook With Miso*, Japan Publications, Japan, 1978.

KUSHI, M., *The Book of Macrobiotics*, Japan Publications, Japan, 1977.

LINDSAY, H., *The Gravy Train*, Ansay Pty Ltd, 1981.

NATIONAL RESEARCH COUNCIL, *Recommended Dietary Allowances*, 1974, p. 44.

NELSON, KANE and BRINSMEAD, *Nature's Way*, Australasian Conference Association Ltd, Victoria, Australia, 1978.

OHSAWA, L., *The Art Of Just Cooking*, Autumn Press, Japan, 1974.

RITCHIE, Carson I. A., *Food In Civilisation*, Methuen, Australia, 1981.

ROBERTSON, FLINDERS and GODFREY, *Laurel's Kitchen*, Nilgiru Press, Petaluma, California, 1976.

SHURTLEFF, W. and AOYAGI, A., *The Book Of Tofu*, Autumn Press, Japan, 1975.

SHURTLEFF, W. and AOYAGI, A., *The Book Of Miso*, Autumn Press, Japan, 1976.

SHURTLEFF, W. and AOYAGI, A., *The Book Of Tempeh*, Harper & Row, New York, 1979.

TALKING FOOD COMPANY, *Salt Walking The Briny Line*, Box 81, Charlestown, Massachusetts, 1976.

TUDGE, C., *Future Food*, Harmony Books, New York, 1980.

VEGETARIAN TIMES, *Radiation—What You Can Do*, Issue Number 52, December 1981, New York.

WHOLE FOODS MAGAZINE, *Whole Foods Natural Foods Guide*, And/Or Press, Berkeley, California, 1979.

NUTRITIONAL COMPOSITION OF FOODS

The following food composition tables, were designed to help you get the maximum value out of each and every meal. If you add up the values given for all the foods in one meal you will see that it is definitely possible to obtain all the nutrients necessary to keep you healthy and full of vigor.

All the figures are based on uncooked foods, so some nutritional loss must be accounted for. The figures are also designed for the total amount of food prepared so they must be divided by the number of meals that each recipe will serve.

SPRING	Kilojoules	Protein (g)	Fat (g)	Carbohydrate (g)	Calcium (mg)	Vitamin A (IU)	Vitamin B (mg)	Vitamin B₁₂ (mg)	Vitamin C (mg)
MONDAY									
Pickled chinese cabbage	567.0	7.7	9.2	25.96	191.66	9888.4	.34	0	138.0
Creme of watercress soup	1967.0	7.09	42.632	45.5	1458.2	560.01	3.5905	2.3	27.13
Stir-fried green beans	2554.0	18.15	76.2	40.5	927.0	3380.0	6.17	0	122.0
Gefilte fish	3787	119.8	12.3	86	399	3360	1.42	1.2	88
TUESDAY									
Muesli	16008.0	190.8	282.0	717.0	2411.5	14120.0	2.53	0	17.0
Samurai soup	1229.2	8.02	16.22	41.9	149.9	6160.0	.44	0	55.4
Rosemary wholewheat bread	2620.0	74.6	8.2	437.5	331.0	0	63.38	0	0
California salad	540.0	13.5	1	25.0	125	300	.5	0	390
Poppyseed dressing	2659.6	5.7	55.9	236.2	103.9	0	.03	0	28
Fresh pea potage	595.0	6.68	.3	32.0	91.0	7490.0	.15	0	39
Almond biscuits	3844.5	52.62	126.4	180.2	378.0	1360	28.885	2.4	.25
Zucchini soup	1418.0	28.7	29.25	15.12	121.0	3620.0	2.6	.03	82.5
Boston baked beans	7985.0	63.2	131.1	296.06	441.2	3168.4	27.78	0	234.0
Parsley rice	2510.0	42.1	27.3	425.0	196.0	1500	.43	0	100.0
Pumpkin pancakes	5424.0	28.1	163.8	34.4	38148.5	5334	6.32	2.4	35
Sesame salt condiment	3304	27	71	31	1756	40	.35	0	0
WEDNESDAY									
Granola parfait	2100	32.3	28.4	40.6	950	3680	.62	.4	15
Walnut balls in creme sauce	1906.0	45.52	42.4	16.9	651.0	1150.0	.75	1.2	25
Stuffed mushrooms	4398.0	27.05	77.4	356.96	427.1	21.405	1.1	0	10
Garden vegetable soup	757.0	13.5	1.5	58.80	1412.0	1610.03	.85	6.4	39.3
Vegetable saute with millet	12210.6	170.04	191.82	343.76	1954.6	39561	16.8018	0	1122.5
Pumpkin salad	2890.0	16.15	103.4	22.2	38298.0	1494.0	3.26	0	88
THURSDAY									
Buckwheat pancakes with apple sauce	4262.0	65.0	28.5	278.9	280.4	2800	1.33	3.6	34
Minstrone soup	7213	45.25	60.9	217.9	5259	11990	2.604	192	244.4
Parsley sauce	423	6.75	7.4	5.2	123	5100	.16	0	103
Rolled sandwich	3668	5.7	66	47.8	251.2	13168	27.6	0	122
Broccoli and onion tarts	6742	81.3	165.4	265.8	1244	25650	31.66	1.2	957
Onion and celery sauce	7045	42.9	146.5	137	1544.5	8650.5	7.43	16	26.5
Creme of rice soup	1834	1.39	12.8	70	99	80	.67	0	45
Sprout salad	920	29	3	0	160	0	1.2	0	90
Mayonnaise	12660.3	7.22	180.41	1.7	80.3	1471.04	1.4304	2	94.2
FRIDAY									
Crepe suzettes	3004	41.1	20.6	260	133	400	28.07	0	0
Apple orange filling	3886	14.2	69	92	225	530	.76	0	36
Millet and vegetable loaf	11756	90.7	171.27	311.98	4115.3	8476	3.45	4.6	92
Carrot and raison salad	1341	13.79	20.7	52.9	299.2	36455	1.49	0	72.75
Lemon-olive dressing	6200.6	2.7	84.3	22.6	51	0	.003	0	22
Split pea pasta	2737	7.91	57.65	38	90	143	184	0	37.06
Turnip pickles	1243	5.7	.1	53.8	234	7900	.72	0	194
Apricot bars	8036	43.65	103.3	467	425.4	28725	18.55	1.2	87.5
Pam's porridge	1591	33	17.7	165	126	0	.48	0	0
SATURDAY									
Alfalfa sprout fritters	4563	39.2	80.45	106.2	123.25	450	5.47	0	21.5
Cucumber topping	232	3.2	.5	12.5	135	1500	.92	0	83
Sweet water pickles	117.3	.03	0	13.6	8.3	0	.003	0	0
Oatmeal bread	4229	77.2	55.53	392.8	331.15	0	49.353	.03	2
Spinach pie	6158.6	78.9	67.3	237.3	970.5	47860	36.27	2.4	250
Steamed tofu a la vegetables	6470	79.46	98.5	106.1	3956	6210	1.07	4.6	86.51
Stuffed onions	4108	45.1	48.6	263.3	630	1087.5	32.693	.8	118.35
Creme of cauliflower and pea soup	2820	41.7	15.68	146.3	1496	8980	3.65	6.4	298.3
Prawn, sweet potato and squash cakes garlic sauce	3700	57.06	74.296	256.68	38363	3519	2.78	0	72.9
Strawberry parfait	2634	3.8	5.2	158	172	120	.24	0	102
SUNDAY									
Broccoli salad/vinegar dressing	17414	37.5	232	71.7	1004	22745	2.03	0	1087
Asparagus crepes	3819	54.6	59.7	85.5	929	6940	1.59	8	160
Tarragon sauce	2518.8	12.7	56.87	23.6	154.2	0	3.556	0	34.25

SUMMER	Kilojoules	Protein (g)	Fat (g)	Carbohydrate (g)	Calcium (mg)	Vitamin (IU)	Vitamin B (mg)	Vitamin B₁₂ (mg)	Vitamin C (mg)
MONDAY									
Gramma pumpkin potage	1479	26.3	20.6	185.6	501.7	10687	.87	0	251.3
Brownies	11352	51.7	133	498	826	60	1.31	.3	4
Strawberry topping	3760	1.06	.75	233.7	352.15	90.5	.05	0	88.01
Steamed fillet of sole	365	102.2	50.48	2222	86.35	30.5	.01	0	8
Olive and orange salad	1824	9.2	10.3	67.5	314	1111	.51	0	263.5
Noodles in sesame hot sauce	1500	10.76	6.95	71.2	148.65	33	1.01	0	.01
Pickled mushrooms	36	6.75	1.3	24.74	66.8	670	.6	0	46
TUESDAY									
Gingered mangoes	880	4.7	2.2	104.4	145	22220	.3	0	180
Egg and tomato	10988	27.6	25.2	65.8	233	6920	.54	3.52	238
Vegetable studel	18317	73.3	145	276.8	1653	20045	3.473	0	142.75
Green bean salad/lemon garlic dressing	1120	33.5	41.55	51.19	8559	2141.36	1.43	248	50.5
Strawberry kiwi cheesecake	11166	121	182	426	1573	2205	641	2.64	140
Summer sardines	12556	217.2	241	8.4	3942	1980	.27	1.8	0
Vegetable curry pie	14448	52.26	192.5	264	458.7	33984	1.43	0	87.1
Watercress and bean salad	1544	27.8	19	93.4	56.4	740	.76	0	88
Tofu stroganoff	1728	155	14.7	40	511.5	450.5	.91	.27	17
Portuguese bridal cookies	4770	32.7	120	115	219	0	.74	0	0
WEDNESDAY									
Fresh fruit salad	8958	46.26	23.36	145.8	708	3856	1.55	.6	101
Almond–peach butter	2976	13.5	38.6	89	176.5	7800	.31	0	55
Sweet and sour dumplings	7212	126.6	98.65	231	2638	788	2.35	.3	26.71
Steamed chicken and melon soup	1600	146.95	39.35	74.5	117.7	21791	.32	0	10
Onion and tomato pizza	12940	110	37.85	376	717.15	4173	3.39	0	321
Orange and onion salad/vinaigrette dressing	6270	19.92	126.4	94.3	350	9720	1.12	0	511
TUESDAY									
Blintzes with cherry sauce	3884	181	1042	4618	170	1965	19.06	2	0
Borscht	832	25	13.5	22.26	173	689	.06	0	96
Strawberry tahini custard	3044	18.08	115.6	1.3747	99	187	.91	0	228.3
Zucchini pasta	3532	38.5	78.7	39.2	252	6380	1.48	0	200
Bulghur pilaf with onion and raisin sauce	10744	153	61.9	459	367	315	1.25	0	73.5
Lentil and silverbeet soup	2979	59.7	70.1	135.7	470	24473	1.02	0	195
FRIDAY									
Vegetable pancakes	4825	50.4	69.37	287.8	166.8	7662	1.81	.8	44.9
Lemon coriander sauce	32	.2	0	2	2	0	0	0	14
Pocket bread surprise	520	.2	0	0	0	23	6	0	8
Alfalfa-almond filling	4955	214.7	49.9	295.6	290.4	12979	6.6	28	59
Sunflower-date filling	5460	45.4	89.4	203.2	1304.1	223	2.836	0	30
Ginger beans	1452	15.9	14.6	69.9	90.2	4558	.55	0	159.8
Mustard pickles	580	1.5	13.2	5.8	42	920	.05	0	19
Scalloped noodles	2845	1672	790	233.45	335.5	7575	2.3	0	343.5
Apricot yoghurt slice	8909	632	198.85	3605.8	10515	15676	.95	2.4	21.5
SATURDAY									
Waffles	1862	40.4	72	275	30	0	1.54	0	4
Orange-almond topping	1848	1462	40.01	61.3	900.7	16	.82	0	34.2
Strawberry melon	2440	14.1	6.0	140.3	272	780	1.5	0	520
Bolghur patties	6064	58.2	11.7	321.25	252	1085	1.96	0	8.4
Mint sauce	2941	19	41.4	7	110	350	.25	0	93
Pea and mushroom aspic	3114	100.45	81.5	2737.6	38.1	14337	2.58	0	4.3
Steamed buns	5319	90.4	19.8	179.2	359	2580	1.29	0	15.8
Black bean sauce	900	2.94	.22	206	220.2	70	.05	0	17.5
Sesame carrot	1842	9.8	25.9	67.4	271.8	30382.5	9.6	0	30.3
SUNDAY									
Zucchini piroski	7732	38.4	140.2	204	96	4000	2.2	0	32.7
Basil and garlic sauce	665	9.0	13	3.04	1	0	18	0	0
Steamed date cake	3599.76	14.4	57	101.1	383.45	4420	22.41	.2	25.75
Green salad	2526	8.5	1.8	87	463.2	12930	.36	0	120

mg = milligrams
g = grams
IU = International Units

LATE SUMMER	Kilojoules	Protein (g)	Fat (g)	Carbohydrate (g)	Calcium (mg)	Vitamin A (IU)	Vitamin B (mg)	Vitamin B$_{12}$ (mg)	Vitamin C (mg)
MONDAY									
Almond bar/carob coating	7750	38.66	111.21	210	749	233.3	1.6	0	6.1
Celery and french bean salad	3178	33.6	40	102	1737	6520	5.72	3.2	230
Orange onion dressing	475	2.8	1.55	23.8	57.15	285	.2	0	72.25
Cous-cous with eggplant and garlic sauce	14702	58.67	292	451.2	703	22127	2.34	.008	65.5
TUESDAY									
Corn fritters	3077	41.25	15.3	215.5	517	2770	6.05	4	109
Russian sauce	987.8	23.18	15.23	9.7	250.5	1623.1	.247	0	35.15
Barley, rice sesame	3903	104	23.6	722	658.5	0	1.49	0	0
Coriander lentils	6908	83.9	55	230	459.6	5608.4	.94	0	99
Late summer fish stew	13672	839	709	119	9432	18025	1837	0	112.2
Hot sauce	1678	6.2	36.85	33.16	27.1	2483.4	.19	0	187
Plenty of pasta	4096	19	80.6	11.36	87.6	8.4	.08	0	0
Walnut and apple salad	7779	35.97	188.7	73.1	295.3	10260	.88	0	113
Corn relish	2550	23.67	6.1	138.3	113.7	12835	19.21	0	897.4
WEDNESDAY									
Tiered pancakes	1507	22	21.0	72	411	770	9.23	5	0
Pumpkin apple jam	927	10.55	1.18	270.7	280.05	40590	80.313	0	.5
Green beans in walnut and dill sauce	3914	31	53.8	85.3	473	5231.2	1.23	0	166
Silverbeet and basil soup	1903	16.1	49.95	21.87	81.4	1596.8	.17	.035	12
Salad in a basket	7026	71.2	39.3	360.88	325.2	3817	1.07	0	24
Vegetables in lemon creme	5608.3	33.6	60.4	163.15	709.89	7589.3	1.173	0	617.41
Burgher wheat	2371	55	35.4	326.7	157.4	800	.636	.031	7.2
Sweet nut rolls	6164	86.93	52.28	281.8	307.3	336.2	3.771	0	10.3
Egg drop soup	3490	44.2	41.85	167.52	390.9	4266.8	16.65	1.235	151
THURSDAY									
Puffed wheat, rice or corn cereal	2480	30.4	33.2	68	1400	3600	2.8	16	0
Carrot slice	15122	71.3	152.6	791	750.5	33620	43.82	2.4	92
Prawns in black bean sauce	3779.6	55.2	52.8	101.16	345.1	160.9	75.16	0	117.5
Peas in a pod	2064	17.9	29	61	339	4000	.64	0	111
Fluffy millet	2763	20	2.0	6.5	40	0	5.87	0	0
Pear pie	9774	46.5	114.4	467.2	334.75	310	4.405	0	28
Mexican beans	8521	99.2	73.35	300.86	583.75	2528.4	1.06	0	90
Mexican rice	1504	22.5	14.1	163.18	189.8	2904.2	.42	0	335
Herb roasted corn	4433	27.2	87.82	64.24	559.9	1722.1	.97	0	28
Mexican tomato sauce	3169	16.1	46.2	71.92	232.2	16877	.54	0	161.4
FRIDAY									
Oat cakes	10471	51.6	259.3	273	251	90	1.93	0	38
Almond-peach spread	1530	13.1	31.8	13	146	0	14	0	0
Almond mushroom sauce	3179.2	22.35	69.3	36.48	272.8	789.2	129.45	0	66.5
Stir fried vegetables	1617.5	7.628	29.684	33.26	1511.1	6298.21	1.4115	2.3	82.83
Caraway onion soup	1564	23.5	24.8	44.5	431.9	8000	.59	0	62
Cucumber pickles	368	5.4	.6	21	172	1500	2.4	0	66
Buckwheat noodle salad	4830	331.23	67	104	1987	17639	.6495	2.3	423.33
Grilled peaches with pecans	3245	10.66	44.718	107.28	92.1	9397	.1138	0	73.3
Dill pickles	1099	16.2	8.3	60.72	920.7	4206.3	.73	0	140
SATURDAY									
Corn pones	4904	22	51.6	180	62	1240	.26	0	0
Apple delight	3196	18.12	31.78	156	401	9683	.943	.27	50.625
Sprout and bean medley	8640	33.36	191.27	74.21	862	28000	27.23	0	722
Treasure triangles	9306	37.2	245	193	672	1587.5	.305	0	37.75
Mayonnaise curry	2030	1	227	5.3	73	750	0	0	29
Pea pate	2562	107.3	42.9	279.66	368.6	2128.4	17.37	0	134
Zucchini and almond loaf	7338	57.9	114.5	184.5	989.25	2920	2.22	2.06	117.5
Spinach lasagne rolls	3530	41.8	99	83.17	848.33	67507	6.688	0	141
Country style fish	6714	135.63	84.2	90.6	406.6	1775	1.565	1.2	86.6
Teriyaki sauce	1732	25.4	26.8	32.56	283.6	8.4	.14	0	0
Date wontons	2930	10.546	24.03	137	106.58	231.25	.29	0	11.4
SUNDAY									
Nut burgers	5045	29.2	249.4	71	321	13080	.8	1.2	17
Spring onion salad	1250	61.3	12.5	92.2	532	9004	.42	0	144
Sweet and sour turnips	733	5.2	2	10.7	229	0	.2	0	189

AUTUMN	Kilojoules	Protein (g)	Fat (g)	Carbohydrate (g)	Calcium (mg)	Vitamin A (IU)	Vitamin B (mg)	Vitamin B$_{12}$ (mg)	Vitamin C (mg)
MONDAY									
Scalloped yams	3348	27.6	26.1	115.0	1156	18670	.37	12.0	50.0
Noodles with caraway onion sauce	1825	13.0	29.0	75.0	244	350	.35	0	185
Radish with miso sauce	1412	20.3	15.1	30.4	291.5	600	.18	1.0	72
Sweet cucumber salad	826	14.15	2.508	42.08	281.335	1615.0	2.81	0	68.35
Fruit and nut bars	7278	69.4	113.14	359	247	750	8.065	0	22
TUESDAY									
Sweet buckwheat creme	2106.3	25.5	22.95	144	194	20	.40	0	5
Tropical chutney	2557	8.08	9.31	136.1	131.95	28842	24.28	0	481.96
Tofu burgers	7174	449	432.6	324	574	1040	1.3	1.76	1.06
Grilled pears/carob sauce	578	5.4	8.18	77.2	54.3	90	.223	0	25
Vegetable chips	2086	13.9	164.2	8.9	350	30262	14	0	30
Chickpea roll	4815	94.5	282.82	63.2	749.8	2630	1.67	0	684.2
Carrot and apple tzimme	2116	8.8	44.1	75.0	186	4990	.3	0	44
Buckwheat stew	4805	49.38	8.3	271	554	2140	12.06	0	66
Coleslaw	323	6.6	.75	82	225.5	12375	1.02	0	141.5
WEDNESDAY									
Creme of wheat, rye and rice	2916	33.8	6.8	170.4	53.7	0	5.67	0	0
Chickpea patties, onion and garlic sauce	3671	45.8	11.22	148.3	348.8	850	26.16	0	16.7
Stir fried chestnuts	525.2	6.14	1.85	31.7	1323.3	778.4	3.721	0	61.3
Chinese cabbage	356	6.7	1.34	17.6	167.6	550	.24	0	97.4
Egg and lemon soup	1332	19.6	14.4	56.6	90.2	1385	3.44	2.4	5
Stuffed envelopes	11603	29.2	145.2	190	266	790	.47	0	56
Okra and tomatoes	18374	41.8	229	150	1492	10620	2.83	0	4.19
Mixed pickles	960	2.72	.62	98.8	156.9	15940	0.12	0	18.22
THURSDAY									
Oatmeal porridge	2300	25.6	5.1	252	161	30	3.12	0	1
Autumn bean salad	7804	129	9.2	354	829	13800	10.23	0	174
Watercress dressing	4028	2.85	114.5	9	94.5	992.2	.185	0	34
Broccoli noodle casserole	3630	36.3	45.2	58.6	1452.5	15805	1.45	0	575.5
Chestnut rice	1614	32.2	12.6	342	165	0	3.38	0	0
Poached snapper in sweet and sour sauce	5655	200.9	135.4	14.4	207.1	5010	2.37	0	262
Bean sprout salad	689.2	15.83	1.4	41	146	12.5	.465	0	37.5
FRIDAY									
Yam crepes	8992	71.4	26	473.2	277.4	860	10.093	1.2	154
Vegetable creme soup	564	2.2	14	6	38	110	.01	0	6
Cabbage and watercress soup	3490	43.5	87.39	77.6	409.15	25580	4.009	0	318
Vegetable croquettes	8514	91.22	157.98	335.05	1694.8	6690	43.975	0	149.2
Miso relish sauce	924	21	8.5	21.5	178	0	.05	0	0
Spinach and pumpkin salad	8362	65	185.2	97.5	1565	38930	1.64	0	278
Plum dressing	3751	4.6	200	1.0	96	1270	3.05	0	41
Clear soup with shredded herbed crepes	4923	26.2	15	10.4	60.5	2600	.03	1	50
Babka	11190	112	188.95	506.5	485.5	9460	55.175	1.4	44
SATURDAY									
Potato cake	9191	29.93	79.48	234.2	107.85	0	.53	0	73.83
Miso topping	997	7.83	15.7	28.03	85.6	0	.01	0	14.6
Pickled red cabbage	954	16.4	1.2	86	383	380.46	.46	0	378
Chestnut balls with creme of cauliflower sauce	1205	12.3	16.3	25.7	151	220	.29	0	181
Pumpkin creme pie	7171	30.75	153.25	99.8	1181.45	32110	3.264	.03	53.5
Chokoes with lemon fish	2475	30.1	30.925	106.72	373.4	762.5	1.815	0	92.3
Bechemel sauce	768	6.34	37	19.8	93	304.4	3.264	0	34.2
Shishkebabs	4978	37.88	73.78	53.87	625	4550	.52	0	230
Baked rice and peas	3055	53.6	12	469	229	860	2.85	0	32
SUNDAY									
Apple marmalade pancakes	43844	73	36.8	694	383	1520	1.07	0	74
Olive bread	4434.5	50.6	65.15	351.9	498	192.6	54.66	1.4	17
Peanut pumpkin spread	1294	15.4	24	15.4	79	50.04	.26	0	20
Apple apricot spread	5007	15.68	3.808	240.18	259.5	559.6	1.31	0	50.3
Almond–mushroom pate	3483	66.72	183.42	86.95	804.9	70	3.9	0	26.22
Tofu–miso pickles	2755	51.3	21.9	54.4	622	480	.21	.004	18
Shoyu pickles	1691	22.1	8	67.7	335	40	.14	.04	17
Lemon pickles	1382	20.82	11.6	45.2	324	225	.15	.34	158

WINTER	Kilojoules	Protein (g)	Fat (g)	Carbohydrate (g)	Calcium (mg)	Vitamin A (IU)	Vitamin B_1 (mg)	Vitamin B_{12} (mg)	Vitamin C (mg)
MONDAY									
Buckwheat nut loaf	8010	300	100	188.64	903.6	3432	2.385	4.64	105.8
Lemon and garlic sauce	1261	18.088	23.038	3.15	689.625	682.5	0.253	.54	32
Caraway salad	264	4.8	.8	26	173	1560	.22	0	135
Yams a la Wakame	3528	31.9	1.6	192	1332	140	.72	0	72
Almond apple mousse	1322.7	4.386	8.133	233.516	90.86	30	.17	.66	13
Mocha crumb topping	6134	60.2	65.5	334.7	398	510	2.17	0	0
Sour dough starter	1524	9.6	1	79.5	22	0	.15	0	0
TUESDAY									
Fresh fruit jam	2805.5	7.636	2.303	4514.695	156.1	212	.85	2	27.3
Oat and barley porridge	8570	59	35.55	309	296	70	5.23	0	0
Four vegetable bake	1250	18.75	2	67.5	178	370	7.685	0	251
Broccoli-miso soup	2404	25.9	37.5	31.74	1343	7820	.98	2	280
Bean and vegetable cassoulet	6383	54.853	12.845	171.598	1495	7469	1.23	4.33	213.93
Boiled watercress salad	117.8	9.7	23.6	16	452.7	10	.482	0	16
WEDNESDAY									
Baked apples	4296.5	10.35	35.3	583.2	469.52	795	1.371	0	37.5
Eggs in the whole	10865	38.9	255.2	54.12	491	2085	.66	0	3.52
Mushroom barley soup	3487	93.8	19.76	551.79	687.66	140.3	3.785	0	35.15
Buckwheat rissoles	8797.9	91.103	14.477	2671.7	830.75	4485	4.285	0	104
Herbed rice	3844.7	23.8	5.8	199.4	271.6	762	.845	0	101
Grilled fish	1465	60	12	0	100	180	20	.4	0
Garlic sauce	1635	.10	42	.45	5.2	0	.05	0	0
Creme of watercress soup	485.6	4.223	1.05	41.1	63.3	993.3	.246	0	7.26
Sesame pretzels	5133.5	41.9	31.8	512	734	0	1.86	0	0
THURSDAY									
Whole grain porridge	8575	82.75	39.07	440	498.5	575	3.82	0	0
Sour dough rye bread	325	3.2	.1	19.5	12	0	.22	0	1
Spiced fruit ring	1954.9	9.1	6.25	446	592	490	.21	0	82
Stuffed peppers	3617	46.4	107.96	113.78	795.6	1654.5	.98	.2	430
Sweet and sour green beans	234	8.6	.9	118.2	259	2720	.36	0	86
Slimmers cabbage pie	1695	35.65	20.25	295	515	2725	.72	2.64	262
Onion parsley sauce	2084	14.4	96.4	108	580.5	2340	.63	0	508
Peanut patties	18693	20.16	23.38	53.415	57.355	4.3	.47	0	1.06
Onion and radish salad	2083	16.97	9.37	24.22	445	1500			
FRIDAY									
Sunflower-sultana porridge	29158	37.5	41	283	1009.5	35	1.48	0	8.5
Turnip slice	5750	35.52	5.475	134.985	904.425	11008	1.097	2	888.12
Broccoli with black beans	669	16.32	1.4	26.8	469	11340	.48	0	513
Tofu whip creme	2684	13.64	22.13	140.2	487.5	2.5	.213	0	2
Tempura (fritto misto)	7537	72.72	61.2	172	429	5721	1.1	2.5	70.4
Sea salad	897.2	10	1.9	92	941.5	910	.42	.3	262
Pear custard	4245	34.21	17.95	223	649	120	1.59	0	49
SATURDAY									
Granola	13405	227.71	317.85	897	3191	130	9.84	0	4.66
Onion and carrot tarts	5758	52.89	32.24	245.27	899.45	1797	2.1	1	63.8
Braised endive and mushrooms	147.2	7	1.35	106.5	64	0	.1	0	3
Anise chicken	15335	199.48	67.556	208.88	589.5	4672	12.18	0	2.8
Apple cake	9003	169.9	111.51	271.15	384.35	842	1.755	1.2	242
Sweet glaze	2804	2.84	7.32	139.4	100.4	300	.09	1.2	11
Leeks in piquant sauce	1265.6	160.6	9.2	29	721.4	80	.34	.2	34
Beetroot vinaigrette	1036.8	157.6	18.85	32	74	520	0	.4	4
SUNDAY									
Sesame-oat waffles	15606	110.5	116.1	544	2098.5	840	42.93	0	13
Lemon meringue pie	13336	37.32	59.18	182.1	245.2	0	9.625	.06	30.5
Danish pastries	5611.75	41.625	91.22	138.25	554.75	1103	1.686	1.2	24

BASIC REFERENCES OF FOOD COMPOSITION

ADAMS, CATHERINE F. Nutritive Value of American Foods in Common Units.
Agriculture Handbook no. 456, U.S. Department of Agriculture. Washington,
Govt. Printing Office 1975.
PHILLIPS, DAVID A. Guide Book To Nutritional Factors In Edible Foods,
The Pythagorean Press, Sydney, Australia 1977.
ROBERTSON, L. FLINDERS, C. AND GODFREY, B. Laurel's Kitchen A Handbook for Vegetarian Cookery and Nutrition. Nilgiri
Press, Petaluma, California 1976.

INDEX